Government in the United Kingdom

The search for accountability, effectiveness and citizenship

Government in the United Kingdom

The search for accountability,
effectiveness and citizenship

DAWN OLIVER

OPEN UNIVERSITY PRESS
Milton Keynes · Philadelphia

Open University Press
Celtic Court
22 Ballmoor
Buckingham
MK18 1XW

and

1900 Frost Road, Suite 101
Bristol, PA 19007, USA

First Published 1991

British Library Cataloguing-in-Publication Data

Oliver, Dawn
   Government in the United Kingdom: The search for
   accountability, effectiveness and citizenship.
   I. Title
   320.941

   ISBN 0–335–15640–1
   ISBN 0–335–15639–8 pbk

Library of Congress Cataloging-in-Publication Data

Oliver, Dawn.
   Government in the United Kingdom: the search for accountability,
   effectiveness and citizenship/Dawn Oliver.
      p.   cm.
   Includes bibliographical references and index.
   ISBN 0–335–15640–1   ISBN 0–335–15639–8 (pbk.)
   1. Great Britain – Politics and government – 1979–   .
   2. Great Britain – Constitutional history.
   3. Great Britain – Constitutional law.
   4. Civil rights – Great Britain.
   5. Political participation – Great Britain.   I. Title.
   JN237   1991   .055   1991
   320.941 – dc20   91–23036
                                                                CIP

Typeset by Type Study, Scarborough
Printed in Great Britain by Biddles Limited, Guildford and Kings Lynn

Contents

List of cases

List of statutes

Preface

This book is about some of the most important criticisms of the United Kingdom constitution and proposals for constitutional reform that are currently on 'the political agenda'.

As the 1990s progress, all of the political parties are developing policies on constitutional reform. These include proposals for decentralization, reform of the civil service, local government reform, a Ministry of Justice, a Bill of Rights, proportional representation, freedom of information and a written Constitution. A number of cross-party campaigning groups are also active in the field, notably Charter 88. And distinguished lawyers and political commentators have contributed to a growing literature on the subject.

This book will discuss the criticisms of the system of government that lie behind proposals for constitutional reform and seeks to evaluate possible reforms in the light of three criteria: the needs to improve accountability in government, to increase efficiency and effectiveness, and to enhance the status and practice of citizenship. The book touches on European law, but it is about government in, rather than in and beyond, the UK. In due course, a book needs to be written that extends the discussion to Europe, but I am not yet ready to undertake such a task.

Inevitably, I have had to be selective in the choice of topics considered and it has been necessary to jettison material that could have been included if space had permitted. Making things shorter has been one of the hardest tasks. Keeping up to date when almost every day new proposals or decisions are being made about constitutional matters has been another. Nevertheless, it is hoped that the discussion presented here will convey a sense of the need for reform of the system of government and offer an approach which could be applied to other topics.

I have been greatly helped by a large number of friends and colleagues, and it would be impossible to acknowledge all of these debts. Questions from students and throwaway comments from colleagues can make as much of an impression as the carefully considered books, articles and official reports that have contributed to this end-product. I would, however, particularly like to thank Professor Bob Hepple, my head of department, for allowing me sabbatical leave in 1990 without which this book might never have been completed, and colleagues who covered for me during that term.

I should also like to express my thanks to the many friends who gave so generously of their time by reading and commenting upon earlier drafts of the manuscript and by recommending further reading: Rodney Austin, Vernon Bogdanor, James Cornford, Gavin Drewry, Nicholaos Emiliou, Cyril Glasser, Stephen Guest, John Gyford, Pam Holt, Nicola Lacey, Anthony Lester, Robert Maclennan, James Michael, Julia Neuberger and William Rodgers. Beverley Crearer patiently and cheerfully helped with endless redrafts and the printing out and photocopying of chapters. David Vavrecka checked many references. The responsibility for shortcomings in this work, however, rests entirely with me.

Above all, I thank Stephen, Beccy, Adam and Rosie for putting up with me so supportively and in such good humour while I have been writing; without their encouragement and patience and the occasional interruption or welcome distraction, I would not have started or finished this enterprise and yet remained, I hope, relatively sane.

Dawn Oliver

PART I

The problems

1

The constitution under pressure

This book is about the reform of the constitution of the United Kingdom. An explanation of what is meant by the term 'constitution' will be helpful before we proceed to discuss its reform. It is important to distinguish two ways in which the word is used, and this will be done by referring to a written document which contains the basic laws relating to the system of government as a 'Constitution'. In other contexts the word 'constitution' will be used. Given that this country does not have a written Constitution, a single document in which the principal rules of the system of government are collected together, one of the definitions proposed by K. C. Wheare (1966, p. 1) provides us with a good starting point: 'The word "constitution" . . . is used to describe the whole system of government of a country, the collection of rules which establish and regulate or govern the government.' He goes on to explain that these rules are partly legal and partly non-legal, the latter taking the form of usages, understandings, customs and conventions.

In this sense, then, the UK constitution is made up of those aspects of the system of government that are subject to rules; much of the discussion about constitutional reform with which we shall be concerned is about changing these rules or changing the nature of the rules. To give an example, the introduction of a Bill of Rights would change quite radically the rules about the protection of civil and political rights that are applied in the UK courts. If a Bill of Rights were to follow the form of the provisions of the European Convention on Human Rights, it would also alter the nature of the rules that govern these issues: at present, that Convention is a treaty, a set of 'international' laws which bind our government in international law, but are not enforceable in our own courts. The 'incorporation' of this international Convention into UK law would give the Convention a dual personality; it would no longer be only an internationally binding instrument, it would also become a set of 'domestic' laws which our courts could enforce.

To illustrate the range of levels at which 'laws' or rules operate in our constitution, we can take a further example from the rules governing Cabinet government. Some of these are unwritten 'conventions'; others are set out in written but unpublished secret documents, notably one entitled *Questions of Procedure for Ministers*. None of these rules is enforceable in the courts, but they should be regarded as rules of the constitution none the less: they have the quality of what we may call 'political enforceability'. But the extent to which ministers are under pressure from the Prime Minister, Parliament, the press and the public to obey those rules, must depend upon how widely those rules are known, understood and obeyed. If the conventions about Cabinet government were written down, and they and the *Questions of Procedure* were published, then these rules would alter in their nature, since the pressures to comply with them or alter them if they appear to be unjustifiable would increase. This book, then, will be concerned with a whole range of rules of the constitution, and a whole range of ways in which they could be reformed.

The issue of constitutional reform

The question of reform of the UK constitution has become a subject of wide-ranging debate among academic political scientists and lawyers and practising politicians in the last 15 years or so. Many activists in the Labour Party and among the Liberal Democrats have expressed their commitment to a range of reforming measures. The Liberal Democrats have published a draft written constitution in *'We, The People . . .' – Towards a Written Constitution* (Liberal Democrats, 1990, app. 2), and the Institute of Public Policy Research too has produced a Constitution (Institute of Public Policy Research, 1991). Tony Benn MP (1991) presented his written Constitution in the form of a Commonwealth of Britain Bill to the House of Commons in May 1991. Cross-party campaigning groups attached to no particular party have also been active. Charter 88, which by May 1991 had 25 000 signatories, was a striking manifestation of the strength of interest in reform of the constitution. Charter 88 and the Human Rights Centre at Essex University are undertaking an *Audit of British Democracy*, financed by the Joseph Rowntree Charitable Trust, which will monitor the system over a five year period.

Interest in constitutional reform has not been confined to the political left and centre. The Conservative government of the 1980s to 1991 introduced extensive reforms in the civil service and local government. Frank Vibert, Deputy Director of the Institute of Economic Affairs, has argued the 'conservative' case for electoral reform, reform of the second chamber and local and regional government, a Bill of Rights and even a written Constitution (Vibert, 1991). Professor Stephen Haseler of the Radical Society has also put the case for 'a new constitutional settlement' (Haseler, 1991).

Public opinion is moving in favour of constitutional change. A MORI *State of the Nation* poll conducted in March 1991 for the Joseph Rowntree Reform Trust found that 40 percent of respondents thought that the present system of government could be improved 'quite a lot' and a further 23 percent felt that it needed 'a great deal of improvement'. Over 50 percent of respondents favoured one or more of a number of reforms including proportional representation, a Bill of Rights and a Freedom of Information Act (MORI, 1991).

Proposals for constitutional reform in the period with which we are concerned have touched on most aspects of the system of government. Many commentators have concentrated on particular problem areas in our constitutional arrangements – the electoral system, the protection of human rights, local government; others have taken a broad view and argued for a new constitutional settlement involving a range of reforms, and even the formulation of a written Constitution that would radically alter the basis of the system of government. It is timely, therefore, to consider the subject of constitutional reform 'in the round'.

Whether advocates of reform are concerned with particular aspects of the system or whether they see the problems in terms of the need for a general overhaul of the constitution, a number of themes tend to recur in the debates. They include the search for ways of making government more effective and efficient in its efforts to meet the needs and wishes of the country; the need to improve the checks and balances in the constitution that are supposed to secure that government is accountable for its work; and the need to define more closely the relationship between the individual and the state and to elaborate a concept of citizenship that is appropriate to conditions in a late twentieth-century European democracy. These are the themes on which the following chapters will focus.

For the most part, the proposals for constitutional reform that have been advanced in the post-war period have accepted the basic structure of the Westminster model – a constitutional monarch as head of state, a parliamentary executive, a permanent, politically neutral public service, and a tier of elected local government. There is no popular pressure to move to a presidential system, a strict separation of powers on the US model, or a politically appointed civil service. The British have not traditionally looked over the parapet provided by the white cliffs towards mainland Europe or the USA to contemplate the remote possibility that other countries might do things better than the British. But some of the proposals that are currently under discussion would radically alter the structure of the UK constitution. This is particularly the case with the proposed introduction of a Scottish Parliament and possibly assemblies for Wales, Northern Ireland and the regions of England. A written Constitution would also be a radical departure from the present system if it limited the legislative supremacy of the Westminster Parliament, for example, by imposing special majorities where legislation is proposed that would alter the provisions of the Constitution.

The rise in interest in the possible reform of the UK constitution is inevitably linked to the history of the post-war period and to the successes and failures of social and economic policies pursued by government, and with developments outside the UK, especially in the European Community. In order to put the debates about reform in context, therefore, we shall start by tracing the history of social and economic policy since 1945 and relating it to the debates about particular aspects of the constitution which will be considered in detail later in the book. It is convenient to start with the aftermath of the Second World War and what has come to be known as the post-war settlement.

The post-war settlement

At the end of the Second World War and for some 20 years thereafter, there was a high degree of consensus over matters of social and economic policy in the UK. The Labour government that was elected to power in 1945 proceeded to give first priority to a policy of full employment and to establish the Welfare State through legislation for the National Health Service (NHS) and for a system of National Assistance to provide a 'safety net' for those unable to provide for themselves.

This set of policies and the other reforms introduced in implementation of the recommendations of the Beveridge Report led to substantial improvements in the standards of living of the poorest in the community, and indeed of the population as a whole, and brought the goal of equality of opportunity closer to realization. The nationalization of major industries (e.g. coal-mining, steel, gas, electricity) heralded efficient planning of the economy and the end of exploitation for workers in those industries. Anthony Crosland's view, expounded in *The Future of Socialism* (1956), that the mixed economy would lead to economic growth which would finance increases in public expenditure and facilitate redistributive taxation seemed to hold good. Keynesian economic theory became the accepted orthodoxy (Keynes, 1936).

As T. H. Marshall (1950) observed, these measures of the post-war period, taken together, introduced a new form of citizenship; they supplemented the civil and political rights of individuals that had been won in the eighteenth and nineteenth centuries with social rights which guaranteed a decent standard of living for all and thus the opportunity to participate in the life of the community free from the barriers that are created by poverty (for further consideration of this work see Chapter 2).

The reforms of the post-war decade were implemented within the existing constitutional framework of a sovereign Parliament, a parliamentary executive and a two-party system. There was no real doubt at that time but that these arrangements were a sufficient guarantee of democracy, accountability and good and effective government.

The liberal-democratic tradition

The Westminster system is an expression of what may be termed the liberal-democratic political tradition. This tradition, though highly political, is essentially non-partisan: the exercise of state power is to be justified primarily in terms of the public interest rather than the interests of particular classes, groups or parties. This doctrine goes back to Athenian political philosophy (Aristotle,

Politics, Book III, ch. VI. For further consideration of what the public interest involves, see d'Entreves, 1967, ch. 8; Barry, 1967; for contemporary discussion of the concept, often referred to as 'the common good', see e.g. Burke, 1774, 'Speech to the Electors of Bristol'; Blackstone, 1825, vol. I, ch. VII). Governments are not supposed to seek to promote the interests of their own supporters, and though they may in practice do so, this is never admitted and would be widely regarded as improper if it were admitted; the permanent civil service and local government officers should be politically neutral. The tradition assumes the fallibility of government (indeed the fallibility of all), and therefore recognizes the need for a system of checks and balances designed to prevent abuses of political power. It accepts that a high degree of individual civil and political freedom, freedom of the press and the toleration of dissent are necessary to protect individuals and the community from misgovernment.

This set of traditions was generally respected in the post-war period by government, Parliament, local authorities and other public institutions. It also commanded broad public support. A striking feature of the period was that the tradition was maintained largely through self-restraint on the part of government and Parliament, and voluntary obedience to unwritten conventions about comity, tolerance and moderation. While the UK doctrine of the sovereignty of Parliament makes it legally possible for measures to be passed that contravene the liberal-democratic tradition, a strong political ethos means that this happened infrequently (see Chapter 11 in particular, but see also Chapter 9). Voluntary observance of requirements of a non-partisan, tolerant approach made possible a low level of legal regulation of state institutions which were regarded as most appropriately controlled through political processes and constitutional conventions rather than through elaborate systems of legal regulation (this point is discussed further in Chapter 5).

This liberal-democratic tradition has come to be questioned in the last 15 years or more, both as a representation of the actual working of the system and as a conception of how a system should operate. The challenge to the liberal-democratic model of the constitution has come about largely as a result of disillusionment with the system and its outputs in terms of the prosperity of the country, the distribution of wealth and the opportunities in fact enjoyed by citizens under the policies of successive governments, which have frequently failed to fulfil their electoral promises.

As we shall see, politicians from both of the two main parties, in central and local government, have felt justified on occasions in breaking with the tradition, adopting highly partisan policies, seeking to suppress criticism and to undermine the system of checks and balances. Such departures from tradition have been particularly noticeable in central–local relations, where goodwill between the parties broke down in the 1980s, with the result that there has been a dramatic increase in central government control and legal regulation of local government; and in relation to civil and political rights, where both central government and some local authorities have sought to suppress freedom of speech, association and opinion in cases like Spycatcher (see Chapter 10), and by discriminating against or 'blacking' their critics (see Chapters 5 and 9). Let us consider, then, the reasons for the challenging of the liberal-democratic tradition and its impact on ideas about the constitution.

The age of disillusionment

A sense of disillusionment with the social and economic policies of the post-war settlement began to take root in the 1960s and 1970s. Although the standard of living of the poorest had greatly improved, Peter Townsend's (1979) national poverty study and other research established that the welfare state had not narrowed the difference in wealth between the richest and the poorest. The health of the poorest was – and is still – worse than the health of the middle and upper classes, despite the NHS (Association of Community Health Councils, 1991). The Education Act 1944 did not produce anything like the due representation of people from working-class backgrounds in higher education or in the professions, management or the higher echelons of the public services.

Although destitution had become virtually a thing of the past by the 1970s, Townsend argued that it was no longer appropriate to define poverty by reference to subsistence: poverty should be redefined to indicate an inability through lack of resources to participate fully in the community. On this definition, many hundreds of thousands of people, including the unemployed, single parents and their children and pensioners, who were unable to afford to share the way of life of the rest of society, were poor. In effect, citizenship in the sense expounded by T. H. Marshall was being denied to these people (see Chapter 2 for an elaboration of the concept of citizenship).

Awareness of the failings of the post-war settlement had begun to become more widespread by the late 1970s as the evidence of poverty and inequality became more visible. From the mid-1970s unemployment began to rise. The standard of living in this country lagged noticeably behind standards in our Western European neighbours, in Japan, the USA or Canada. Private industry in the UK was not competing effectively with overseas companies, and foreign goods periodically flooded our markets. In the 1970s, the balance of payments was usually in deficit. Inflation began to rise in the early 1970s. For the most part, the nationalized industries – perhaps because of the lack of any coherent ideas as to the rationale of nationalization – had not been innovative or competitive when viewed in an international context.

Is the system to blame?

The failures of the post-war settlement began to be laid in part at the door of the political system: there must be something wrong with a system under which government seemed unable to formulate and then to implement policies that would solve the country's problems, especially since our European neighbours were prospering so much more than we were.

Concern that the system might be in part to blame was reflected in the institutional reforms of the 1960s and 1970s; these touched local government, the civil service, the public expenditure process, the select committees of the House of Commons. But they effected relatively modest improvements in the system of government and these areas were again undergoing quite radical reform only 20 years later.

Among those who blame the system, opinions differ as to what it is that makes it so difficult for governments to solve social and economic problems. One version blamed the ability of the trade unions and industry and other centres of power to frustrate government policy by withholding their cooperation; the activities of pressure groups in the 1960s and 1970s made it difficult for government to adopt and implement policies that damaged vested interests (see, e.g. Miliband, 1961, 1972; Rose, 1976; Smith, 1976). As a result, the public interest suffered from a form of creeping paralysis. The pressures on government not to act without first achieving agreement from those affected produced what Rose (1976, p. 414) has called a 'directionless consensus'.

Awareness of the influence of powerful corporations over government, of the 'corporate bias' which has been identified by Middlemas as having its origins earlier in the century, contributed to the loss of legitimacy of governments in the eyes of the general public (see Middlemas, 1979). The resulting partisanship in government, with Labour administrations bowing to the unions and Conservative governments favouring industry and financial interests, seemed to represent a departure from liberal-democratic constitutional values.

Beer (1982a, b) has explained the problems of the 1960s and 1970s in terms of the breakdown of the foundations of the collectivist polity, the balanced civic culture, the class system and the two-party choice mechanism. He has argued that the disintegration of these foundations led to 'pluralist stagnation', a paralysis of public choice, which contributed to disillusionment with the political system and the constitution. The rise of group politics and pluralism fragmented the decision-making system, impeding its ability to produce choices in the long-term interests of the population. Government was largely concerned with crisis management rather than with long-term strategic planning.

Marquand (1988) has argued that one of the problems in the system is the inability to adjust to the changed conditions of the late twentieth century: this is contributed to by the 'unprincipled' nature of the system which has no tradition of an active role for the state – a 'developmental' state. The suspicion of state power that is implicit in the liberal-democratic tradition contributes to the negative attitude to the role of the state.

Attention came to focus on the machinery within government for facilitating strategic planning and preventing governments from being blown off course by political pressures. The political parties came to recognize that the effectiveness, the authority and the legitimacy of government needed to be enhanced.

The impact of social and political change on the constitution

Other influences have been at work on the operation of the political system which raise issues about the working of the constitution. The two-party system, linked to the class system – identified by Beer as the foundations of the polity – has altered in its operation. As the living standards of the majority of workers have improved, and home ownership and the ownership of cars and other major items of property has increased, manual workers have ceased to see themselves as 'working class'. Beer argues that this process of class decomposition undermines the social foundations of the country, the two-party system and party government. As increasing numbers of voters come to regard themselves either as belonging to no class or as being middle class, Labour has experienced increasing difficulties in winning overall majorities in Parliament (for further consideration of this topic, see Chapter 8). Their ties with the increasingly unpopular trade unions have become electoral liabilities.

But Labour has not been alone in losing popular support. Both of the two main parties began to experience increasing difficulties in mobilizing consent to government in the 1970s. The Heath administration was defeated by the miners' strike in 1974; the Callaghan government by public revulsion at the strikes in the Winter of Discontent of 1978–79. As Labour and the Conservatives experienced these problems, support for the Liberal Party began to rise. And, at the same time, a new populism, in Beer's (1982b, p. 111n) words 'an exaggerated assertion of the values of democracy', undermined the traditional authority of rulers over the ruled. Beer (1982b, ch. V) uses student protests, strikes, claims for worker participation in decision making and worker self-management, intra-party democracy in the Labour Party, the collapse of class deference and dissension in the House of Commons as examples of this new populism. By 1979, there were real crises in the authority of government, and in social and economic policy.

The overload problem

A major problem that has undermined the effectiveness of government has been one of 'overload' at the centre: this is contributed to by the highly centralized nature of the system with only a weak local authority tier below central government. It has been exacerbated by the progressive increase in government functions, particularly in the post-war years when responsibility for major aspects of the welfare state were taken on by central government. Acknowledgement of the problems that this overload causes has been reflected in a range of proposals for reform, from decentralization to the nations and regions of the UK of much of the work currently performed by Whitehall (see Chapter 6), to the hiving off of functions from central government to autonomous executive agencies that has been taking place since 1988 (see Chapter 4); from increasing support for the Cabinet in its role as strategic planner to providing ministers with 'cabinets' of political and other advisers (see Chapter 4).

Politicians have seemed to be unable to plan in opposition policies that they could realistically seek to implement in office. Election promises have all too often turned out to be harder to implement than anticipated. Inadequate preparation for office by opposition parties has often meant that there have to be reversals of policy after a period when a government comes 'face to face with the realities of its economic, industrial and social environment and has to reexamine those policies produced with a greater regard to ideology than to their practicability' (Garrett and Sheldon, 1973; quoted in Rose, 1976, p. 436).

The inability of parties in opposition to plan for power is in part due to the Opposition's lack of resources and access to official information. And the Opposition devotes much of its energy to opposing the government of the day, often a more pressing task than planning for power in the future. Hence proposals came to be heard in the 1970s for the public funding of political parties; other suggestions for enabling the Opposition to prepare for office include the establishment of a Department of the Opposition (see Chapter 4).

Blame for the failures of the post-war settlement have not fixed solely on the parties and their leaders; the efficiency and effectiveness of the civil service has attracted adverse criticism, and acknowledgement of the need for improvement here is reflected in measures such as the setting up of executive agencies, referred to above (see Chapter 4; see Rose, 1976, p. 409; see also Hoskyns, 1983; Meacher, 1979; Miliband, 1982).

Adversarial politics

Another line of criticism of the effectiveness of the system focuses on the instability of policy that results from the adversarial nature of British politics. The two-party system, which has dominated politics in the UK since the Second World War – subject to what may have been a 'blip' in the 1980s with the rise and fall of the Liberal–Social Democratic Party Alliance – has meant that governments of differing complexions alternate in power, each seeking to reverse many of the policies pursued by its predecessor. This tendency has been particularly marked in industrial policy, with major industries nationalized, denationalized, renationalized and, more recently, privatized. The prospect of such changes being implemented by the next government cannot be good for the long-term planning of investment in industry. Regional policy has changed with each change of government and this again has affected industry's performance and forward planning.

These aspects of adversarial politics would be constitutionally unobjection-able if changes of government and pendulum swings in policy reflected the will of the people and the considered judgements of politicians. But it is argued by supporters of this 'adversary politics' thesis (see Finer, 1975; Bogdanor, 1981) that the first past the post electoral system operates so as to exaggerate both the gulf between the two parties and the electoral support which each enjoys, and so prevents the moderate middle ground of views in the electorate – for example, the views of what is now the Liberal Democratic Party, and of its predecessors – from receiving the representation in Parliament that their electoral support in the country would seem to merit. From this position, the argument is put for electoral reform to secure proportional representation of the parties in

Parliament which might result in coalitions and thus, it is hoped, greater stability of policy (see Chapter 8).

Accountability

During the period of the Wilson and Callaghan administrations from 1974 to 1979, a new concern emerged about the machinery for securing accountability and responsiveness in government. This too raised the question of the electoral system. Labour won the election in February 1974 on 37.1 percent of the votes cast; in the election of October 1974, its share of the vote increased to 39.2 percent. So it had nowhere near the support of a majority of the voters. It proceeded to implement a range of policies many of which were highly controversial; some were partisan or arbitrary, or both (the 'social contract' with the unions and the non-statutory 'blacklisting' policy designed to keep private sector wage rises down to the government's norm); others were unpopular with the party's own backbenchers and voters (the cuts in public expenditure from 1976, which were imposed by the IMF as a condition of their support for the economy).

Backbenchers in the House of Commons began to feel that the government was insufficiently accountable to the House for its policies. Perhaps the most colourful expression of the concern was Lord Hailsham's phrase 'Elective Dictatorship', the title of his Dimbleby lecture of 1976. So accountability became an issue in politics.

The House of Commons' response was to refer the matter of ministerial accountability to the Select Committee on Procedure, which reported in 1977 with recommendations for reform of the select committee system. These reforms were implemented in 1979 when the Conservative government came to power. The select committees – Public Accounts and Treasury and Civil Service – also pressed successfully and, in the face of government opposition for reform of parliamentary scrutiny of public expenditure, this resulted in the passing of the National Audit Act 1983. But these procedural reforms have not satisfied those concerned about the accountability of government and further measures that would increase accountability by revitalizing the political process, for example through proportional representation, reform of the second chamber or public rights of access to official information, have begun to gain support.

1970–90: Political polarization

The post-war consensus began to crack in the 1970s. Nineteen seventy-four may be regarded as a key date, for the defeat of the Heath government in the election in February of that year marked the end of consensual Conservatism and in due course led to the election of Margaret Thatcher as leader of the party. But 1974 also marked a growing tension in the Labour Party between its socialist or left wing, and what came to be recognized as its social democratic wing. Eventually, some of the members of the social democratic wing were to leave the party and form the SDP in 1981, but this was preceded by a period of conflict in the party and, eventually, its move sharply to the left in the aftermath of the 1979 election defeat (Seyd, 1987).

This polarization of the two main parties affected party policies and attitudes not only on substantive social and economic issues, but also on constitutional matters – relationships between Parliament, central and local government, and the civil service, and the rights and obligations of citizenship.

For some commentators, failure in the sphere of economic and social policies was in part due to an institutionalized resistance in the system to thoroughgoing socialist policies. The common assumption of liberal-democratic theory that the constitution is neutral between the parties was challenged from the left. Tony Benn (1981, p. xiii) suggested that the current constitutional arrangements were 'institutional devices that merely siphon off public discontent by providing a "constitutional" remedy' and that 'this is not what democracy is all about'. Miliband (1984) argued that, contrary to popular assumptions, a liberal-democratic constitution such as that of the UK is effective in controlling, absorbing and withstanding popular pressures from below, rather than in accommodating and giving in to pressures for fairer opportunities to participate in political life and to share in the national wealth; it has an in-built resistance to socialism. These views challenged both the theory and the operation of the liberal-democratic tradition and implied a need for alterations to the constitutional ground rules that would, for example, provide greater opportunities for expressions of popular discontent to influence government policy.

On this approach, the task for socialists was to strengthen the power of the Labour Party and the Labour movement in order to secure that a Labour government was accountable to them and could not be deflected from pursuing socialist policies by pressure from 'the Establishment' – the City, the civil service and other capitalist institutions. This pressure led to reforms of the Labour Party's constitution which had clear constitutional implications (Oliver, 1981). They affected the method of choosing the Labour leader and thus indirectly a Labour Prime Minister, giving a major role to the extra-parliamentary party. They linked the party more explicitly than before to the trade unions and thus undermined any claim it might make to be the promoter of the general public interest. Indeed, many on the left expressed scepticism about the very existence of such a thing as 'the public interest'. This attitude would, in turn, affect the legitimacy of a future Labour government in the eyes of supporters of other parties.

But the Labour Party was divided internally over these issues and about the substantive policies that a Labour government should pursue, many of which had constitutional dimensions. Until the mid-1980s, the terms of the policy debate in the Labour Party were dominated by the view that the economy needed to be centrally controlled by the state and the state should have a providential role for the benefit of its citizens. In the late 1980s, the Labour Party leadership came round to the view that a properly regulated market economy was a more efficient generator of wealth than a centrally planned or state-owned economy could be. In response to the spirit of the age, Labour began to think in terms of consumer rights. The terms of the policy debate in the party changed subtly from being worker-oriented to being consumer-based and this focus on consumerism in the field of public services introduced a new dimension to the debates about the nature of citizenship (Plant, 1988).

The role of the state

Labour's attitude to the role of the state as provider also altered as Conservative policies in the 1980s won support from members of the public, including Labour or former Labour voters. A view of the state as 'enabler' rather than provider gained currency. Many people had benefited from policies of the Conservative government replacing state provision with self-help, or treating recipients of state services as consumers and customers rather than recipients. The right to buy accorded to council tenants by the 1980 Housing Act and the introduction of increased parental choice in education, were broadly popular with the electorate. Other policies, of course, were less popular, but the shift in the attitudes of citizens to themselves, as active rather than passive, customers rather than claimants, came to be reflected in Labour Party policies too. A new concept of citizenship began to gain ground in the party.

During this period, an opposite view to that of the Labour Left in the late 1970s and the early 1980s, which also had a constitutional dimension, gained currency on the Right: socialism or social democracy was the problem, not the solution. Attention focused on what was regarded as an overactive state and overregulation of the private sector: if the state interfered less in the operation of the market and concentrated on providing a framework within which competition was assured, the economy would thrive and produce the wealth the population needed. Although this would increase inequality, the poor would benefit from a 'trickle-down' effect. Nationalized industries should be freed from political interference and exposed to the market (Veljanowski, 1987); this would compel them to increase their efficiency and effectiveness. Competition has been characterized by Galbraith (1983) as an 'ideology'. For this same reason, public services should be privatized (housing, bus services) or freed from political management (schools, rented housing, NHS hospitals) and exposed to market-type forces. Hayek (1961) sees capitalism and the 'free market' as essential both to economic prosperity and individual freedom of activity (see also Johnson, 1977; Graham and Clarke, 1986).

A strong theme in Conservative policy was the need to remove many functions from the political sphere to the market, and this implied mistrust of the mechanisms of political accountability as controls over the performance of the services and industries in question, and confidence instead in market mechanisms. To the extent that members of the public were to have a greater degree of choice and influence in the provision of public services, this set of policies treated them as active citizens rather than passive recipients of benefits, a shift which marked a changing conception of citizenship in the Conservative Party. The state would have an enabling rather than a providential role. After the acute political polarization of the late 1970s and most of the 1980s, a new consensus began to develop around these themes of enablement and active citizenship.

The New Right element in the Conservative Party has been influenced by 'public choice' theory (Buchanan, 1965; Breton, 1974; Downs, 1967; King, 1987; Laver, 1981; McAuslan, 1988; Mueller, 1979; Niskanen, 1971; Olsen, 1965; Schelling, 1978; Self, 1985, 1990; Tullock, 1965, 1976); this has affected policy towards local government and the civil service. According to this somewhat cynical set of beliefs, individuals and organizations, including public institutions, are merely self-interested 'utility maximizers' always seeking more satisfaction of their own demands and needs for the same or smaller outlay. Translated into constitutional terms, this means that, unless they are constrained by enhanced systems of accountability and legal regulation, civil servants and local authorities will tend to put their own interests and convenience before those of the community they are supposed to serve. This theory has been partly responsible for the government's privatization of services, especially in local government, and the introduction of market disciplines into service delivery (for example, in the NHS and education) in order to counteract the dominance of bureaucracy and trade unions and party interests (for a legal analysis of public choice theory, see McAuslan, 1988). It is significant again that the government has substituted non-political for political mechanisms of accountability in these areas.

Conviction politics and the constitution

The Conservatives' response to the crisis of authority and the pluralist stagnation and directionless consensus of the 1960s and 1970s was to substitute conviction for consensus politics and to go for 'a strong state' alongside 'a free economy', to adapt the phrases employed by Andrew Gamble (1988).

The Conservatives' strong 'law and order' policy has been intolerant of opposition and dissent, and their hostility to criticism from the press and to the publication of embarrassing revelations by the media has led to a series of confrontations with the media (see Chapters 9 and 10). The government has employed a range of measures to restrict the freedom of local authorities to pursue policies of which they disapproved, thus abandoning the tradition of minimal legal regulation of the state (see Chapter 5).

Partisanship became increasingly obvious in political life in the 1980s, and it was by no means the prerogative of the Conservative Party; many Labour-controlled councils also adopted a highly intolerant, partisan style. Some local authorities made what appeared to be political appointments and discriminated against political opponents (see Chapter 5); central government ministers invited accusations that they were manipulating statistics for party political advantage, discriminating against local authorities that were under Labour control, and channelling funds to areas where they needed to increase their political support. The reasons for the increase in partisanship are complex: they were partly a reaction to the end of the post-war settlement, to the end of the comity between the parties that went with it, and the adoption of a 'conviction politics' style after the long period of consensus by Mrs Thatcher's adminis- tration. But the increase in partisan activity fuelled concern about the weaknesses of the political and legal systems in controlling the exercise of public power and protecting the liberal-democratic tradition. That tradition was under attack from both ends of the political spectrum and it became clear that it had rested on a political and constitutional consensus that had been destroyed with the end of the post-war settlement.

Constitutional reform moves up the political agenda

Illiberal, intolerant actions in central and local government added fuel to the heat of a debate which had started in the 1960s, about the legal protection of civil and political rights. The legal protection that is offered to freedom of ex- pression, association, conscience and freedom from discrimination serves to underpin the liberal-democratic tradition. In granting constitutions to former dominions and colonies, the UK has commonly included a Bill of Rights. The European Convention on Human Rights, to which the UK is a party, is in effect an international Bill of Rights. And yet the UK has no such charter of its own. As politicians have become more authoritarian, illiberal, even chauvinis- tic, the arguments for a Bill of Rights have become stronger and the weak- nesses of the legal system and the political process in protecting these rights more obvious.

The Conservative response as far as partisanship and authoritarianism in local government is concerned, has been to subject this tier of government to increased legal regulation; but they have resisted both political and legal control of these political practices by central government, and they have shown no interest in enhancing the legal protection of civil and political rights – quite the reverse.

Both the two main political parties have resisted claims that the problems in social and economic policy reflect fundamental defects in the constitutional and political system. Labour has tended to the view that the best way to get rid of a bad government is to elect a better one, which Robertson (1989, p. 402) in *Freedom, the Individual and the Law* describes as 'a counsel of despair'. And the Conservatives claimed a mandate for their policies and seemed blind to the constitutional implications of their own authoritarianism and partisanship or the need to improve accountability in central government.

Nevertheless, in the 1980s, a number of reforms of a constitutional kind was introduced. Reforms of local government have increased efficiency and effectiveness, but they have also undermined that tier of government, reducing the degree of pluralism in the system and the scope for local accountability (see Chapter 5). Current reforms of the civil service through the establishment of executive agencies are designed to improve efficiency, but they too create problems over accountability (see Chapter 4).

In 1990, Labour's attitude to constitutional reform began to change. The party reacted to pressures from Scotland for a Parliament by adopting a policy of decentralization to Scotland, Wales and the regions of England (see Chapter 6). Labour, the Conservatives and the Liberal Democrats agree that decentralization to Northern Ireland would be desirable, but is impossible unless the people of the province are willing to acquiesce, which for two decades they have not. Labour also advocates reform of the second chamber (see Chapter 3) and of local government (see Chapter 5). But the party remains opposed to a Bill of Rights, preferring a series of specific measures for the protection from discrimination, freedom of information and other reforms, which it calls a 'Charter of Rights' (see Chapter 9). The party began to consider electoral reform for regional and national assemblies and the reformed second chamber. But it has been reluctant to contemplate proportional representation for the House of Commons or local government (see Chapter 8).

Northern Ireland

Northern Ireland is a part of the UK which suffers from special problems, deriving from its history and the divisions between the communities there. Alone among the countries of the UK, Northern Ireland had a system of devolved government from 1925 to 1972 (Buckland, 1981). In practice, the system was dominated by one party, representing one section of the population, the Protestant, unionist majority. The majority exercised their powers so as to exclude the Catholic population from political influence, and to discriminate against them in employment, housing and other services (for an account, see McCrudden, 1989). Many members of the Catholic minority identified with the neighbouring Republic of Ireland rather than with the community in the province. The province, then, has been plagued by sectarian divisions and, since the 1970s, by sectarian violence. Divisions have been such that direct rule has had to be imposed from Whitehall since 1972. Successive efforts to secure agreement on government in the province foundered because of the lack of a sense of common citizenship between the Protestant and Catholic communities (Bew and Patterson, 1985; McCrudden, 1989, pp. 323–41). The outcome of the Government's initiative in the summer of 1991 was failure.

It should not surprise readers to know that it is not one of the purposes of this book to put forward a solution to the Northern Ireland problem. But experience of the implications of a divided community in the province serves to highlight the responsibility of government to adopt policies that will promote a sense of citizenship and community – antidiscrimination legislation and proportional representation for example – and the tragic consequences that can flow from the absence of such a sense. The importance of effective mechanisms for holding government to account for its actions in such a way as to promote the welfare of the whole community and not the interests of particular sections, is also illustrated by experience in Northern Ireland.

International dimensions

It is important to put debates about the UK constitution and possible reforms in an international context. The failures of the post-war settlement, though they were important influences in bringing into question the workings of the UK constitution, have not been the only factors at work. The international climate has played a major role. The formation of the United Nations Organization in the aftermath of the Second World War, followed by the adoption of Covenants on Civil and Political Rights, emphasized international interest in political systems. The adoption of the European Convention on Human Rights by the Council of Europe, in the drafting of which the British played a major role, was another landmark in the process of internationalization of constitutions, which has been reflected in a growing interest in the protection of civil and political rights in the UK from the mid-1960s. These developments in the international scene have affected not only the international obligations of the UK, but also the climate of opinion at home, by raising concern and consciousness about civil, political and social rights.

The European Community, subsidiarity and the constitution

In 1973, the UK joined the European Economic Community. This was another major milestone in the internationalization of UK constitutional law. It had the immediate effect of bringing a large body of law made outside the realm into the legal systems of the Kingdom. It brought those systems into contact with the quite different European legal tradition. These changes have had a profound impact. In particular, they have undermined the 'cornerstone' of the UK constitution, the legislative sovereignty of Parliament.

Although there are complex legal arguments about whether or in what sense the Westminster Parliament retains its legislative sovereignty since the UK joined the European Community (Bradley, 1989; Collins, 1990), the practical reality is that it is now no longer politically or economically possible for the UK to behave as an entirely independent sovereign state for as long as it remains in the community. This, in turn, raises issues about the institutions of the European Community, their accountability and effectiveness, since they exercise considerable power over the policies of member states. These issues took on major political significance from the autumn of 1990 when the Conservative government appeared divided about the degree to which it was prepared to progress towards economic and political union with other Community states given the difficulties experienced in the Community in agreeing on policies and reforming agricultural policy and other areas. On the one hand, the Prime Minister was unwilling to abdicate sovereignty to an organization which seemed unable to act effectively, while on the other, the Deputy Prime Minister, Sir Geoffrey Howe, who resigned over the matter, did not want to see the country missing the European train.

The UK's membership of the European Economic Community, then, has transferred some of what were the powers of the government and Parliament 'upwards' to the Community institutions. This raises questions about a principle that is influential in the Constitutions of some member states and in the thinking of the Community, i.e. 'subsidiarity' (Wilke and Wallace, 1990; House of Lords Select Committee on the European Communities Twenty-Seventh Report, 1989–90, paras 23, 24, 165; Kapteyn, 1990; Pontier, 1986). This is essentially a socio-political term rather than a legal or constitutional principle (Wilke and Wallace, 1990. para. 13). Although there are a range of ways of expressing the principle (see, e.g. Kapteyn, 1990), it is sufficient for our purposes to adopt the *Oxford English Dictionary* definition: 'a central authority should have a subsidiary function, performing only those tasks which cannot be performed effectively at a more immediate or local level' (OED definition adopted by the House of Lords Select Committee on the European Communities). Although this cannot yet be said to be a principle of Community law, it is recognized in, for example, Article 130 of the Treaty of Rome, which allows the Community to act only where this would achieve the relevant objective better than action by individual member states. The principle is based on the assumption that government can be both more effective and more accountable to those affected by its actions if its functions are discharged at the lowest possible level.

The principle of subsidiarity is not only a consideration in relations between member states and the Community; it also plays a part in the constitutions of some member states, particularly that of Germany, where the *Länder* are guaranteed the right to regulate on their own responsibility all the affairs of the local community within the limits set by law (Article 28 of the German Basic Law). Article 91a of the German Basic Law provides that the Federation shall participate in the discharge of certain responsibilities of the *Länder*, provided that such responsibilities are important to society as a whole and that federal participation is necessary for the improvement of living conditions. Otherwise, by implication, the federal government may not interfere in *Land* government (for a discussion of subsidiarity in the French Constitution since the reforms of 1982, see Pontier, 1986, pp. 1533–7).

The principle of subsidiarity is influential in the discussions about decentralization to national and regional governments in the UK (see Chapter 6). It also appears in consideration of local government – there is no reason why the levels of government to which functions may be devolved in accordance with the subsidiarity principle should be limited to central and national or regional levels. But we have to bear in mind that the principle is easier to state than to apply; it does not provide us with the means for deciding whether any particular function – education for example – is better performed at a central or local level. And many of the functions of government have a range of aspects, some of which can be performed more effectively at one level than another. For example, the raising of revenue to finance education and the setting of standards could arguably be better done by central than local government; but the actual provision of schools might be better left to the localities.

Another problem with this subsidiarity principle is that the mere allocation of functions to a lower tier of government rather than to the centre cannot prevent the centre taking an interest in how the functions are discharged. In the UK system, it is legally possible for central government to use its majority in Parliament to intervene in the conduct of local government, thus undermining (or even increasing) subsidiarity. Without some constitutional protection in the form of entrenchment (see Chapter 11), a commitment on the part of a government to subsidiarity could not be guaranteed any permanence or stability, since a later government could always go back on it. Despite the difficulties with this principle, it has the endorsement of the Liberal Democrats (1991, p. 15).

A 'Europe of the Regions'?

There has been a strong trend towards regional or subnational government in a number of the member states of the European Economic Community as minorities in Belgium, the Basque country and other areas have asserted their rights to self-determination, and as regional populations, notably in France and Spain, have demanded a greater degree of control over their own affairs. The pressure for decentralization in the UK has parallels in other European countries. But an interesting dimension to regionalism in Europe which bears on the subsidiarity principle is the possible evolution of what has been called 'a Europe of the Regions' (Daltrop, 1986, ch. 9; de Rougemont, 1983).

To put this in context, there are a number of strands to thinking about regionalism in Europe. On one view, it is simply a development within member states, a tier of government activity below the European and national tiers, which reflects the subsidiarity principle, recognizing that the interests of effectiveness require that government should be conducted at the lowest level possible. On another approach, however, put most forcefully by Denis de Rougemont (1983), the nation state is the enemy of both local regionalism and European federation, imposing artificial frontiers which cut across the natural boundaries of language and culture. On this view, the nation state should be bypassed, and the principal relationships in the Community should be between regions and the institutions of the Community.

Hence regionalism is an issue both in the European Economic Community and for the member states. Some commentators feel that the Community is better placed than the national governments of member states to take an overall view of regional needs and to provide for them (Armstrong, 1989); national governments may be forced to adopt policies which are effective nationally but are not in the interests of their regions (Daltrop, 1986, p. 112).

In the long term, a system of 'international regionalism' (Daltrop, 1986, p. 119) may develop within the Community, and it could accommodate the small nationalities as well as regional interests. But despite the strong arguments in favour of European regionalism, this view of the future is highly controversial; it would further undermine the 'sovereignty' of member states and, given the 'democratic deficit' in the Community, it could leave the nations and regions exposed to decisions and policies for which there was little institutional accountability (Spencer, 1990, pp. 22–8; Toussaint, 1988). Such a development would clearly have important implications for government in the UK, some of which are considered in Chapter 6.

The 'external constitution' of the UK

Although the workings of the internal constitution of the UK – the subject of this book – remain important, they need to be seen in the context of the 'external constitution' (I am grateful to Simon Lee for this phrase) formed by our international obligations. The UK is economically, morally and, in terms of international law, legally bound by a whole host of other international treaties and obligations, relating to such matters as defence, the environment, human rights, social rights, aviation and taxation. In effect, these undermine the very concept of the sovereign nation state (Held, 1989, ch. 8). Yet the institutions of international constitutionalism are not, and do not claim to be, democratic in any sense in which domestic institutions are. Even the Parliament of the European Community, which is elected, leaves a 'democratic deficit': it has very limited powers to control the Commission and the other institutions of the Community and it has no real legislative initiative. This lack of democracy in international organizations has been a source of conflict between the UK and international organizations, especially the European Communities.

Our themes

Since accountability, effectiveness and citizenship are the themes chosen to draw together the discussion of particular aspects of the constitution in the second and third parts of this book, the next chapter will prepare the ground further by exploring the meanings of these terms. The chapters in Part II are concerned with the scope for reform of important institutions in the constitution, and look separately at Parliament, the civil service, local government, devolution to a Scottish Assembly and assemblies in Wales, Northern Ireland and English regions and the system of justice.

Running parallel with proposals for institutional reform, there is another debate about the need to revitalize and reform the political process itself. The chapters in Part III are concerned with that aspect of the subject, and consider the three main issues in this area – electoral reform, a Bill of Rights and open government.

The final part considers some of the issues raised by proposals for the adoption of a written Constitution; and in the last chapter the threads of the arguments about the need to improve accountability, effectiveness and citizenship in the UK will be drawn together.

2

Accountability, effectiveness and citizenship

As indicated in Chapter 1, a number of themes recur in the criticisms of the system of government that have emerged since the Second World War and the proposals that have been advanced for constitutional reform. Of these, the most prominent are the need to enhance responsiveness and accountability in government, a desire to increase effectiveness and efficiency, and the search for a modern concept of citizenship.

Given the importance of these three themes in discussions of the constitution, it will be helpful to consider what accountability, effectiveness and citizenship involve and why they are important, indeed central, to the UK constitution, before proceeding in the next two sections of this book to discuss particular aspects of the working of the system and proposals that have been made for its reform.

Accountability

Accountability has been said to entail being liable to be required to give an account or explanation of actions and, where appropriate, to suffer the consequences, take the blame or undertake to put matters right if it should appear that errors have been made. In other words, it is explanatory and amendatory (Turpin, 1990, pp. 421–2). Accountability is therefore closely related to responsibility, transparency, answerability and responsiveness, and these terms are often used interchangeably.

Accountability is the solution to the problem of fallibility referred to in Chapter 1 around which the liberal-democratic tradition has been built up: if nobody is infallible and no particular substantive policy can be assumed to be right, then it is essential that the constitution and the processes – the rules of the game – that it entails, recognize these factors and provide safeguards against bad government. Decision makers must be obliged to justify their acts and not be allowed to rely on claims that their rightness is to be assumed. Alternative policies must be permitted to be advanced to highlight the fact that claims that 'there is no alternative' may be flawed. There must be provision for matters to be put right when things have gone wrong. The procedures and mechanisms for making processes of accountability effective are therefore central concerns of a liberal-democratic constitution.

An important question that needs to be addressed before we turn to discuss different forms of accountability is: What is a public body or organization accountable for? It is a constitutional commonplace that ministers are accountable, in the senses that they must defend and justify, explain and make amends for, everything that happens in their departments. But accountability furthers important objectives. It is supposed to promote wise government, efficiency in policy implementation and success in achieving the objectives set by government. On yet another level of abstraction, we should ask: To what ultimate end is accountability imposed on government? What does wisdom in government mean? What sorts of rationales for government policy and action are regarded as legitimate? Does policy have to be humanitarian, popular, egalitarian, just?

The answers to these questions depend on the subject matter of the policy at issue. The values of egalitarianism, popularity and justice will frequently clash. Some decisions may be justified simply by reference to whether they are popular or not – what name should be given to a new parliamentary constituency or a local authority for example. But 'the wishes of the majority' or the popularity of a policy is often a dangerous basis for state action. And any suggestion that it is legitimate for a government to do whatever it wants to do simply because it has been elected or because those policies were set out in its manifesto, is bound to be met with powerful and plausible objections on liberal-democratic grounds.

So, ultimately, as suggested in Chapter 1, in the British liberal-democratic tradition it is for their stewardship of the public interest that state institutions are in practice most commonly accountable, and by this criterion that they are judged. So in considering questions such as 'to whom is a minister to be accountable and by what mechanism is accountability to be imposed?', it is important not to lose sight of the fact that the public interest is the ultimate legitimating justification for government, and accountability should promote this.

Political accountability

It is helpful when analysing accountability to distinguish four classes of body to whom accountability is owed. First, there is accountability to the politicians of this world – ministers, the Houses of Parliament and their committees, and local authorities. Ministers are accountable to Parliament, the prime minister and the Cabinet; civil servants to ministers; local authorities to government and Parliament. The point about this form of accountability is that it exposes the bodies to politically motivated control, to public censure through elected institutions – the House of Commons or local authorities – or to electoral risk.

We should also note that the sanctions where the machinery of political accountability imposes a duty to make amends are not generally legally coercive but political: a minister's duty to undertake to put things right or to resign is a matter of convention rather than law.

It is necessary to distinguish between different subcategories of political accountability, particularly between accountability to ministers and accountability to Parliament and its committees. Accountability to ministers (of civil servants and local authorities for example) is open to be used, or abused, by ministers for partisan purposes – to protect their own position or that of the government for example – unless there are effective checks in place to prevent such abuses, which under the system as it operates at present there are not. The accountability of bodies to Parliament (for example, the accountability of bodies in receipt of public funds to the Public Accounts Committee), on the other hand, is less likely to provide opportunities for the promotion of partisan interests and more likely to be directed towards promoting the general public interest.

It will be one of the arguments in this book that political accountability is not always as effective as it should be. It is too easy for public bodies to avoid giving an account of their actions or making amends if found to be at fault. Many of the reforms discussed in later chapters are designed to improve political accountability – electoral reform, access to official information, decentralization and other measures would all have this effect.

Political accountability, as it operates in the UK, is not always the most suitable form of accountability. Although under the rubric 'ministerial responsibility' it is supposed to be a cornerstone of the constitution, it has had both a centralizing and a politicizing effect on the system of government (Johnson, 1977).

The responsibility of the UK Government to Parliament is supposed to secure that the general public interest is promoted: it is not sensitive to the fact that the nations and regions of the UK may have differing public interests. A wider range of public interests could be accommodated if there were elected organs representing the nations and regions; if, in other words, the principle of subsidiarity were recognized in the system (see Chapters 1 and 6).

Through the convention that bodies exercising functions on behalf of government or financed from government funds should be accountable to Parliament through a minister, Whitehall and Westminster have gathered increasing powers to themselves. These have all too often been exercised for party political and partisan purposes or in ways that undermine their efficiency and effectiveness. Government and, to a lesser extent, Parliament have the power to assert authority over many institutions that do not strictly form part of central government – local authorities, nationalized industries, the British Broadcasting Corporation (BBC) – and these 'intermediate institutions' have all had their autonomy, efficiency and effectiveness eroded, directly or indirectly, through the constitutional attachment to ministerial accountability (Grant, 1989).

The point that political accountability is by no means always appropriate is well illustrated by the case of the judiciary (see Chapter 7). The judges are constitutionally insulated from political accountability for the way in which particular cases are decided and this position is a well-learned lesson from constitutional history. But it does not follow from this that no accountability should be imposed on judges, or on those responsible for the system of justice. There are, as we shall see, a range of forms of accountability and within each form a variety of particular mechanisms, and an important aspect of the constitution is securing that the most appropriate forms of accountability are applied to public bodies.

Public accountability

Secondly, there is accountability to the general public or to interested sections of the public. Ministers, Members of Parliament, councillors and other public officials are in practice under obligation to explain and justify their actions to the public, and may find themselves obliged through pressures of criticism and embarrassment to make amends where errors have been made. Elected bodies are publicly accountable through the ballot box.

But 'the public' is not monolithic. There are different publics with different needs and wishes in the nations and regions of the UK; and yet, with the exception of a weak tier of local government, there are not in the political system the institutions to respond to these different publics. This is one aspect of the systems for imposing public accountability, to which we shall return in Chapter 6.

The effectiveness of accountability to the public or publics depends on the availability of information. An ill-informed public cannot hold government to account for its care of the public interest. Hence the freedom of the media to report on matters of public interest, public rights of access to official information and freedom of speech are crucial to the effectiveness of this form of accountability (see Chapter 10).

'Consumer' accountability is a relatively new form of accountability to the public that has been developing in the last decade or so. As we shall see in Chapters 4 and 5, the Conservative government took steps in the 1980s to increase the influence of consumers of public services over their quality and method of delivery, e.g. by introducing choice, providing information and giving consumer representatives (parents of school children) rights to participate in decisions (on school governing bodies for instance). The desirability of strengthening the position of consumers of public services is now recognized across the political spectrum, with Labour and the Liberal Democrats both putting forward proposals to improve this form of accountability (see Chapter 5) and the Conservatives producing *The Citizen's Charter* which prescribes standards of service and even entitles consumers to compensation if services do not come up to an agreed standard (1991).

The sanctions available to the public through which they can give 'teeth' to mechanisms of public accountability range from transfer of 'custom' elsewhere ('exit'), the withholding of electoral support, which can effectively deprive government of its majority, and even payment of compensation.

As with political accountability, public accountability is not always the appropriate form. Some matters must be kept confidential and therefore immune from public scrutiny (certain matters to do with national security, the detection and prevention of crime, sensitive foreign relations). Consumer accountability can undermine the ability of government to provide services efficiently and effectively if it subordinates the general public interest to the interests of consumers (see discussion in Chapter 5). Nor is it necessarily in the public interest that a government should owe particular duties of accountability to sectional interests within the public. So the design of constitutional mechanisms should be such as to secure that public accountability does not undermine efficiency and effectiveness, and that it does not promote sectional interests at the expense of the general public interest.

Legal accountability

Thirdly, there is accountability to the courts. The legal accountability of public bodies is an important aspect of the rule of law in the UK constitution. The duty to obey the law, enforceable by action in the courts at the instigation of those affected by the actions of public bodies, imposes an obligation on a public body to explain and justify its actions in legal terms if sued in the courts and to make amends if found to have transgressed.

This is not the place for an exposition of the complex subject of judicial review (see Wade, 1988; see also Chapter 7), but the legal accountability of public bodies needs to be put in perspective in this discussion. In important respects, it differs from that of the private sector. Public bodies, or more precisely bodies exercising public functions, have many special legal powers – to grant and refuse licences, to levy taxation, to acquire property compulsorily and so on. But they are also subject to special legal duties to secure both that their actions are lawful in a narrow, technical sense, and that their discretionary powers are exercised fairly and rationally (per Lord Diplock in *Council of Civil Service Unions* v. *Minister for the Civil Service* [1985] AC 374; see Chapter 7). This duty extends to private bodies exercising public functions, such as professional organizations and regulatory bodies in the City of London (*R*. v. *Panel on Takeovers and Mergers, Ex parte Datafin* [1987] QB 815), but it does not generally bind private bodies: I am happily under no general legal duty to be rational or fair in my relations with my family and friends, with shopkeepers or in my commercial transactions. Public bodies and other exercising public functions also enjoy certain privileges from legal actions that are not enjoyed by private bodies (Woolf, 1986).

An important respect in which legal accountability differs from other forms is that the remedies and sanctions are coercive: although the sanctions are discretionary, generally public bodies can be compelled by the courts to perform their legal duties and to refrain from unlawful acts.

As with political and public accountability, legal accountability is not always the appropriate form. There are, as we shall see in Chapter 7, problems over whether judges are competent to decide on the legality of government action and whether political accountability is therefore more appropriate (discussed in Chapters 7, 9 and 11). Certain matters are said not to be 'justiciable' (*Council of Civil Service Unions* v. *Minister for the Civil Service* [1985] AC 374) – for example, disputes about national security, diplomatic matters, foreign affairs – and this is generally recognized by the courts.

Administrative accountability

Finally, there is administrative accountability: what is embraced under this head is the duty to account to non-political bodies such as the Commissioner for Local Administration (the local government 'Ombudsman'), the Audit Commission, the Efficiency Unit and various other bodies concerned for the most part with matters such as efficiency, effectiveness, value for money and fairness to consumers. Other administrative bodies – for example, the Comptroller and Auditor General, the National Audit Office, the Parliamentary Commissioner for Administration – are linked in with political accountability: the Comptroller and Auditor General works with the Public Accounts Committee and the Parliamentary Commissioner for Administration with a select committee on the PCA. Here the link between accountability and our second theme, the need to improve efficiency and effectiveness, is clear, and administrative accountability will therefore be discussed further in the next section of this chapter.

As we shall see, especially in Chapters 4 and 5, this form of accountability relies on the development of administrative law, not of the kind that involves judicial review, as with legal accountability, but other mechanisms such as the use of standards, guidelines and codes of practice, tribunals and inquiries and various forms of audit, internal review, appeal and complaints procedures and performance indicators.

Administrative bodies often have coercive powers to gain access to documents and information about the matters under investigation. But the sanctions in administrative accountability are not generally legally coercive: the recommendations of the Parliamentary Commissioner for Administration and the Commissioner for Local Administration (the Ombudsmen) are advisory only. The Comptroller and Auditor General and the National Audit Office, in their reports on value for money, cannot impose legal sanctions. But they are taken very seriously by government departments. The principal weapons of these agencies are publicity and embarrassment, and so there are links here with public and political accountability. These are often backed up by political pressures. The Select Committee for the Parliamentary Commissioner can apply pressure on ministers to comply with the Commissioner's recommendations, and in practice this is usually effective. The Public Accounts Committee also has strong influence in securing that notice is taken of the reports of the National Audit Office.

Often, accountability is imposed in more than one form and to several bodies, e.g. local authorities are publicly accountable to their electors, politically accountable to central government (which provides the bulk of their funds), administratively accountable to the District Auditor and the Commissioner for Local Administration, and legally accountable to the courts.

Accountability, then, is about constructing a framework for the exercise of state power in a liberal-democratic system, within which public bodies are forced to seek to promote the public interest and compelled to justify their actions in those terms or in other constitutionally acceptable terms (justice, humanity, equity); to modify policies if they should turn out not to have been well conceived; and to make amends if mistakes and errors of judgement have been made. The question of to whom accountability is owed is often crucial, as is the design of the mechanisms of accountability, to the good working of the constitution. Choices have to be made about the balance between the different forms of accountability – whether legal accountability is to be preferred to political accountability, or whether a number of forms of accountability can operate in parallel.

Efficiency and effectiveness

The second theme in discussions of reform of government has been the need to increase the efficiency and effectiveness of the system. But before discussing the place of efficiency and effectiveness in the constitution, a preliminary point needs to be got out of the way – the fact that these two desiderata have found a special place in the debates about constitutional reform should not be taken to mean that they are necessarily to be regarded as more important than, for example, accountability, citizenship, substantive social rights, or civil and political rights. Although some of the reforms introduced by the Conservative government in the 1980s in the name of efficiency and effectiveness were primarily aimed at cost-cutting rather than promoting quality and they arguably undermined citizenship or public accountability (the increased legal regulation and erosion of the financial autonomy of local government for example), it is not inevitable that efficiency and effectiveness should only be achievable at the expense of other important values; indeed, they should enhance them.

Sir Douglas Wass (1984, p. 5) has eloquently placed what might seem a tedious aspect of the constitution in place in the debates about the constitution in the following terms:

> As I pondered over the essential requirements of a good system of government I found I could narrow them down to two ideas, efficiency and responsiveness. It may seem odd to elevate efficiency to such a level of importance in considering anything so fundamental to the human condition as government, but I am using the term in a very broad sense. For me

efficiency means that actions, decisions are taken in a rational and systematic way; that internal conflicts and inconsistencies are brought to the surface and resolved; and that objectives are defined and optimal means employed to secure them.

The implication is that unless a process is adopted that conforms to these criteria, the impact of policy in the sense of its success in achieving ends will be weakened.

Wass has also looked at the efficiency of the policy-making process which, as indicated in Chapter 1, has not produced solutions to many of our worst problems since the end of the Second World War. He has emphasized how important it is that there should be effective safeguards against 'arbitrary and inefficient policy-making by the government' (Wass, 1987), and as we shall see in Chapter 4 he has put forward a number of proposals for improving the safeguards, including a Freedom of Information Act to make public comment and participation in the policy process possible, official help for the Opposition, reformed parliamentary procedures and independent administrative bodies (a proposal the spirit of which is reflected in the setting up of *Next Steps* agencies by central government; see Chapter 4). We can see from these examples that effectiveness and accountability are closely related.

Looked at from these perspectives, efficiency is clearly critical to the operation of government – there is no point in having a government whose task is to solve the problems of the nation if it does not adopt working practices which promote that objective.

What are efficiency and effectiveness?

There are differences of usage in employing the terms 'efficiency' and 'effectiveness' in the literature. In the passage quoted above, Sir Douglas Wass uses the term efficiency where others might prefer effectiveness. The Widdicombe Report (1986) on the 'Conduct of Local Authority Business' uses the terms the other way round from Wass. It points out that 'there is an important distinction between efficiency and effectiveness. Efficiency is concerned solely with output, effectiveness is concerned also with the meeting of needs' (Widdicombe, 1986, para. 3.26). The Sub-Committee of the Treasury and Civil Service Committee adopted similar definitions and distinctions in using the terms. By the effectiveness of a programme, the sub-committee understood 'such matters as the definition of objectives, the measurement of progress towards achieving these objectives and the consideration of alternative means of achieving objectives'. This approach resembles in some respects that of Sir Douglas Wass to what he called efficiency. Effectiveness was distinguished from efficiency by which the sub-committee understood 'given the objectives and the means chosen to pursue the objectives the minimising of inputs to the programme in relation to the outputs from it' (HC 236, 1981–82, para. 1). Here efficiency is not at all what Sir Douglas Wass intended in his use of the term. On the sub-committee's definitions, effectiveness is concerned with the policy-making process, strategy and the monitoring of policy implementation where successive governments have had a poor record, being ill-prepared for office while in opposition and unable to develop successful policies while in office (see Chapter 4). Efficiency is largely an operational matter of institutional design and control.

The definitions used by the sub-committee will be broadly adopted in this work. But despite the range of meanings that are attached to these concepts, precision in their use is not essential if one keeps in view the reasons why they are important to the system. These are to secure that the efforts to solve national problems have a chance of success, and to protect organizations and individuals from misguided government activity.

Effectiveness and accountability

A range of approaches to promoting efficiency and effectiveness has been developed; as with accountability, it is important that inappropriate mechanisms should not be applied, that the right techniques should be found for each particular body. One method of promoting effectiveness is to increase accountability. However, as we saw in the previous section, certain forms of accountability can have negative as well as positive implications for effectiveness in administration. On the positive side, the pressures imposed on institutions by the need to justify their actions politically, administratively, publicly or legally should secure that they take care to be efficient and to identify their objectives and pursue them effectively. But on the negative side, political accountability, if it is taken to justify or excuse ministerial or party political interference in the operations of institutions, can damage the efficiency of the performance of the body under scrutiny, since it is not always in the interests of politicians that bodies under their direction perform efficiently and effectively. The point may be illustrated by reference to experience with the nationalized industries in the post-war period up to the 1980s: ministerial powers to give directions to these bodies as to their investment, purchasing and pricing policies often interfered with their profitability and their ability to produce efficiently (National Economic Development Office, 1976; Redwood and Hatch, 1982). The desire to get away from this interventionist relationship, together with the belief that the status of management needed to be enhanced, formed part of the rationale for the privatization of industries in the 1980s (Veljanowski, 1987, ch. 1).

The establishment of executive agencies in Whitehall (see Chapter 4), which will immunize administrations from ministerial meddling, reflects acceptance of the disadvantages of some forms of political accountability. So attention has turned in the last decade to the development of various forms of administrative accountability, using internal and external audit of matters of value for money, efficiency and effectiveness which can improve performance outside the sphere of political accountability. *The Citizen's Charter* (1991, Cm. 1599) uses consumer accountability to promote efficiency and effectiveness.

Subsidiarity – the allocation of responsibility to bodies as close to the people affected by actions as possible – also has implications for effectiveness. In theory, it should promote accountability; the assumption is often made that it should also increase efficiency and effectiveness. But here, too, accountability and effectiveness can undermine one another. To devolve responsibility to small units of or within local government, for example, should increase the accountability of those bodies to local people; but it could also increase costs and make for inefficiency if it meant that a full range of services (e.g. for the disabled, the homeless, problem families) could not be provided within a small locality or that they could only be provided at a high price. As we shall see in Chapter 5, these considerations have arisen in relation to decentralization in local government.

The 1980s, then, saw the development of a range of processes for improving the efficiency of central government and other public bodies outside the conventions of ministerial responsibility (Drewry and Butcher, 1988, ch. 10). It is too early for these to be assessed, but they raise issues about the relationship between different forms of accountability, and its relationship with efficiency and effectiveness which will be discussed in Chapters 3, 4, 5 and 10.

Citizenship

Citizenship, the third theme that runs through discussions of the working of the UK system of government and how it might be reformed, has a wide range of meanings. It is a social, political and legal status: in common usage, it describes the relationship between the individual and the various communities that make up the nation and involves rights and duties. But it is not simply a matter of status; it is also a practice, in the sense that it implies the active participation of the individual in the community, and especially in the political process (Oldfield, 1990a,b; Fishman, 1989).

Our concern in this work is primarily with the role of the law and the design of political institutions, and how they can promote a conception of citizenship that is appropriate to the needs of the UK. We cannot discuss except in passing other ways in which citizenship may be promoted, for example through education, important though this is (see Heater, 1990, chs 5, 9; Speaker's Commission, 1990, esp. pp. 37–8, apps E,H; National Curriculum Council, 1990).

It will be convenient in this discussion to consider separately what is involved in citizenship as a practice, the sense of citizenship and national identity, and the rights and duties of the citizen and the state as they bear on the institutions and political processes of the constitution and issues of accountability and effectiveness.

The practice of citizenship

The individual who participates in local or national politics, through membership of a political party or a pressure group, for example, is practicing citizenship in a political sense. But much activity in the community is of a non-political kind – membership of rugby clubs, churches, school and university communities is not in the ordinary way political in nature. Activity in such organizations has relevance for citizenship none the less, since it serves to give the individual experience of participation in group and communal activity which is useful when it comes to political participation; and it also serves to foster senses of social cohesion and solidarity which are vital to citizenship. It is important, too, in establishing a 'civil society' independent of the state, thereby contributing to pluralism and a dispersal of power, important attributes of a liberal-democratic system.

Citizenship, then, can be practised on a wide range of levels: nationally or locally; through political parties or pressure groups and campaigning organizations; in the public or private sphere. Our prime concern will be with the public aspect of citizenship, but we must bear in mind the importance not only of the ways in which citizenship may be practised in these private activities, but also of the importance of reserving certain aspects of the individual's life to a 'citizenship-free zone', where he or she is free of duties to the community. In a liberal-democratic system, a line needs to be drawn between the individual's public life, his or her relationship with the state and the community, and his or her right to a private life, free from state intrusion: 'A society which inflates citizenship so that it expands to occupy the total area of an individual's life is indeed in danger of becoming totalitarian' (Heater, 1990, pp. 319–20). It is in recognition of the dangers of this that certain legal rights or freedoms (to marry, to practise religion) protect the dignity and autonomy of the individual in a field which does not raise issues about the relationship between the individual and the community.

The relationship between citizens and the state should be such as to promote accountability and effective government; the mechanisms for promoting accountability and effectiveness depend for their effectiveness to a large extent on 'political due process', the involvement of members of the public, and the willingness of government to permit and respond to their involvement (Fishman, 1989, p. 442). The rights of citizens to vote in elections, to comment critically on government policy and to put forward alternatives should all promote accountability and effectiveness. If citizens do not contribute in these ways, we cannot expect good government. It is important, then, that citizens exercise these rights and make use of opportunities to participate in the political process.

Citizens also have a role to play in giving service to the community; this is most obvious in the willingness of individuals to stand for election to Parliament and in local government, but it is also found in the magistracy, and in work in voluntary agencies. If there is not a strong body of citizens prepared to give their services in this way, we would find ourselves governed by bureaucrats and limited in our ability to affect the way the system worked.

But for there to be a sufficient supply of citizens willing to discharge these functions, there has to be what Heater (1990, ch. 5.2) has called a sense of 'civic virtue', a moral sense of duty to the polis and commitment to the community. Another way of expressing it is 'active citizenship', which has become a favoured expression among Conservative politicians since the late 1980s (see, e.g. D. Hurd, *The Independent*, 13 September 1989; J. MacGregor, *The Independent*, 17 February 1990; J. Patten, *The Guardian*, 5 May 1990). This brings us to the important subject of the rights and duties involved in citizenship.

The rights and duties of the citizen and the state

'Active citizenship' is a controversial subject. For Douglas Hurd, then Home Secretary, it involved 'the free acceptance by individuals of voluntary obligations to the community of which they are members. . . . Freedom will flourish where citizens accept responsibility' (*The Independent*, 13 September 1989). He cited 'neighbourhood watch' schemes as useful examples of active citizenship, which could 'rekindle a sense of local identity and a belief that determined action can reduce crime' (ibid.). Hurd argued that while public service may once have been the duty of an élite, now it was the responsibility of all who have time or money to spare. He traced active citizenship back to 'the traditions of civic obligation and voluntary service which are . . . rooted in our history'. They were also 'central to the thinking of this government' (ibid.).

While there is in this conception of citizenship a welcome recognition of the effectiveness and importance of community spirit and self-help on the part of individuals and groups, there is reason to fear that a strong attraction of the idea was that it provided an alternative to state provision of benefits and essential services, what Marshall has termed the 'social element' of citizenship (see Chapter 1 and below). Looked at in this way, it could be a controversial party political conception of citizenship, since it raises issues about the duty of the state to its citizens.

Despite the fact that the Conservative version of 'active citizenship' has these controversial overtones, the members of the Speaker's Commission on Citizenship, a cross-party group, agreed that it was the duty of government to provide a 'floor of entitlements' (Speaker's Commission, 1990, p. 21), and asserted that 'in no sense should voluntary bodies partly or wholly reliant on fundraising and voluntary help take over elements of the core work of the public services' (ibid., p. 36). The area of dispute between the parties is probably more about what the floor and the core are than about the existence of the duty in principle.

Hurd rejected the claim that the encouragement of voluntary service amounted to a 'shuffling off' of state responsibilities. His case was that there are a myriad of needs that are *not* best met by the state bureaucracy; that voluntary schemes can be more precise and flexible than state schemes. There is, it is suggested, considerable truth in this. Other Conservative spokespersons have expressed similar views (J. MacGregor, *The Independent*, 17 February 1990; J. Patten, *The Guardian*, 5 May 1990), and in principle Labour and the Liberal Democrats also accept the importance of the citizen's willingness to be active in the community.

But although Hurd's vision of citizenship had many positive qualities, it was only a very partial vision. No attention was paid to the citizen's rights, or to the obligations of the state to the citizen in providing protection for civil, political and, as indicated above, social rights. Nor was there recognition of the importance of the 'private' side of the life of the individual and the need for this to be free from undue burdens which remove from people the opportunity for personal fulfilment: one implication of the merits of self-help might be that the care of the old and ill should fall on individuals, not on the community in any real sense. It is this aspect of 'active citizenship' that has attracted most controversy.

What of the legal rights and duties of the citizen? There is no explicit legal status of citizenship in the UK in the sense in which we are considering it here. In English legal usage, citizenship is connected with immigration law (the British Nationality Act 1981 established the following categories: British Citizen, British Dependent Territories Citizen, British Overseas Citizen, British Subject and British Protected Person; the Immigration Act 1971 distinguished between patrial and non-patrial immigrants; for a discussion, see Dummett and Nicol, 1990; for a brief summary of the position, see Wade and Bradley, 1985, ch. 25). The various grades of British citizenship are concerned with the right to enter and remain in the UK. These rights do not themselves give even the full British citizen any rights other than the right to come and go from the UK and, in certain circumstances, to vote – even that right is shared with many who are not British citizens. The legal status known as 'citizenship', then, is negative rather than positive, and Gardner (1990, p. 65) has gone so far as to suggest that 'immunity from the various disabilities which attach to alien status provides a "definition" of the content of British citizenship'.

Individuals benefit from many rights regardless of whether they are legally British citizens (see Chapter 9). Non-British citizens living in the UK (EC nationals and others) receive public services such as education, health services and housing. Citizens of the Republic of Ireland have the right to vote in UK elections. Rights to participate in the political process do not depend to any great extent on being a British citizen. In this respect, '. . . during the last forty years the United Kingdom has moved away from the nationality citizenship model' (Gardner, 1990, p. 68). This trend reflects what may be termed the 'internationalization' of citizenship and the constitution, referred to in Chapter 1.

Despite the absence of an explicit legal status of citizenship outside the ambit of immigration law, citizenship in our sense does have considerable legal content. In identifying that content, it is convenient to go back to what is still the seminal work on the subject, the set of lectures delivered in 1950 by T. H. Marshall, Professor of Social Institutions in the University of London, entitled *Citizenship and Social Class* (see also Giddens, 1981, 1982, 1984; Held, 1989, ch. 7). Marshall divided citizenship into three parts: political, civil and social. By the political element of citizenship he meant the right to participate in the exercise of political power as a voter, or as an elected member of Parliament or a local authority. By civil citizenship he referred to the rights necessary for individual freedom – liberty of the person, freedom of speech, thought and faith, the right to own property, and the right to justice or access to the courts.

Marshall's third aspect of citizenship was the social element, 'by which I mean the whole range from the right to a modicum of economic welfare and security to the right to share to the full in the social heritage and to live the life of a civilised being according to the standards prevailing in society' (Marshall, 1950, p. 11). Marshall saw the welfare state as the guarantor of this social element. It was legally enforceable social rights which gave practical content to the legal and political rights of the citizen, by making it possible for civil and political rights to be exercised and for the citizen to participate in society. It is this social element which many feel to be under threat from government exhortation to 'active citizenship'.

Marshall's version of citizenship has come to be referred to as 'the citizenship of entitlement', since it lays stress on the importance of the citizen's rights to these elements. As Dahrendorf (1988, pp. 117–18) has put it, citizenship 'is above all a set of entitlements, rights. Rights lose their quality if they become conditional . . . citizenship rights . . . stipulate unconditional entitlements, and . . . any condition detracts from their quality.

Although as indicated above aspects of the social element of citizenship have been eroded in the last decade or more, there is renewed interest in the three main political parties in finding ways of improving the quality of public services. Leaving aside issues about how much should be spent on these services, an issue on which the parties are divided, there is growing recognition of the scope for improving quality by various forms of audit (a form of administrative accountability discussed above) and by giving members of the public express rights through the use of devices such as 'consumer contracts'. The Conservatives' *Citizen's Charter* (1991, Cm. 1599) borrows ideas from practice in some Labour-controlled local authorities, notably York (Chapter 5).

Hence citizenship, public accountability and efficiency and effectiveness are linked in this area. It is interesting to note, too, the way in which the conception of the citizen has changed from the passive recipient of public largesse of the post-war period to the active consumer, customer or client of the late twentieth-century state. But the fear is that overemphasis on the consumer-citizen may undermine the role of the individual as a member of the community and foster a sense of selfish individualism. It makes for 'happier subjects, not true citizens' (Liberal Democrats, 1991a).

Citizenship is not simply a matter of entitlement; it also involves duties to the community, and this is a controversial subject. The principal, and well-recognized, duties of the citizen include the payment of taxes, jury service and service in the armed forces. These duties are, if it comes to the crunch, legally enforceable. But in the changed political climate of the 1990s, new obligations of citizenship are being mooted, e.g. the duties to work (Mead, 1986) and to bring up one's children in acceptable ways (Oldfield, 1990b, p. 181). These duties might not be directly legally enforceable through sanctions imposed by the courts, but they could be just as effectively made compulsory through techniques such as the withholding of benefits by the state from those who do not perform them to its satisfaction.

'Civic virtue' and active citizenship are also about the duties – both social and moral – of the citizen to the community. Though in principle these are, as suggested above, necessary in a community, we must be wary of allowing enthusiasm for encouraging the acceptance by citizens of 'voluntary obligations' to the community to trespass on their individual autonomy; if, for example, eligibility for housing, or for a place at a local authority school of one's choice, or for a discretionary grant for further education, were to be conditional on the individual's performance of the 'voluntary obligations' of citizenship, we should be moving towards a very intrusive system of government. This is an area in which education and institutional design are more appropriate techniques than the imposition of legal obligations.

At the time that Marshall was writing, the civil, political and social elements of citizenship were well protected in law and respected in practice: the post-war consensus on social and economic policy extended, as indicated in Chapter 1, to constitutional matters, and the liberal-democratic tradition treats the civil and political freedoms of citizens as central to the system. However, in the last two decades or so, the elements of the citizenship of entitlement as conceived by Marshall have been eroded and the weakness of the legal and political foundations of that conception of citizenship has been exposed. As we shall see in Chapter 9, many of the civil and political rights of citizens – especially freedom of speech and association and the right of peaceful demonstration – have been limited by government legislation (the Public Order Act 1986), and by a series of decisions by the courts in the miners' strike of 1984–85 and in the Spycatcher (see Chapters 9 and 10) and Ponting (see Chapter 4) cases. The value of the right to vote has decreased, not as a result of any deliberate action by the government, but because of the changing operation of the electoral system and the distribution of support for the political parties (see Chapter 8).

The social element of the citizenship of entitlement has been eroded in various ways in the years since Marshall was writing. Attempts by government to reduce public expenditure have resulted in the reduction in the value of some cash benefits (child benefit, unemployment benefit and so on) and in the availability of others to certain classes of claimant (unemployed young people for example).

It would be inappropriate in a book about the constitution to take a view about the wisdom of substantive policy on public expenditure and the economy, and it is not suggested that these policies are 'unconstitutional'. However, it is important to recognize the implications for citizenship, especially for social cohesion, of policies that deny some members of the community the opportunity to participate in the political process and the life of the community, especially if those policies also result in the alienation of sections of the population. The phenomenon of 'Cardboard City', of homeless, penniless people sleeping rough in large numbers in the cities, suggests that there is a problem of exclusion from society by poverty. Examples could be multiplied. Any government in a free society needs to rely on voluntary cooperation with the state and obedience to the law by its citizens, and care must be taken by government that reductions in the social element do not result in alienation, which can produce in turn a subculture of crime and disorder.

The sense of citizenship and national identity

A modern concept of citizenship has to include a sense of belonging to the national, local and functional communities in the country – in other words, social cohesion. This is linked to 'active citizenship.' As Heater (1990, p. 182) has put it: 'He who has no sense of a civic bond with his fellows or of some responsibility for civic welfare is not a true citizen whatever his legal status.' We can see the implications of a lack of this sense in the troubles in Northern Ireland, and in the alienation of some members of the ethnic minorities from the mainstream of national life.

The problems posed by the need to promote this sense in the UK as a whole are likely to increase rather than decrease in the next decades. The point is illustrated by the fact that the publication of Salman Rushdie's *Satanic Verses* inflamed relations between sections of the Muslim and ethnic English, Scottish and Welsh communities. The crisis in the Gulf in 1990–91 could well have caused damaging rifts in the community. We may be embarking on an age of mass migration as famine and civil war in the Third World drive people to seek refuge in the more prosperous European countries; the opening of borders in the USSR and Eastern European countries could lead to large numbers of people seeking a future in the West. If some of these emigrants are to settle in the UK as citizens, sensitive policies will be required to foster their sense of belonging, without at the same time interfering in their rights to their own culture and way of life. Here the importance of drawing a line between the individual's life as a citizen and their private autonomy, referred to above, is clear.

But how to encourage a sense of national identity and social cohesion are complex problems for government. The extent to which the law or institutional arrangements can be drawn into the process is limited. Attempts to compel members of minority communities to abandon their own cultures and conform to local ways would both deny to individuals their right to autonomy and privacy and almost certainly be counter productive in generating resentment and alienation. A middle way between absorption and rejection has to be found. Anti-discrimination legislation and the provisions for its effective enforcement are of central importance.

Institutionally, local authorities would have a role in promoting social cohesion and good relations between communities in their areas if they were allowed the resources and freedom of action to do so. A system of decentralization to national and regional assemblies (see Chapter 6) would promote a sense of identity with the communities in those areas.

The importance of citizenship in these senses has only been recognized relatively recently in the UK legal system. The precursor to citizenship in English law was the relationship between the sovereign and the subject, which represented a form of contract under which the King gave his protection in exchange for the subject's obedience (Blackstone, 1825, vol. I, ch. 10; see also Dummett and Nicol, 1990). This relationship has now only a residual place in English law, but it has not been replaced by any very developed understanding of what the relationship between the citizen and the political community is or should be. This is a gap which needs to be filled; institutional arrangements, improvements in the rights of individuals and the openness of the political process, all have a contribution to make.

It is part of the argument of the following chapters that despite changing social and economic conditions, the civil, political and social rights of citizens remain central to the institution of citizenship. It also has an important role in promoting the other ingredients of citizenship, especially the sense of national identity and social cohesion. Access to the courts, as Marshall stressed, is a vital guarantee of rights, and often more effective than political and other forms of accountability can be in these matters. Effective antidiscrimination legislation is crucial in promoting social cohesion. As we shall see in Chapter 9, the case for a Bill of Rights rests largely on recognition of the need to enhance these aspects of citizenship. The arguments for reform of the electoral system (see Chapter 8) are based in part on recognition of the need to restore the value of the citizen's right to vote, which in turn is linked to the subject of accountability discussed above.

Institutional arrangements also have an important role in promoting citizenship, especially 'civic virtue', social cohesion and the sense of national identity. It is not easy for central government to provide the opportunities for citizen participation in the political process and community service that can promote these senses. Local government, however, is well placed to play a role here, and in Chapter 5 we shall see how it is possible for local authorities to organize themselves in a way that both fosters a local sense of community and provides an outlet for it, e.g. through the institution of neighbourhood committees. Local authorities are also in a position to encourage active citizenship, by providing the framework for 'community care' and other activities.

The relationships between accountability, effectiveness and citizenship, then, are complex. In many respects, they are mutually reinforcing, but in others one can undermine the other. In discussing constitutional reform in the following chapters, we shall be looking for ways of achieving a workable balance between them. Having sketched out what accountability, effectiveness and citizenship involve, why they are important criteria against which to measure the constitution and proposals for its reform, and how they are interrelated, we can now turn to consider the working of the system and particular proposals for institutional and political reform.

PART II
Institutions

3

Parliament

'The House of Commons needs to be impressive, and impressive it is: but its use resides not in its appearance, but in its reality' (Bagehot, 1963, p. 150). It is clear that the reality has changed in many respects since Bagehot wrote these words in 1867.

The ability of Parliament to perform its roles in protection of the citizenry and promoting effectiveness and accountability in government depends in large part on two factors. First, the procedures of the two Chambers: do they afford opportunities for backbenchers to influence government and do they give the necessary powers, coercive if need be, to enable Members of Parliament to scrutinize and criticize (or even praise) government effectively? Secondly, what may be termed the politics and the ethos of the two Houses: is there the will on the part of backbench members to exercise influence over government and what pressures are there on ministers to respond to Parliament? Party discipline is central here, for so long as one party has a majority, it can in practice count on its backbenchers to secure the winning of any vote.

We shall consider these factors in turn, but before we do so we must bear in mind that the composition of the House, particularly the balance between the parties, is crucial to the relationship between government and Parliament. This balance depends upon the level of support for the parties and the working of the electoral system, matters considered in Chapter 8. Much of our discussion in the next section of this chapter will assume that the first past the post electoral system will continue to be used for House of Commons elections. If proportional representation were to be introduced, then this would alter radically the workings of the party system and the relationship between backbenchers and government.

Our discussion of the House of Commons also assumes that no attempt will be made to entrench legislation, a Bill of Rights for example. The implications of entrenchment for the operation of Parliament are included in consideration of the second chamber, and in Chapters 9 and 11.

Parliamentary procedures: the select committees

The important role of scrutinizing government policy and administration and holding government to account for its stewardship of these functions is discharged in Parliament through a range of procedures. Policy issues are discussed in debates on the Queen's speech, ministerial statements, and on 'Opposition Days' when the opposition parties may choose the subject for debate; in the reading of bills, the policy which the bills seek to promote will also come under scrutiny. The parliamentary question is a useful device for raising individual grievances and matters of policy and administration (HC 178, 1990–91). These are used by backbenchers to extract information from departments that they would prefer not to disclose. A knowledgeable MP can use the parliamentary question to good effect.

A new balance between Parliament and the executive?

Our discussion will focus on the role of the select committees of the House of Commons in holding government to account for its policies and administration. One of the first steps taken by the House of Commons after the 1979 general election was the introduction of a new system of departmentally related select committees. The Select Committee on Procedure in its Report of 1978 (HC 588, 1977–78) had expressed the view that a new balance needed to be struck in the relationship between the executive and the House of Commons; however, they were cautious as to the extent of the shift of power from the government that should be sought. The general aim was to enable the House as a whole 'to exercise effective control and stewardship over Ministers and the expanding bureaucracy of the modern state for which they are answerable, and to make the decisions of Parliament and Government more responsive to the wishes of the electorate' (HC 588, 1977–78).

The system set up in 1979 represents an advance on what had been the patchy coverage of government business by House of Commons select committees that had grown up on an incremental basis in the late 1960s and the 1970s. But it should be seen as an evolutionary development rather than a sudden change of direction in parliamentary scrutiny of government. Under the 1979 system, there is a committee 'shadowing' most of the main government departments, and this secures nearly comprehensive coverage of government business. However, the security services are excluded from the jurisdiction of the committees. (Ewing and Gearty, 1990, pp. 175–88). The Lord Chancellor's Department and the Law Officers Departments were originally excluded because of a fear that this might lead to politicization of the judicial system. However, in 1991 the Government conceded that the orders of reference of the Home Affairs Committee should be amended to include certain matters within the responsibility of the Lord Chancellor's Department and the Law Officers, the Crown Prosecution Service and the Serious Fraud Office (Cm. 1532, p. 20. For further discussion of this point see Chapter 7).

The departmentally related select committees are supposed to enjoy a greater measure of independence from the executive than their predecessors, the idea being that independence should enhance their ability and willingness to insist that government give an account of its actions and policies and make amends or take corrective action where appropriate. Committee members are appointed by the House of Commons following selection and nomination by the Committee of Selection. However, a convention has developed that the members of the two main parties in the Committee of Selection decide which of their parties' nominees go forward for approval and they consult the whips on appointments (Drewry, 1989a, pp. 424–5). The chairman of the Liaison Committee has expressed concern that debates on the floor of the House have given the false impression that in some cases internal party discussions and the influence of the whips may have had a decisive influence on the choices made by the Committee of Selection (HC 19–i, 1989–90, Memorandum from the Chairman of the Liaison Committee, para. 16). The Procedure Committee felt that the only effective safeguard of the independence of Select Committees in the face of attempted interference from any quarter was the strength of purpose and resilience of individual Members (HC 19–I, para. 173). No better alternative system has been devised.

The members of these select committees are appointed for the duration of a Parliament and are therefore not dismissible by the whips as was the case under the previous system. Some of the committees are allowed to have one sub-committee, thus enabling them to broaden the range of issues that they can examine. And they have the right to appoint specialist advisers. This is not entirely new – the old Expenditure Committee had such a power for example. They, like the old committees, have powers to send for persons, papers and records.

By convention, the chairs are shared out between the governing party and the opposition in proportion to party strengths in the House. But, subject to prior agreement as to which party they are to be drawn from, the members of the committees elect their own chairs. It will be seen, therefore, that the system is overlaid with conventions which undermine the independence of the committees from government and party.

Some of the recommendations of the Procedure Committee were not implemented when the new select committees were set up, and these omissions mean that the committees are weaker in their relationships with government than the Procedure Committee would have wished them to be. The government was not prepared to allow the 8 days per session for the debate of committee reports sought by the Procedure Committee, although they did undertake to give greater priority to such debates. The fact that reports are not aired in the Commons means that the government can get away with ignoring unwelcome recommendations without undue embarrassment. But this problem must not be exaggerated: government generally responds to reports in writing, and the committees' recommendations may register with departments concerned and in due course be reflected in later policy (HC 92, 1982–83, para. 13).

The procedure for compelling the attendance of persons and the production of papers before the committees is problematic (Liaison Committee, HC 100, 1986–87, para. 2). While the government has conceded a power on the part of committees to compel the attendance of civil servants (Treasury and Civil Service Committee, HC 260, 1989–90, paras 21–2), it does not concede a duty on the part of civil servants to answer questions (Cabinet Office, 1980, rule 10). This is set out in HC 617, 1989–90, para. 8: 'In all circumstances the official would remain subject to Ministerial instructions as to how to answer questions.' Nor does the government concede a right on the part of committees to compel the attendance of ministers (or MPs), though in theory the House may do so (Cm. 1532, pp. 8–11; Doig, 1989). In the Westland Affair, the civil servants directly involved in the leak of the Solicitor-General's letter were not even permitted by ministers to attend the investigation of the affair by the Defence Committee, and the committee decided not to insist (Drewry, 1989a, pp. 411–17; Oliver and Austin, 1987). There was some speculation that the committee might seek to compel attendance in the face of government refusal to allow civil servants in the Department of Trade and Industry and Number Ten Downing Street to give evidence, but the committee drew back from this confrontation and accepted instead evidence from the Cabinet Secretary, Sir Robert Armstrong. The episode highlighted the inability of the committees in practice, despite the formal position, to compel the attendance or testimony of civil servants without the permission of ministers (Cabinet Office, 1980; Head of the Home Civil Service, 1987; see further Chapter 4 on this point).

The effectiveness and coverage of these committees have been hampered by political considerations. After the 1987 general election, there were insufficient Conservative MPs for a Select Committee for Scottish Affairs to be set up. After the 1983 and 1987 general elections, there were delays of some 6 months in forming the committees for the new Parliament. The delays were contributed to by the Labour Party taking time over election of the shadow cabinet, since, again by convention, Opposition front benchers do not sit on these committees, membership could not be fixed until the front bench was appointed. The Study of Parliament Group regards this delay as a party political problem that is not readily susceptible to procedural solutions (Procedure Committee, HC 19-i, 1989–90, Memorandum 17, p. lviii). By contrast, the chairman of the Liaison Committee has recommended that the Commons' Standing Orders should impose a deadline of 30 sitting days for nomination of select committee members (Procedure Committee, HC 19–i, 1989–90, Memorandum 29, para. 23). This would mean that the Labour Party would have to revise its rules for election of shadow cabinet members.

The main usefulness of the committees has been in extracting information from a secretive government (Liaison Committee, HC 94, 1982–83, paras 7–15) and in producing reports which bring together not only official information but also the evidence of experts presented to the committees (HC 19–i, 1989–90, Memorandum 17 submitted by Drewry for the Study of Parliament Group, p. lvi). Drewry (1989a, p. 426) pinpoints the value of 'nagging away repeatedly at the same issue' until the government takes some notice.

The Study of Parliament Group has been complimentary about what it saw as the non-partisan spirit and non-party character of the committees (Procedure Committee, HC 19–i, 1989–90, p. lvi). But the performance of the committees is regarded by some commentators as disappointing. Sir Douglas Wass (1984) criticizes their partisan composition and concern with the short term (pp. 71, 115), the quality of questioning by members, and the quality of their advisers, some of whom in his view are politically committed and seek to put forward a personal viewpoint (pp. 64–75).

The new select committees have not radically altered the relationship between the executive and the House of Commons. The Study of Parliament Group expressed the view emphatically that 'reform of the committee system cannot by itself achieve major change in the "balance" between Executive and Legislature' (HC 19–i, 1989–90, Memorandum 17, p. lvi). Whether this is to be regarded as a criticism must depend on what one expects Parliament to do. The fact of the matter is that despite the rise of the centre parties in the 1980s, the political system seems to have settled down again into a two-party system with one party having a safe majority for the duration of a Parliament, while the other waits in the wings for its turn. That being the case, it is not to be expected that select committees, which reflect the balance of the parties in the House, will be able, or even wish, to secure major changes in government policy. What can be expected is that they should be willing to be critical and this has been the case in many of their reports (Drewry for the Study of Parliament Group, HC 19-i, 1989–90, Memorandum 17 p. lvi). If anything more is expected of them, the politics and ethos of the House would have to change, a matter discussed below. The Procedure Committee's own conclusions are that the system as a whole has proved itself 'a valuable and cost-effective addition to the House's ability to perform its proper function of holding Ministers to account' (HC 19–I, 1989–90, para. 363), and they were surprised how few witnesses had been keen to take a basically critical or sceptical line about the Committees (HC 19–I, 1989–90, para. 365).

The Public Accounts Committee

The Public Accounts Committee (PAC) was set up by Gladstone in 1861 and deals with accounting matters which, for the most part, have little party content. In this respect, it is quite different from the departmentally related select committees. The PAC has a special status among select committees, quite distinct from that of the departmentally related committees, in seeking to impose real accountability for public expenditure. In this area, too, the 1980s saw reform. The National Audit Act 1983 sought to improve parliamentary control of expenditure by increasing the powers of the Comptroller and Auditor General (AG) and the National Audit Office to secure the propriety of government expenditure and the economy, efficiency and effectiveness with which a department has used its resources. His power extends to bodies and institutions which are wholly or mainly supported from public funds. The CAG is an Officer of the Commons, accountable to Parliament in the shape of the PAC, and is independent of government. The considerable influence of the PAC has been attributed to its working with the CAG and to the fact that the Treasury pressurizes departments to implement the PAC's recommendations (Drewry, 1989b, p. 157). Other departmentally related select committees do not have the advantage of this kind of back-up to increase their influence.

Reform of the select committees, then, has achieved some improvement in the ability of the House of Commons to impose political and public accountability, efficiency and effectiveness on government; but the scope for using parliamentary procedure to this end is severely limited by other factors to which we now turn, i.e. the politics and ethos of the two Houses.

The politics of Parliament

In the 1950s and 1960s, governments tended to regard it as unacceptable for a backbencher to vote against the whip or dissent from the party's line on even the most insignificant matter. In order to avoid the embarrassment of defeat, ministers were generally careful to take account of the views of their backbenchers and to avoid if they could putting forward proposals that would meet opposition from their own party. But in the period since the late 1960s, there has been a substantial increase in the number of government defeats in the House of Commons at the hands of the government's own backbenchers and the other parties (Norton, 1980; Griffith and Ryle, 1989, pp. 118–30). This has been put down to the decreased concern of governments to take account of the wishes of their backbenchers (Norton, 1978, ch. 9; Benn, 1981, ch. 2) and the fact that more independent-minded MPs have been elected in recent years as the two main parties have sought candidates outside the ranks of trade unionists and the 'knights of the shires' who tended to regard their first duty as loyalty to the party leadership.

As a result of governments having had to learn to live with the possibility of parliamentary defeats in the 1970s, conventions also changed. The view that a government should resign or go to the electorate if defeated in the House of Commons was modified, as in the 1970s the Labour government faced many defeats, some of them at the hands of its own backbenchers, and yet carried on in office until eventually defeated on a vote of confidence in May 1979.

A count of government defeats does not give a full picture of the relationship between ministers and the House. Each party when in government is primarily dependent on its own backbenchers, and ministers regularly temper their proposals or even withdraw them in response to pressure from this quarter. But what of government accountability to Parliament as a body?

Norton has argued that the attitudes of MPs are crucial to the question of whether the House of Commons can or will exercise any effective control over the government (Norton, 1981, pp. 219–35). Writing in 1980 and basing his case on the record of increased backbench dissent in the 1970s (at a time when the Conservative government was in power with a majority of 43 seats), Norton argued that backbenchers already had the power which they could and should exercise to influence government. By implication, no procedural or other reforms were necessary. All that was required was that MPs change their attitudes to government and to their own roles.

The 'Norton view' leaves unanswered the question of why backbenchers should change their attitudes and behaviour. For many years now, MPs have been drawn from a wider spectrum of the population and not all aspire to the front benches – and yet the dissident remains the exception. Norton's conclusion that no reforms are necessary and that we should expect attitudes to change under the present rules, seems somewhat complacent.

But would further reforms of House of Commons procedure make any difference? As early as 1967, when procedural change was widely regarded as something of a panacea, Butt (1967, p. 444) was sceptical:

> In short, the question of procedural changes still revolves round the ancient dilemma of how far they should be designed to make it easier for the Member to call the Government to account, and how far to enable Government to conduct its business more efficiently. In the end, it is unlikely that the balance of power will be markedly altered as a result of procedural changes.

Professor Bernard Crick's book on *The Reform of Parliament*, first published in 1964, was very influential in the decision to introduce the so-called 'Crossman reforms' of the 1966–70 Parliament in the shape of functional select committees. But even this champion of procedural reform has expressed the view that the parliamentary reform movement of the 1960s was 'largely a waste of time and effort' (Crick, 1989, p. 396; see also Crick, 1977). He and other commentators in the Labour camp have come to the conclusion that the politics of Parliament need to be changed; procedural reform cannot itself achieve this. There are signs here of the convergence of views between some sections of the Labour Party and the Liberal Democrats, who argue that the way to shift the balance in favour of Parliament, thereby strengthening political and public accountability, lies in fundamental constitutional reform that would revitalize and reshape the political process (see Part III for a discussion of the reforms that are designed to alter the operation of the political process).

It must indeed be the case that the politics of Parliament, based as they are in party discipline and the patronage in the hands of the party leaders, can only be altered if the political relationship between backbenchers and frontbenchers is changed. This will only happen if the balance of representation in the House of Commons is changed and brought more closely into line with support for the parties in the electorate. This in turn is an argument for proportional representation (see Chapter 8). Without this sort of political reform, the select committees and Parliamentary Procedures cannot effect a change in the balance of power between Parliament and government.

The parliamentary ethos

The relationships that exist between MPs and outside bodies have been causing concern for a number of years. The practice by which MPs are sponsored by or act as consultants and parliamentary spokespersons for sectional interest originated before they received salaries. Its existence and the conflicting loyalties that it engenders contradict the Burkean theory of representation, according to which MPs represent and have duties to all their constituents and the general public interest:

> Parliament is not a congress of ambassadors from different and hostile interests; which interests each must maintain, as an agent and advocate, against other agents and advocates; but parliament is a deliberative assembly of one nation, with one interest, that of the whole; where, not local purposes, not local prejudices, ought to guide, but the general good, resulting from the general reason of the whole (Burke, 1774).

The House of Commons has sought to deal with this problem of conflicting interests by emphasizing that a MP's first duty is to his or her constituents and the country as a whole, and by requiring MPs to declare their personal pecuniary interests before speaking in a parliamentary debate or in transactions or communications with ministers or other MPs (Wade and Bradley, 1985, pp. 224–6; Griffith and Ryle, 1989, pp. 55–60) and to register their interests (Select Committee on Members' Interests (Declaration), HC 57, 1969–70; see also Wade and Bradley, 1985, pp. 226–8). There are weaknesses in this approach: the amount involved does not have to be disclosed, nor the commitment in time that is involved. The Select Committee on Members' Interests investigated a number of complaints in 1989–90 and recommended that the rules be reviewed since the requirements as to registration of interests were not sufficiently clear or detailed [Select Committee on Members' Interests, HC 561, 1989–90 (*re* Mr Michael Grylls, MP); see also HC 506, 1989–90 (*re* Mr Michael Mates, MP); HC 135, 1989–90 (*re* Mr John Browne MP)].

The question arises whether a spotlight, even a stronger one, is a sufficient protection against MPs allowing their allegiances to sponsoring agencies to cloud their judgements on decisions to be taken in Parliament, and whether a new set of rules needs to be devised. Any scheme has to take into account that it would be politically difficult to prevent MPs from having financial relationships with outside interests unless the House of Commons and the government were prepared to authorize the payment of substantially larger salaries to MPs. Some MPs have jobs and professions and it might seem unduly restrictive of their freedom of action if any rules designed to prevent MPs from being subjected to sectional pressures prevented them from pursuing these. In many cases, connections with outside interests enable MPs to speak with authority on matters of general concern and in this respect they can be beneficial. In any event, a prohibition against links of this kind would be difficult to enforce.

Ryle (1990, p. 321) has suggested that MPs be required to disclose the amount of money involved and the amount of time spent on sponsors' business in the Register of Members' Interests. The assumption is that a stronger spotlight would be sufficient. Charter 88 has recommended that the influences of outside financial interests be curbed 'so that MPs are fully accountable to their electorate'. Hugo Young (*The Guardian*, 21 February 1990) suggested at the time of the John Browne affair that MPs should be excluded from any political function which directly bears on an outside interest; they should not be able to speak, lobby or vote on anything to do with the affairs of a sponsoring body; but MPs should remain free to assist anyone who did not pay them. This proposal would in effect stop the paid sponsorship of MPs as there would no longer be any benefit to sponsors in these arrangements.

The Select Committee on Members' Interests has considered the problems that arise for select committees in particular from the relationships of MPs with outside bodies. Its members have recommended stricter rules about disclosures of interests in select committees. They also propose that MPs having pecuniary interests as contractors of a government department or similar financial relationships should not be nominated to membership of select committees concerned with that department. The committee further recommended that the chairmen of select committees should divest themselves of any direct personal pecuniary interest or benefit which might reasonably be thought to influence their judgement or from which the chairmen might reasonably be thought to benefit directly from their position as chairmen. This quite radical proposal would extend to backbenchers some of the restrictions that apply to ministers (HC 108, 1990–91).

The second chamber

The preamble to the Parliament Act 1911 made clear that the measure was intended to be temporary. The long-term aim was to create a new second chamber not based on the hereditary principle. But a major constitutional reform of this kind would be hard to justify to the public without consensus between the parties, or a strong electoral mandate, or a groundswell of public pressure for change. Attempts were made to secure inter-party agreement in 1918 (Bryce, 1918, Cd. 9038), 1948 (Cmd. 7390) and 1968 (White Paper on House of Lords Reform, Cmnd. 3799; see Morgan, 1975), but they failed, and the electoral mandate or groundswell of public pressure have not materialized. Instead, the only reforms to the second chamber have been the reduction of the period of delay of legislation to 1 year by the Parliament Act 1949 and the introduction of life peerages by the Life Peerages Act 1958. The House of Lords remains, therefore, a partly hereditary, partly appointed body with no claim to democratic legitimacy.

A constitutional watchdog?

The House of Lords is well aware of the weakness of its position, and it has for the most part exercised voluntary self-restraint in the post-war period. It has assumed a role as constitutional watchdog, as scrutineer of government policy and as a forum for discussion of matters of public concern. The life peers in particular are able to bring experience in government, the House of Commons and other walks of life, and this combination of knowledge and wide experience gives authority to debates in the House. Its position in the constitution is nevertheless precarious.

In the 1980s, with a government in power throughout the decade with very substantial majorities, with the official opposition in disarray for much of the decade and with unpopular and sometimes seemingly authoritarian policies being promoted by the government (see Chapters 5 and 9), the House of Commons' inability to oppose the government effectively became obvious. In some respects, the Lords were more representative of public opinion than the Commons. They felt confident about asserting themselves against the government on matters where public opinion was behind them or where the government seemed to them to be acting counter to democratic principles. They took some of the role of opposition upon themselves, and the respect in which they were held rose accordingly. They had in many respects a more forward-looking attitude to their role than the Commons, introducing the televising of the House in 1985, 4 years before the Commons.

The House has sought to keep a balance in the constitution between the world of party politics and democratic principle. It has been one of those anachronistic institutions of the constitution, like the monarchy, that has worked relatively well in the post-war period.

But there have been occasions when the action of the House of Lords has seemed most undemocratic, and its lack of accountability to the public has seemed a severe defect; this has been particularly notable when the government has called out the 'backwoodsmen' to support controversial legislation such as the community charge, when the Conservative majority in the Lords defeated an amendment that would have related liability to ability to pay – this backbench Lords amendment was defeated by 317 votes to 183 and of the 317, 233 were hereditary peers.

The future of the second chamber remains an issue that attracts attention from the other political parties and from academics. A range of proposals for reform has been made over the years. Until recently, most of these have seen reform of the second chamber in isolation and have assumed that other aspects of the constitution will not also be reformed. But it is unrealistic to approach the subject in this way, since there is also currently discussion of regional and national decentralization which could well affect the role and composition of a second chamber; and in other measures, such as the introduction of a Bill of Rights where some form of entrenchment might be thought desirable, the second chamber might have an important role.

Proposals are generally directed to reforming the composition of the second chamber; its functions – debate, revision of legislation, delay, veto, even the initiation of certain legislation – are generally accepted (e.g. Vibert, 1991, p. 12; the Commonwealth of Britain Bill, clauses 10, 11 (Benn, 1991); Liberal Democrats 1990, pp. 40–3, 45; Labour Party 1991b, p. 50. See also discussion in Chapters 9 and 11). It could have a role in protecting important constitutional legislation, for example a Bill of Rights and national and regional assembly laws, from repeal (Labour Party 1991b, p. 50; Liberal Democrats, 1990, p. 45). Given that there is no real support for outright abolition of the second chamber, leaving a single-chamber legislature, proposals may broadly be divided into three groups: those which see a new second chamber having a role in functional representation; those that see it as an outlet for national and regional representation; and more conservative proposals which prefer to retain the present House of Lords as the basis for a second chamber but would like to see its composition more fairly reflecting the population and possibly representing national and regional interests.

A functional second chamber?

Proposals for a functional second chamber first surfaced seriously in the inter-war years (Smith, 1972, pp. 132–4) when Beatrice and Sidney Webb were suggesting two parliaments, one for industry, health and education, and the other for the traditional functions of defence, foreign affairs and the administration of justice (Webb and Webb, 1920, pp. 93–5). In the 1940s, L. S. Amery put forward proposals to separate economic and industrial responsibility from other aspects of public policy, though he felt that a new economic parliament must not compete with the House of Commons in the field of finance or general legislation (Amery, 1947). Christopher Hollis (1949) suggested a House of Industry.

In 1974, Political and Economic Planning, in its publication *Reshaping Britain: A Programme of Economic and Social Reform*, again proposed a House of Industry. This would have been based on a reformed House of Lords in which the representation of industry was formalized and extended, but not in such a way as to challenge the authority of the Commons or to confuse it with the normal party political process (Coombes, 1982, p. 145). The idea of a separate legislative chamber with different functional responsibilities from those of the House of Commons lingered on, and as late as 1978 Butt was advocating a separate economic and social chamber (Butt, 1978, p. 197).

The conviction behind proposals along these lines was that it was necessary, and possible, to isolate industrial and economic policy from other aspects of government, and it was hoped that the former could operate in a non-party atmosphere. In the climate of the 1990s, it seems unrealistic to suppose that these issues can be separated from party politics or indeed foreign policy.

More recently, there has again been renewed interest in a functional chamber, but of a different kind. Hirst (1988, pp. 190, 202) has suggested that the House of Lords should be replaced with a corporatist second chamber and sees a benefit in that 'such a continuously functioning chamber would permit continuity, consensus and co-ordination in policy, a programme which could pass such a chamber would have a much higher chance of lasting than any proposal of a party government'.

There are several difficulties in functional chambers. As Coombes (1982, p. 146) has observed: 'There is a danger . . . of confusing two separate issues: the need for the direct representation of industry and the need to maintain, if not strengthen, constitutional checks and balances against party government.' It would not be a simple matter to design a system of election or appointment to such a chamber that produced a fair representation of the interests that would wish to participate. A rough and ready system would have to be devised for deciding which interests should be represented (trade unions, industries, artists, women, ethnic minorities, the elderly, the disabled and so on). Who would choose the representatives – the interests themselves (and what if there are several organizations representing particular interests?) or the Crown? Would interests be guaranteed a certain number of 'seats' in the chamber? If so, then unlike members of the House of Commons, representatives of the corporations would not have to face the electorate and run the risk of being deprived of their seats. Their public accountability would be defective.

Would the members owe their duties to the bodies that they represented or to the general public? If to the former, it is unlikely that what would emerge from the deliberations of such a body would promote the general interest. It would be more likely to reflect the balance of power within the body and could well mean that the power of the already powerful was enhanced and institutionalized, while the weaker were outvoted. If members were supposed to be putting the general welfare before the interests of the bodies that they represented, this would be inconsistent with their general duties to those bodies. Representatives of trade unions and of industry would naturally regard it as their duty to look after the interests of workers and companies rather than of the country as a whole. This was a problem experienced during the course of the 'social contract' from 1974 to 1976, when many unions found it difficult to deliver the wage restraint they had promised in the public interest if their members were in a strong position to obtain larger rises from their employers than the agreed norm (Daintith, 1989).

In other words, a corporatist second chamber would increase the power of the corporations and legitimate it, while what is required is that this power be more responsibly exercised and its illegitimate exercise be subjected to some kind of accountability.

An alternative approach for those who would wish to see a greater element of functional representation and participation in policy making and public administration would be the establishment of a new 'forum' with no role in the legislative process and operating outside the parliamentary system and independently from government. Coombes, for example, is in favour of the establishment of an Economic and Social or Industrial Council, which would give the representatives of industry an opportunity to question in public the attitudes of both the party machines and the leaders of industry and trade unions. Such a body would impose a form of public accountability. This arrangement would support a form of pluralist representation and indeed counter any drift to corporatism (Coombes, 1982, p. 189). The idea could be expanded to include in the membership of the forum representatives of other groups and interests such as consumers, women and ethnic minorities. But whether a body with no role in the legislative process and no powers to compel the attendance of witnesses and the production of papers would command the necessary respect and authority is doubtful. In any event, it would not be a second chamber.

National and regional representation in a second chamber

Another approach to reforming the second chamber would be to give it a role in the representation of national and regional interests (see Chapter 6). Charter 88 has suggested a second chamber consisting of representatives from the nations and regions, together with elected representatives of vocational groups; the latter would raise all the problems outlined above in the discussion of a functional chamber.

The Liberal Democrats' Working Group on Constitutional Reform propose a Senate of about 100 voting members directly elected by the citizens of the nations and regions. Each of the nations and regions would elect the same number of members, each member serving for 6 years with one-third retiring every 2 years. To retain a degree of continuity, for a transitional period existing peers would retain their seats and be able to speak and participate in the activities of the Senate, but not to vote. Ministers in the House of Commons would attend and participate without votes. The powers of the Senate would be similar to those of the House of Lords except that the delaying power would be increased to 2 years from the present 13 months under the Parliament Acts, and it would have a decisive role in the process of amending a written constitution, since this would require the support of two-thirds of its members (Liberal Democrats, 1990, p. 13).

There are a number of problems with these ideas. If the second chamber were composed solely of representatives of the nations and regions of the UK, then it is doubtful whether they would wish to, or be qualified to, continue to perform the present roles of the House of Lords in the scrutiny of Bills bearing no regional or national implications, and of European and subordinate legislation, which the second chamber currently performs well. The members of the Senate would not have the same range of expertise as the present House does. If national and regional interests were dominant, they might not be sufficiently detached from the system to act as constitutional watchdogs except to the extent of protecting the interests of the nations and regions. Minority interests would continue to be unrepresented even in a rough and ready way. If ministers attended the Senate other than as members, as the Liberal Democrats' working group suggests, the process of ministerial responsibility would not operate as it does under present arrangements, and this would have important implications for the ability of the nations and regions to influence central government. Further, the populations of the nations and regions might be widely different in numbers and if each nation and region had the same representation in the second chamber, this would produce disproportionate representation; or it would provide an incentive to draw the boundaries of English regions so that the population of each was similar in size, and this could lead to artificial boundaries that cut across natural communities. And, finally, an elected second chamber would have a claim to legitimacy equal to that of the Commons, and this could lead to deadlock in conflicts between the two Houses in which even the power to delay legislation for 2 years might seem an unreasonable fetter on the second chamber if public opinion were on its side.

The Labour Party has proposed a variant on the elected chamber representing the nations and regions of the UK, a new elected second chamber with the power to delay, for the lifetime of a Parliament, changes to designated legislation dealing with individual or constitutional rights. The party established a working party 'to consider what electoral system is appropriate' for the second chamber but no firm recommendation of proportional representation was made (Plant, 1991). This extremely vague proposal is open to all the same objections as the Liberal Democrats' proposals, plus the objection that it would rival the House of Commons if it were elected on the same franchise and representing the same interests, and if it were elected by proportional representation and the Commons were not it would have a greater claim to legitimacy than the Commons.

An evolutionary approach

Another approach to dealing with the problems posed by the House of Lords is to retain the present chamber (possibly renamed) with its existing powers, but to reform its composition so as to remove the hereditary element and make it more democratically accountable, even if it is not, or not entirely, democratically elected.

A solution along these lines was attempted in 1968 in the aftermath of the failure to reach inter-party agreement on reform. The Labour government introduced a Bill to reform the House of Lords. After a transitional period, hereditary peers would have lost the right to attend or vote, so that the voting membership of the House would consist of life peers appointed as at present by the Prime Minister, subject to a retiring age of 72, plus the Law Lords and some Anglican bishops. New life peers would be created at the start of each Parliament to secure the government approximately 10 percent more members than the other parties. This meant that, in practice, the balance of power would have been held by cross-bench peers. The actual powers of the reformed House would have remained broadly as at present except that the power to delay Commons legislation would have been reduced to 6 months.

The Bill had the broad support of the House of Lords and of the leaders of the Conservative, Labour and Liberal parties, but there were reservations on the part of a number of backbenchers from all parties, and the Bill made such slow progress through the House of Commons that the government eventually abandoned it (for an account of this attempt to reform the House of Lords, see Wade and Bradley, 1985, pp. 194–6).

Although the precise terms of this proposal no longer meet the case for reform of the second chamber, an approach that is evolutionary and retains the good points of the present House of Lords has attractions. Any reform of the second chamber should allow for government ministers to be members of the House and therefore accountable to it, an important element in the constitution which would not be readily achieved in the options discussed earlier. Despite its undemocratic composition, the present House performs the functions of scrutiny of legislation (especially European legislation) efficiently and effectively and these qualities should not be lost in reform. A second chamber also has an important role as constitutional watchdog, which is particularly necessary for so long as we have no written constitution and subscribe to the doctrine of parliamentary sovereignty. Even if this were to go with the adoption of a written constitution with entrenched provisions, a constitutional watchdog would be required and a second chamber could perform that role.

There are also advantages in having a second chamber that does not have the same democratic legitimacy as the Commons, and this implies some merit in a chamber that is not entirely elected. If the second chamber were entirely elected, whether on the same electoral system as the House of Commons or on some form of proportional representation, then there could be clashes between the two chambers, since each could lay claim to an electoral mandate and democratic legitimacy.

The following proposals could form the basis for a reformed second chamber that meets these points. Hereditary peers should lose the right to membership, but life peers should continue to be members. The process for creation of peers in the future should be removed from prime ministerial patronage, possibly through a reformed Political Honours Scrutiny Committee. These appointments need not be called peerages: 'senator', 'counsellor' or 'elder' would be alternatives. The range of these appointed members of the second chamber could be widened to make the House *de facto* more representative, even though not elected, through the adoption and publication of guidelines regulating the award of peerages or senatorial status to include people with expertise and special interests in both sides of the major industries, in the arts, science, the academic world and the professions, and in sections of the population that are generally not well represented in the Commons or by pressure groups, such as the religious and ethnic minorities, the disabled, women and single parent families. Tenure could be limited to, say, 15 years.

An elected element should be introduced if a scheme of decentralization to the nations and regions of the UK were undertaken (see Chapter 6). National and regional senators should be directly elected from equal-sized constituencies in those areas to sit alongside the other members. This would give these areas representation at Westminster, and enable them to participate in the process of holding central government to account on behalf of the nations and regions. The numbers could be such as to give elected senators more than half the seats. They would be in a strong position to bargain in favour of national and regional interests with central government, and this would be an important ingredient in any decentralization scheme (see Chapter 6).

A chamber composed in this way would enable the government to appoint ministers to sit in the House as members from among the senators, so that the processes of ministerial responsibility to the House could operate. If the government did not have a majority in the Senate, it would face a delay of, say, 6 months (save on constitutional issues), which should enable it to reconsider its position but then to proceed on the consent of the Commons alone if felt appropriate.

On constitutional issues, the second chamber could have either a veto or the right to delay legislation until after an election, or be subject to a requirement of a special majority, such as two-thirds.

A scheme of this sort should secure the continued existence of a body of people with expertise in important areas, willing to perform a role in the scrutiny of policy, legislation and administration, with clout where necessary but without the democratic legitimacy to enable it to challenge the Commons and therefore cause deadlock, except on constitutional and national and regional issues.

An approach along these lines to reform of the second chamber should enable progress to be made without sacrificing the considerable contributions that the House of Lords has been able to make to justify its existence in recent years. It is also likely to be more politically acceptable to a broad spectrum of opinion than any of the other approaches.

4

Government and the civil service

As the discussion in Chapter 1 indicated, the ways in which the institutions of central government operate – the Prime Minister, Cabinet and government, and the civil service – have attracted much of the blame for the country's ills. Criticisms focus on weaknesses in the mechanisms for imposing political and public accountability on government, and the ineffectiveness of central government policy making and administration, which mean that policies are often ill-thought out and doomed to failure, or poorly administered and doomed to only partial success. Problems are caused by ministerial overload; by the lack of sense of long-term strategy in the Cabinet which results from the pragmatic, evolutionary ethos of British policy making; excessive partisanship among politicians; and a lack of resources for the Opposition. The civil service is also open to criticism for its lack of specialism and, at the highest levels, lack of interest in administration as opposed to policy making.

The Prime Minister and Cabinet government

The Cabinet system is highly adaptable. It is not regulated by law (and it is not suggested that it should be), but nor is it regulated in its *modus operandi* by any published set of guidelines or standards which require a collective style of decision making. The conventions of collective responsibility operate to protect its operation from public scrutiny and comment rather than to expose it to public or political accountability for these matters. In the last 25 years or so Prime Ministers have increasingly adopted presidential styles, and this has led some commentators to seek ways to limit or control the power of the premier in order to rehabilitate Cabinet government: the aim would be to enhance collective discussion and decision making in government, but without emasculating the Prime Minister and tying the hands of government as some proposals would do (see, e.g. Benn, 1981, ch. 2). In the absence of any such method of regulation, the Cabinet system suffered from stresses in the 1980s manifested in the resignations of Michael Heseltine in 1984, Nigel Lawson in 1989 and Sir Geoffrey Howe in 1990. These led, finally, to the replacement of Mrs Thatcher as Prime Minister by John Major in 1990.

Promoting collective decision making

The system does, then, have a 'safety-valve' mechanism which means that eventually a collective system will reassert itself (Marshall, 1991). But the question arises of whether a more orderly, collective process could be encouraged that would avoid subjecting it to stresses of the kind experienced in the 1980s and promote a more responsive style of government.

One approach would be to follow the Australian example. Openness about the way in which an institution should operate can encourage conformity: the Australian *Cabinet Handbook* sets out the rules of Cabinet government and acts as an aid to efficient and effective collective decision making. It lists the names, tasks and membership of Cabinet committees and sets out their objectives. For example: 'The committee system is designed to ensure that outcomes are reached after thorough discussion and on the basis of consensus.' Cabinet members are entitled to receive copies of committee documents. The *Handbook* affirms Cabinet as opposed to prime ministerial government (Hennessy, 1989b). It is published and regularly updated. Mrs Thatcher was invited to disclose the nearest equivalent in the UK, *Questions of Procedure for Ministers* in January 1989, but refused to do so (Hennessy, 1989b). The publication of this document would, it is suggested, expose it to public criticism and increase media, public and parliamentary pressure on a Prime Minister to adopt a collective Cabinet style (for some extracts from *Questions of Procedure*, see Hennessy, 1986, pp. 8–4, 110).

Improving strategic policy making

Another problem with Cabinet government has been its seeming inability to develop and pursue a coherent, effective strategy. Much of the problem over strategy is due to ministerial overload, which means that ministers have difficulties both mastering the briefs from their own departments, and taking a view of the overall strategy of the administration (Hennessy, 1986; Hoskyns, 1983; Wass, 1984). As far as the mastering of policy within departments is concerned, this could be improved if ministers had 'cabinets' or ministerial policy units, groups of specialist advisers, possibly a combination of civil servants and political advisers recruited from outside the civil service. This solution has been proposed by a number of commentators, including the Treasury and Civil Service Committee (TCSC, HC 92, 1985–86, paras 5.21–5.30) and more recently, John Smith, Shadow Chancellor of the Exchequer (Smith, 1991).

The defects in the policy making system mean that details of policy are not considered in Cabinet and, as Sir Douglas Wass, Permanent Secretary to the

Treasury from 1974 and Joint Head of the Home Civil Service from 1981 to 1983, contends: '. . . the general thrust of the government's policies is seldom if ever reviewed and assessed by Cabinet' (Wass, 1984, p. 25).

Wass considers two possible ways of dealing with the lack of strategy: to bias the composition of the Cabinet away from the departmental ministers, by setting up an 'inner Cabinet' of ministers without departmental responsibilities who could take responsibility for strategy; or to supply the Cabinet with a staff whose job would be to identify the issues and choices which the Cabinet must face as a collective entity. Members would then be briefed on these matters and should be able to take informed collective decisions on them. This body, which Wass christens a 'Cabinet Review Staff', would have to be involved in Whitehall's day-to-day business (the fact that the Central Policy Review Staff, the 'Think Tank', abolished in 1983, was not so involved was one of its weaknesses) and participate, for example, in the annual bilateral negotiations between the Treasury and the spending departments: 'A unit like this would force ministers in their collective embodiment to realise that they have to make choices, and that by facing the issues which those choices impose, they stand only to gain' (Wass, 1984, p. 40).

Although this approach has much to commend it, it is not easy to see how it would work effectively unless the problem of ministerial overload were tackled at the same time. The setting up of executive agencies (see below) should reduce the ministerial workload. Decentralization of power to national and regional assemblies would relieve the problem even more. Here, as in most areas, remedies often depend on what other reforms might be introduced.

Even if Wass's reforms were instituted, it would remain difficult for departmental ministers to take a strategic view of overall policy without access to additional advice. This point supports the view that the Prime Minister should have a department, more substantial than the Downing Street Policy Unit, that would enable the head of government to fulfil this role effectively (for accounts of the resources available to a prime minister in the field of policy, see Callaghan, 1987, pp. 404–408; Donoughue, 1987, pp. 16–26, set out in Brazier, 1990, pp. 224–34).

Ministerial accountability

The weak accountability of ministers, both individually and collectively, to Parliament is yet another dimension of the problem of Cabinet government. Accountability is limited by the highly secretive way in which Cabinet government is conducted, and the ability of ministers to avoid answering parliamentary questions. There is no express recognition in constitutional law or in the *Questions of Procedure* referred to above, of a duty on the part of ministers to account to Parliament (but it was explicitly acknowledged by the government in *Civil Servants and Ministers: Duties and Responsibilities*, Cmnd. 9841, 1986, at para. 11). If a written constitution were adopted, it could include an express duty to be accountable to Parliament. The Institute of Public Policy

Research Constitution (Institute of Public Policy Research, 1991) includes just such a duty. But in the absence of such a measure, the publication of *Questions of Procedure*, as suggested above, would have the added advantage of attracting constructive proposals for improvement, including no doubt the addition of an express duty on ministers to give a full account to Parliament of their conduct and that of their departments and in relation to all matters for which they have responsibility. In other words, a published set of guidelines, though not legally binding, would serve to regulate the *modus operandi* of Cabinet and of ministers and thus increase political and public accountability. They would provide the criteria against which the operation of the system could be judged.

The opposition

Lord Rothschild (Rothschild 1977, pp. 173–4, quoted in Hennessy, 1986, p. 184) wished that 'there could be a law against a new Government doing anything during its first three or so months of existence'. Of course, nothing can be done to prevent governments from acting in their first 100 days, but something could be done about the quality of opposition policies for the longer term.

A major problem is that those who take on the work of policy preparation in opposition do not have access to the official information which is necessary if realistic policies are to be developed. One of the benefits of a public right of access to official information would be in the improvement of policy making in opposition (see Chapter 10). But there are other problems too. Consultations do not, of course, take place with interests outside of or hostile to the party. Often, there will be covert pressures from sectional interests, e.g. the trade unions in the Labour Party, for policies to be adopted which might not be in the general public interest. And resources for policy preparation in opposition tend to be very limited.

Whether it is for these reasons or others, the quality of the work done by the parties in preparation for office is often inadequate, sometimes of a 'back of the envelope' kind. And the policies promised in the party manifestos and programmes are often unwise, unrealistic or uncosted. Once in office, a party may proceed to implement its policies without reconsidering them in the light of official information and advice, and rash steps are taken. This has caused problems which have surfaced in the courts in a number of cases (see *London Borough of Bromley* v. *Greater London Council* [1983] AC 768; see also Oliver, 1988, 1989).

Sir Douglas Wass sees a need to provide opposition parties with the staff to do the job of policy preparation effectively. He considers a number of possibilities, which include a 'Department of the Opposition' or the secondment of career civil servants to the Opposition (Wass, 1987, pp. 191–2).

The idea of a Department of the Opposition has the disadvantage that if there were only one it would institutionalize the two-party system and make it even more difficult than at present for new parties to enter the political arena. If there were more than one it would be expensive. It would pose problems for the career structures of civil servants working in the Department of Opposition and those working in government departments, since there would be inevitable difficulties about where civil servants working in the Department of the Opposition should go once the Opposition took office.

Sir Douglas, therefore, has reservations about this solution, and prefers an experiment under which a small number of civil servants would be seconded to the opposition party or parties for up to 5 years; on return to the civil service, they would be given a purely managerial post away from the political stage (Wass, 1984, pp. 75–80). But if this were to be tried, there would continue to be problems about access to official information (though this would be mitigated if a Freedom of Information Act were introduced; see Chapter 10) and the high fliers in the service would not be attracted to a secondment which promised a return to a backwater of the mainstream civil service. The Treasury and Civil Service Committee (TCSC) was of the view that a Department of the Opposition 'would raise complex constitutional questions and would lead to great practical difficulties' (TCSS, HC 92, 1985–86, para. 5.34).

Another solution, and in my view the most promising, would be to offer public funding to the political parties, or only opposition parties in Parliament, over and above the 'Short' money that they already receive for parliamentary work, which they could use to hire policy makers with experience in particular areas (these could include retired civil servants or those who desired secondment). The payment could be earmarked for policy work rather than campaigning. Whatever system is adopted, there is clearly a need to improve the policy-making capacities of the parties.

The loyalties of civil servants

'The duty of the individual civil servant is first and foremost to the Minister of the Crown who is in charge of the department in which he or she is serving' (Armstrong, 1985, amended 1987, Cmnd. 9841). This rule raises a number of questions. First, the points raised by the Ponting case (*R. v. Ponting* [1985] Criminal Law Review 319; see Chapter 10) and the Westland affair (for accounts of this affair, see Hennessy, 1989a, pp. 302–307; Oliver and Austin, 1987; Dunleavy, 1990): What if a minister is acting improperly in some way? Does, or should, a civil servant have a right or a duty to bring the matter to the attention of the public or Parliament? Does a civil servant owe any loyalty to the general public? What if a minister uses civil servants for party political purposes?

The legal position after the *Ponting* case is in effect that it is not for civil servants to take a different view of the public interest from that of their minister (see discussion of this case in Chapter 10). But, like the jury in that case, public opinion was unsympathetic to the judge's direction in *Ponting*: an opinion poll conducted in the wake of the case found that 55 percent of respondents felt that civil servants owed their main duty to 'the state as a whole', while only 34 percent thought they owed their main duty to the government of the day (Gallup poll, February 1985).

In the Westland affair, it will be remembered, the head of information at the Department of Trade and Industry had disclosed the contents of a confidential letter from the Solicitor General to the Secretary of State for Defence. She had doubts about the propriety of this action and had tried to contact her permanent secretary to clear it with him, but had been unable to do so and had gone ahead and made the disclosure.

Given the legal position, the question arises whether the political process can provide for cases such as these where civil servants are concerned about the propriety, as opposed to the wisdom, of their minister's activities, or whether some other process of accountability should be introduced.

This question and the circumstances of the Westland disclosure were investigated by the Defence Committee (Defence Committee, HC 519, 1985–86). But the Prime Minister refused to allow the civil servants involved to give evidence to the committee on the grounds that to do so would have major implications for the conduct of the government and for relations between ministers and their private offices. In the absence of full evidence, the select committee had difficulty in ascertaining the facts against which to make judgements about proprieties and form a view as to whether any further mechanism for accountability was required. The committee criticized the ministers involved for failing to accept that they had a duty to account fully to Parliament (a matter discussed above), for leaving their civil servants in the lurch, and for refusing to allow them to testify to it. The civil servants who had master minded the leak were also criticized for adopting a method of disclosure that was improper, authorized or not. They were further criticized for not owning up when the Prime Minister had asked Sir Robert Armstrong to investigate the circumstances of the leak.

Civil servants' dilemmas

One point that emerges strongly from the Ponting and Westland affairs is that there were serious lacunae in the procedures for dealing with ministerial impropriety. Sir Robert Armstrong, Head of the Home Civil Service, issued a Note reiterating the duty of civil servants to their ministers but suggesting a form of appeal: an official having 'a fundamental issue of conscience' should take the matter to the permanent secretary who could if he or she felt it necessary to do so refer the matter to the Head of the Home Civil Service (Armstrong, 1985, cols 128–130, Written Answers; Marshall, 1989, p. 140). Under pressure from the TCSC, the government later changed its position and agreed that civil servants had a right to appeal directly to the Head of the Home Civil Service if they alleged illegality, impropriety or maladministration on the part of a minister, and the government gave an assurance that such complaints would not damage a civil servant's career prospects unless they were frivolous or vexatious (TCSC,

HC 617, 1989–90, paras 16–18). The Civil Service Pay and Conditions of Service Code would make this clear.

Sir Douglas Wass has proposed an independent quasi-judicial 'Inspector-General' for the civil service to deal with complaints of ministerial impropriety, with power to report *in camera* to the relevant select committee (TCSC, HC 90–II, 1985–86, Q.179). The First Division Association had argued for a right to refer complaints about improper instructions from ministers to an independent body which would report to the chairman of the appropriate Commons select committee (TCSC, HC 92–II, 1985–86, paras 64–6; TCSC, HC 260, 1989–90, paras 39–43). The TCSC has not accepted the need for an independent body (TCSC, HC 260, 1989–90, para. 43).

There could be problems for the Head of the civil service (who is also the Cabinet Secretary) if her or she received a complaint of ministerial impropriety, for example through misleading Parliament or authorizing leaks of confidential communications. The Head of the civil service is hardly in a position to remonstrate with the minister, or authorize the civil servant to refuse to comply with instructions. Nor can he or she lawfully disclose these matters to a select committee, or MP, or the press.

If the 'appeal' system does not work satisfactorily, a complaints procedure could be introduced, perhaps in the shape of a civil service ombudsman along the lines of the Parliamentary Commissioner for Administration, responsible to the TCSC, who could take up cases that the government was not prepared to deal with to the satisfaction of the committee. This would introduce a measure of independence into the process of holding ministers and civil servants accountable for their methods of operation.

Discipline and the civil service

Another point that was highlighted by the Defence Committee in its report on the Westland Affair is the inadequacy of the machinery for dealing with allegations of improper actions by officials whether taken with the authority of their minister or on their own initiative. As the committee observed, the position is supposed to be that ministers discharge their obligations to those officials by satisfying the House of Commons that they have behaved properly; officials have a right to expect that support from their minister; but where the conduct of individual officials is a matter of general comment and controversy, those officials are not permitted to defend themselves; if a minister cannot satisfy the House that an official has behaved properly, the question of disciplinary proceedings should arise. In the matter of the leak of the Solicitor General's letter in the Westland affair, ministers had not satisfied the committee about the propriety of officials' conduct. But the committee was informed that no disciplinary action was to be taken against any of the officials concerned. It commented, 'we find this extraordinary' (HC 519, 1985–86).

To the extent that there are uncertainties as to what a minister may demand of civil servants, this could be clarified if there were a Code of Ethics governing the matter. There is such a code in the USA. The First Division Association has argued for the introduction of a code, and produced a draft of one (TCSC, HC 92, 1985–86, paras 4.8–11), but ethics on these matters are still not collected in one document; instead, they are to be found scattered in the Civil Service Code and in guidelines, assurances and undertakings given by government and the Head of the Home Civil Service from time to time (see, e.g. TCSC, HC 260, 1989–90, paras 23–30, on political neutrality, the use of press and information officers, and public activities of civil servants; on civil service ethics, see O'Toole, 1990).

Improving management in government

Concern about efficiency and effectiveness in the civil service goes back many years. One of the main themes of the Fulton Report (1968) was the lack of effective management in the civil service. The committee felt that the service was based too much on the philosophy of the amateur or 'generalist' and 'all-rounder', especially in the administrative class; scientists and other professionals in the service were not given enough responsibility, opportunities and authority; too few were skilled managers, and personnel management and career planning were inadequate; and that there was no real system of accountable management in the departments.

A number of steps has been taken in the last 20 years to meet some of the criticisms of management in the service made in the Fulton Report. These have included the introduction of 'Rayner Reviews' by Sir Derek Rayner, the government's Efficiency Adviser from 1979 to 1983, which achieved some success in cutting waste and improving efficiency. In the early 1980s, the introduction by Michael Heseltine in the Department of the Environment of MINIS ('management information system for ministers') improved the ability of ministers to keep track of work in what are often vast departments with responsibilities for a range of almost unrelated activities. This laid the basis for the Financial Management Initiative (FMI) introduced in 1982, which involved devolving authority within departments and setting up a system of accountable management (but the FMI also encouraged ministers to get involved in management, thus adding to the overload). In some departments, cost centres have been established with managers having responsibilities for their budgets. Some management training has been introduced. In sum, 'A series of developments has taken place in the systems and procedures of departments, and in the policies for career management and training, in an attempt to encourage cost-consciousness and to allow civil servants to have a clearer view of their policy objectives' (Drewry and Butcher, 1988, p. 207).

The Next Steps

A radical proposal to devolve responsibility to managers and hive off certain functions from central government to executive agencies was made by the Prime

Minister's Efficiency Unit in 1988 in a paper entitled *Improving Management in Government: The Next Steps*. The idea had its origins in the Fulton Report of 1968, but it had not been implemented. The ultimate objective is that the central civil service should be reduced in size to 'a relatively small core engaged in the function of servicing ministers and managing departments, who will be the "sponsors" of particular government policies and services' (Efficiency Unit, 1988, para. 44). The rest of the business of government will be hived off.

Government plans were spelt out in more detail in the White Paper *The Financing and Accountability of Next Steps Agencies* (1989, Cm. 914). Since then, there has been a succession of papers issued by government, and reports by the TCSC on these agencies. A number of the agencies is already up and running.

The bodies charged with these hived-off functions are known as 'executive agencies' (often referred to as 'Next Steps' agencies). They have at their heads professional managers with authority over their budgets and organizations, who are to concentrate their efforts on the effectiveness and quality of their service delivery. They have a duty to get value for money from assets and run their offices on profit and loss account lines, and they are expected to improve their service to 'customers'.

A sharp distinction is made in this scheme between administrators and those concerned with broad policy issues. The relationship between the government department and the agency is more transparent than relationships within a department can be. The agencies operate through framework documents, reviewed every three years, which specify the policy that the agencies are to implement. This creates a 'quasi-contractual' relationship between ministers and the chief executives. They state clearly who is responsible for doing what, and set out the ways in which the performance of the agency is to be measured (TCSC, HC 481, 1989–90, paras 14–24). The framework documents are supplemented by 'annual performance agreements' which detail the requirements of the agency. The chief executive of each agency proposes targets, which are subject to ministerial approval. These targets are supposed to be 'an effective management tool'. Output targets measure the quality of customer service and financial performance. They are part of the Conservative Government's *Citizen's Charter* (1991, Cm. 1599). Agencies also have their own performance indicators, for internal management purposes (Efficiency Unit, 1991, p. 3. For discussion of performance indicators, see Carter, 1991). 'The overall objective should be to improve performance, efficiency and effectiveness by switching the focus of attention away from process towards results' (TCSC, HC 481, 1989–90, para. 1).

Considerable progress has been made in implementing the programme (Goldsworthy, 1991). The Government Trading Act 1990 has expanded the powers of ministers to set up large parts of Whitehall on company lines. Among the first batch of agencies set up to be run on *Next Steps* lines were the Royal Mint and the Stationery Office. The Vehicle Inspectorate, Companies House and the Employment Service were others. By the end of 1991 there will be 50 agencies with more than 200 000 civil servants working in them.

Transferable technology: Will it work?

These reforms have won cross-party support (see Smith, 1991), being seen as 'a piece of transferable technology' (Hennessy, 1990) which, if carefully managed, should improve efficiency and effectiveness for governments of all colours. It should be a simple matter for an incoming government with different policies from those of its predecessor to change the terms of the framework document, and so the reforms are seen as being politically neutral (TCSC, HC 481, 1989–90, para. 20).

Nevertheless, there are reservations about how successful the reforms will be. The Efficiency Unit recommends that, to secure that the best people are recruited as chief executives, these posts should be filled by open competition. Pay arrangements should have incentives and penalties built in (Efficiency Unit, 1991). Managers will be limited in their ability to improve the service to their consumers if the Treasury does not allow them the freedom to fix their staffing levels and terms and conditions, and if the agencies are under-resourced, so much will depend on the attitude of the Treasury and the freedom of action that the chief executives are given. The Project Manager, Mr Peter Kemp, has expressed the wish that the Treasury should adopt a 'sum of money' approach and give the chief executives considerable freedom of action within the sum allotted to meet the costs of administration. The Efficiency Unit recommended in 1991 that the terms of the Civil Service Order in Council be altered to reduce the powers of Treasury and Civil Service ministers and to allow more flexibility to departments and chief executives (Efficiency Unit, 1991).

One important objective of *The Next Steps* is supposed to be to encourage the recruitment of good managers into government. As the Fulton Report (1968, para. 18) put it, civil servants '. . . tend to think of themselves as advisers on policy to people above them, rather than as managers of the administrative machine below them'. *The Next Steps* seems to envisage at some points a separate career in management for those who do not see themselves as policy advisers; at other points, management is seen as a first step for those who do. The TCSC in its response to the report, which was favourable in principle, recommended that 'the golden route to the top' should combine management experience within agencies with experience of policy work (HC 494, 1987–88, para. 26).

Although Sweden was the model on which *The Next Steps* report and the Fulton Committee drew, the career structure envisaged in *The Next Steps* is different from – and, in some respects, the reverse of – that in Sweden. There the pattern is for very able people to be recruited into the small central government civil service early and to rise to the top as policy advisers by their early or mid-40s. From there, they progress in their late 40s to become heads or senior officers of executive agencies. They do not receive professional management training before moving to the agencies (Fulton, 1968, app. C). Management is seen as a matter of career development to which high-fliers progress, rather than a stage on the way to the top policy advice level jobs in the mainstream civil service.

Parliamentary accountability in executive agencies

The issue of accountability has caused considerable concern in the setting up of these agencies. The Swedish agencies, on which *The Next Steps* agencies are supposed to be modelled, do not allow for ministerial responsibility for agencies at all. They report to Parliament and to a number of administrative agencies. By contrast with Sweden the government envisages that ultimate accountability should remain with ministers through the conventions of ministerial responsibility. Executive agencies would be bound by the Osmotherly Rules, which prevent civil servants from answering questions about policy, and treat civil servants as answering on behalf of, and therefore at the direction of ministers. The government's theory is that heads of agencies are to be accountable to their ministers and, ultimately, with the Permanent Secretary, to the Public Accounts Committee of the House of Commons: 'The Permanent Secretary's role would be to justify and defend the framework; the manager would have to answer for his or her performance within that framework' (Efficiency Unit, 1988, para. 22).

The Next Steps report itself was not specific on the forms of accountability, except that it proposed that in hearings by the Public Accounts Committee, the Accounting Officer (who would normally be the Permanent Secretary in the department) should be accompanied by the manager of the agency. The Accounting Officer would answer questions about the framework within which the agency operated, while the manager would answer questions about operations within the framework (Efficiency Unit, 1988, Annex A, para. 7). The government later agreed that the chief executive should be the Agency Accountancy officer and this will increase his or her accountability to the PAC (HC 348, 1989–90, para. 60).

The TCSC expressed regret that the government had paid insufficient attention to the role of Parliament in holding these agencies accountable (1988, Cm. 524; TCSC, HC 348, 1988–89; 1989, Cm. 841; 1989, Cm. 914; H.C. Deb., 21 December 1989, Written Answers, cols 367–8; TCSC, HC 481, 1989–90). They felt that 'giving managers a sense of personal responsibility for improvement is a key step in securing the cultural change in the Civil Service, which is essential to the success of *The Next Steps*' (TCSC, HC 494, 1987–88, para. 39).

The committee felt that the chief executives of the agencies should be directly responsible to House of Commons select committees and not, even theoretically, responsible only through the minister (TCSC, HC 494, 1987–88, para. 46). The FDA agreed (ibid., para. 47) – ministerial responsibility should remain only to the extent that if things were to go badly wrong, Parliament would expect the minister to put things right, possibly by dismissing the chief executive or revising the terms of the framework document.

The Procedure Committee has taken the view that 'as their numbers and scope grow, scrutiny of the executive agencies ought to play an increasingly important part in the work of Select Committees.' (HC 19–I, 1989–90, para. 44). In its response the government agreed (Cm. 1532, p. 2) and this marks a move away from the traditional approach to ministerial responsibility.

The setting up of these executive agencies has the potential for giving the select committees of the House of Commons an important new role in the scrutiny of public administration. Peter Hennessy, in his evidence to the TCSC, saw them as having a role that was crucial to the durability of the reforms (Hennessy, 1990). The TCSC gave them its blessing in 1990, expressing the view that the process was crucial for governments of whatever political colour, and should help to transform the civil service into a more efficient deliverer of public services (TCSC, HC 481, 1989–90). The *Steps* were regarded as 'politically neutral' and the committee saw itself as having a 'unique involvement' in monitoring these agencies (reported in *The Independent*, 30 July 1990).

However, concern remains about the ability of individual MPs to raise questions about the conduct of these agencies if the traditional relationship of civil servants with the minister is broken. Framework documents make some provision about this, and the position varies from agency to agency. For example, if the Secretary of State for Employment were to receive a question about the Employment Service, he or she would have to decide whether it was a matter to do with strategy or resources, in which case he or she would deal with it, or an operational matter, in which case it would be passed on to the chief executive. The executive's reply would be placed in the House of Commons Library. If the MP asking the question was dissatisfied with the executive's reply, he or she could table a further question to the minister, who could press the executive on the matter. As far as questions directly from MPs to chief executives are concerned, the position is unclear and the TCSC is pressing for machinery for publication of chief executives' replies and their placing in the House of Commons Library (HC 260, 1989–90, paras 63–70). The Procedure Committee is pressing for these replies to be published in Hansard (HC 178, 1990–91, para. 125). Clearly, there is less direct and wide publicity for this sort of correspondence than for normal parliamentary questions, and the opportunities to press ministers to secure that administrators deal with complaints are fewer under *The Next Steps* reforms than hitherto. There is a need here to strengthen the machinery for 'redress of grievances', traditionally the role of Parliament, but one which these reforms undermine without making proper provision for alternatives. But we should not be starry eyed about the efficacy of traditional provisions for redress of grievance (Birkinshaw, 1985). *The Next Steps* both exacerbate and highlight the deficiencies in the system and the need for measures to deal with them. One possibility would be for ministers to appoint agency 'ombudsmen', charged with investigating complaints from individuals and reporting to the minister and to Parliament. But a step of this kind would be a departure from the present system under which MPs act as filters and the Parliamentary Commissioner for Administration cannot deal with complaints direct from citizens.

Administrative law: Controlling technology transfer

The Next Steps has thus focused attention on the need to develop mechanisms for holding civil servants to account outside the conventions of ministerial responsibility. This means that, as Drewry (1990, p. 328) has perceptively observed, 'a much stronger system of administrative law' is required, which could provide both legal and administrative accountability (see also discussion in Chapters 2 and 7). In this important respect, the UK differs from Sweden, since that country has a developed system of administrative law and a powerful Ombudsman (Elder, 1973), thus providing a range of means both for dealing with individual grievances and for ensuring efficiency and effectiveness in public administration.

The Next Steps report listed a number of possible administrative law alternatives or supplements to ministerial responsibility: statutory definition of legally enforceable responsibilities; the discipline of the market; and the use of tribunals, an important process for impartial review of decisions in many of the areas of government activity that could be given to executive agencies, notably in the field of welfare benefit payments.

Other supplementary forms of accountability to which executive agencies will be exposed include the Parliamentary Commissioner for Administration (the Ombudsman), who has power to investigate complaints of maladministration by government departments and to recommend redress. These complaints must be referred to the Commissioner by MPs. Maladministration includes 'bias, neglect, inattention, delay, incompetence, ineptitude, arbitrariness' (Richard Crossman on the second reading debate on the Parliamentary Commissioner Bill: HC Deb., vol. 734, col. 51, 18 October 1966). This is commonly referred to as the Crossman catalogue. The National Audit Office and the Comptroller and Auditor General have powers to audit expenditure for value for money and propriety (see the National Audit Act 1983). These are all forms of administrative accountability. Legal accountability via judicial review is available to a person affected by a decision that is alleged to be unlawful (in this context, unlawfulness includes unfairness, unreasonableness, inconsistency and certain other failures of good administrative practice – see Jowell and Lester, 1987, p. 368; for further discussion, see Chapter 7).

So even at present, ministerial responsibility is only one of a range of mechanisms for securing the accountability of the civil service for its performance (see Birkinshaw, 1985, for a full discussion of these mechanisms). The hiving off of agencies, even if they were then removed from the ambit of ministerial responsibility, would not leave those agencies free from checks. *The Citizen's Charter* (1991, Cm. 1599) imposes accountability to consumers through openness, explicit standards and, sometimes, compensation. Administrative law has discovered new territory in the no-man's-land that will be left when ministerial responsibility no longer reaches into executive agencies, and it is preparing to colonize it.

The TCSC, in its response to *The Next Steps*, mentioned further possible reforms, including the formulation of codes of administrative practice. This form of accountability and structuring of discretion was also endorsed by the Justice-All Souls Review of Administrative Law (Justice-All Souls Review, 1988, ch. 2).

In assessing the chances of *The Next Steps* succeeding both in increasing the efficiency and effectiveness of the public service and making it genuinely accountable for operations, the Swedish experience is again instructive. As indicated earlier, the civil service proper in Sweden is a small band of high-flyers dealing only with policy. Ministers are not regarded as bearing responsibility for the autonomous agencies. Instead, a range of independent effectiveness, auditing and programme review mechanisms is employed to secure their public and administrative accountability; these are backed up by the duty of agencies to report directly to Parliament: so administrative and political accountability reinforce one another; the freedom of information regime that has been in operation in Sweden since the eighteenth century also enhances public and consumer accountability.

The independent auditing agencies in Sweden include parliamentary auditors, who are principally concerned with effectiveness; the Association of Swedish Local Authorities, which reviews the implementation of national policies by local government; and, most importantly, the National Audit Bureau (the RRV), which gives a central position to elucidating the goals of the agency, examining its activities and evaluating its system of control. The Swedish Agency for Administrative Development (SAFAD) is primarily concerned with organizational problems, the development of administrative methods and automatic data-processing systems. Although these arrangements have their shortcomings, there are lessons to be learned from the Swedish experience as *The Next Steps* are taken. In particular, the National Audit Office, the rough equivalent of RRV, with its links to Parliament, has an important role (Richardson, 1982).

The British system is evolving in the direction of using a range of auditing procedures as a means of holding executive agencies accountable. The TCSC has emphasized the need for 'evaluation programmes' to assess how far agency status has changed the effectiveness of the operations hived off to *Next Steps* agencies (TCSC, HC 481, 1989–90, para. 12). The Treasury is developing 'a suitable "portfolio" of output and performance measures' (TCSC, HC 481, 1989–90, para. 21). The project manager is conscious of the need to measure both quality and productivity in the performance of the agencies (TCSC, HC 481, 1989–90, para. 22). The TCSC has urged the need to find ways of evaluating customer satisfaction (TCSC, HC 481, 1989–90, paras 49–57). There continues to be scope for evaluation through 'Rayner scrutinies' and other processes.

There is, then, awareness of the need to replace or supplement ministerial responsibility with a range of other mechanisms, and in time these may come to be more effective than ministerial responsibility could ever be. They will need, however, to be backed up by direct political accountability to Parliament, as in Sweden. But while the need for various kinds of 'audit', the developing form of administrative accountability, is acknowledged, it is clear that these must not be so intrusive as to undermine the ability of the chief executives to perform efficiently and effectively. The TCSC saw this danger and warned that departments must learn to exercise a self-denying ordinance to ensure that review arrangements are not used as a vehicle for interference with the running of the agency: departments must learn a 'hands-off' management role (TCSC, HC 481, 1989–90, paras 19, 58–62). The Efficiency Unit (1991) endorsed this approach.

Conclusions

The various proposals for reform of the civil service that are currently under discussion challenge in a number of ways the principles laid down in the Northcote-Trevelyan Report of 1854. The introduction of special advisers and outsiders on secondment, and the potential for recruitment of managers of executive agencies from outside the service modify the principle of a permanent, professional career service; executive agencies may break up the civil service, especially where the agencies operate outside departments, the more so if, as the government envisages, pay scales vary from agency to agency according to the area in which they operate and the state of the labour market. Hence the principle of a unified service will have to be adjusted to take account of modern conditions. The civil service unions are anxious to retain mobility and transferability between different parts of the civil service, and so the new catchphrase is 'unified, not uniform'. In effect what binds these civil servants together is 'certain common codes and principles of doing business and . . . the unity of its purpose in serving collective Cabinet government' (Efficiency Unit, 1991, foreword). The convention that ministers are alone responsible for the conduct of civil servants must give way to various forms of direct accountability to Parliament, the public, a range of auditing agencies and the courts.

The rule, asserted by the government, that civil servants owe their loyalties exclusively to ministers, is under challenge in its present form, which impedes Parliament's ability to hold ministers to account for what they or their officials do. The TCSC sees itself having an important role here, and this suggests a new set of functions for Parliament in the direct scrutiny of the public service – a function already well established through the Parliamentary Commissioner for Administration and the Select Committee, and the Comptroller and Auditor General and the Public Accounts Committee. These parallels suggest that there is a case for establishing an Officer of the House of Commons with a special relationship with the TCSC similar to those of the PCA and the CAG, with responsibility for standards in the civil service.

While the efficiency and effectiveness of the civil service are undergoing reform, that of government and the Opposition remains in need of improvement. The policy-making process has to be better funded and the processes of information gathering and consultation directed to securing the adoption of policies with a greater chance of success and subject to continuing review. The wider questions of government strategy need to be given greater attention and the Prime Minister and ministers need more resources to secure that these issues do not disappear in a problem of overload. As with reforms in the civil service, openness through the publication of codes and handbooks has a role here.

5

Local government

Local government is one aspect of the British system of government that has been subjected to repeated reform since the end of the Second World War. Reforms have affected the finance, functions and structure of local government and most recently the operation of political processes within authorities. In particular, the 1980s saw a series of important measures that radically affected the powers of local authorities. These raised issues about the proper constitutional role of this tier of government and whether there are, or should be, limits to central government interference in local government.

Given the history of efforts over the last 150 years to improve local government and to find the right balance in central–local relations, we should have a picture of the rationales that are advanced for this tier (see Jones and Stewart, 1985) (for a brief history of local government, see Kilbrandon, 1973, ch. 7, paras 189–98; Hart and Garner, 1973, ch. 1; Jackson, 1966, introduction and chs 1 and 2). One is the value of political pluralism as a safeguard against the abuse of power. The over-concentration of power at the centre paves the way for abuse, and so the existence of other institutions, responsible for the provision of public services and possibly under different political control, acts as a counterweight against abuse by the centre. In effect, pluralism enhances public accountability.

Next is the recognition of the value of the responsiveness that comes from service delivery being operated locally, a version of the 'subsidiarity' principal recognized in European Community law (see Chapter 1) and in the European Charter of Local Self-Government (see below). As the Conservative government has itself acknowledged, for central government to seek to run the delivery of local services would involve increased employment of civil servants and increased bureaucratism. It would also mean that responsiveness to local needs would suffer. That is not to say that local government has proved itself to be always responsive to local needs; but it has greater potential for responsiveness to local needs than central government.

Then there is the 'diversity and difference' argument that bringing power and decisions closer to the people who will be affected by them secures improvements in the quality of decisions and greater flexibility: services can be delivered more efficiently and effectively at a local level.

Lastly, local government should have a central role in acting as promoter of local community development, and a training ground for citizenship (see Chapter 2). It can facilitate experimentation and 'social learning': Participation in local government can encourage citizen assertiveness and efficacy and thus form part of the 'civic culture'. Rhodes (1987, pp. 63–73) argues that local government should be regarded as a means for emancipating the individual and creating a free society through citizen participation. He suggests that local government is the most appropriate agency for giving citizens the opportunity to participate in and influence the process of government and self-government, outside Parliament (see also Hambleton, 1988). This is not a role that central government can perform.

These arguments for local government are, in effect, versions of the case for accountability, effectiveness and a contemporary concept of citizenship. They imply that local authorities and local communities should enjoy a real degree of autonomy, both financially and in the making of choices between possible policy options.

The importance of local government is recognized by the international community. The Council of Europe's European Charter of Local Self-Government 1985 (Treaty Series No. 122) aims to protect local authorities from encroachment by central government by ensuring that they have their own adequate financial resources and providing that financial equalization processes are not to be used to diminish the decision-making powers of local authorities (Article 9). Nor should their powers be undermined by administrative action by central government (Articles 4 and 8). Authorities should have powers of general competence (Article 4), unlike those in the UK who are enabled to do only those acts for which there is specific statutory authority. They should have freedom of choice as to the manner of provision of services and in their internal organization (Article 6). They should also have the power to determine the rate of their own taxes (Article 9). The UK has not ratified the Charter, so it is not binding on the government. The Labour Party has promised to sign the Charter once in government (Labour Party, 1991a, p. 29).

Local government in the 1980s and 1990s

The Conservative government that took power in 1979 was concerned about the impact of local government activity on central government policy, and about inefficiency and ineffectiveness in local government services. Local government was believed to be undermining Conservative macro-economic policy and its desire to roll back the frontiers of the state. Central government felt justified in imposing its own version of the public interest in local government, and was able to do so because of the fact that local government has no secure constitutional position, but is subject always to the possibility that Parliament will alter its position at the behest of the government of the day.

Part of the government's diagnosis of the problem was that local authorities were not under sufficient pressures from their electorates and ratepayers to keep spending down and to be effective and efficient in their delivery of services. This was attributed to the influence of trade unions representing local government employees over Labour authorities, and to the fact that the majority of electors were not ratepayers and therefore did not have to meet any part of the costs of the increased local expenditure that they voted for. Public choice theory was influential in this, as in other aspects of government policy (see Chapter 1).

There was some force in the Conservatives' scepticism about the efficacy of the political pressures to which local government is subject in promoting accountability and efficiency. One of the problems about local elections is that the turn out is usually low and they are often treated by the parties and by the electorate as barometers of the level of support for the parties nationally rather than true measures of the performance of the parties locally. These influences undermine the effectiveness of the ballot box in imposing accountability.

The impact of this admitted weakness in local government elections can, however, be exaggerated. Rallings and Thrasher (1988, p. 188) have examined voting behaviour in local elections and have found that there are differences of voting behaviour between local and national elections and that communities within the same authority are influenced by their particular characteristics and by local issues. Nevertheless, they acknowledge that the turn out is unduly low, averaging only 40 percent, and they argue that interest in local politics must increase if the turn out is to increase and if local elections are to be seen as important and real political checks on these bodies.

The government's efforts to control local government in the 1980s met with resistance from many authorities, and this in turn inflamed relations between the two tiers of government. Some authorities pushed their legal powers to and beyond the limit, using what came to be known as 'creative accounting' to enable them to continue with their expenditure policies; government retaliated with increased legal regulation of their activities and rate-capping (Lansley *et al.*, 1989; Parkinson, 1986; Grant, 1986).

It will be convenient to consider the techniques employed by the Conservative government for increasing efficiency, effectiveness and accountability and for enhancing active citizenship under the following heads: financial reforms; removal of functions; increased legal regulation; and the promotion of consumerism and active citizenship. Another, less controversial device, increasing openness and public rights of access to information in local government, is discussed in Chapter 10.

Financial reforms

The last decade has seen a dramatic increase in local government accountability to central government through the financial control of local authorities, and a reduction in their freedom to raise taxation independently of Whitehall. This problem of central government financial control is not new and it is inherent to some degree in the reliance of local authorities on the centre for a large part of their financial resources. The reliance flows from the need for equalization of resources between authorities through government grants. As far back as the 1930s, William Robson (1931, p. 36) was anticipating that local government would come under central government control via the block grant which met a large proportion of its costs (Local Government Act 1929, s. 104). It was Robson's (1931, p. 42) view that local authorities were themselves largely responsible for this state of affairs: 'They have for many years, through their associations, insistently demanded more money from central government regardless of the consequences to their own dignity and freedom.' The dependence of local government on Whitehall, which inevitably results from central government subsidies, means that the authorities' accountability to their own electors takes second place to their accountability to the centre, and this trend has accelerated in the last decade.

By the 1970s, local government expenditure accounted for about 30 percent of total public expenditure, some £15 billion per annum. The proportion of this expenditure that was financed by central government grants had increased steadily until it reached about 48 percent in 1975. In that year, local authorities were informed by Anthony Crosland for the government that 'the party is over' as a result of Treasury decisions that overall public spending and borrowing should be reduced, and thereafter subsidies from central government fell. However, it remained open to local authorities to maintain their spending levels by raising money through borrowing or through raising their own independent tax base, i.e the rates, and this many authorities did. While this did not increase central government expenditure, it interfered with government policy on public expenditure cuts, designed to encourage private sector investment and enterprise. In the 1980s, the government acted against the use of the rates by local government to finance higher expenditure than the government felt necessary by a series of legislative measures designed to penalize authorities that spent beyond government-imposed limits, and ultimately by the device of rate-capping (see Rates Act 1984; see also Grant, 1986). Thus the financial autonomy of local government came to be severely restricted.

The Conservative government sought to justify its desire to increase pressure on local authorities to keep their spending down on the grounds that these authorities were inefficient and wasteful, and that local authority revenue expenditure damages the economy (*Paying for Local Government*, 1986, Cmnd. 9714, paras 1.13–1.18). The evidence for this latter point is unconvincing (for an analysis of the case, see Loughlin, 1986, chs 2 and 7, and the literature referred to therein). Loughlin, among others, takes the view that the true explanation for government measures to reduce overall public expenditure flows not from economic policy but from public choice theory (see Chapter 1): 'the government's objective has been to expand the sphere of society subject to market disciplines' (Loughlin, 1986, p. 22).

On another interpretation of Conservative policy, it was the fact that some local authorities were under the control of parties other than the Conservatives and that some of these wished to pursue policies that were inconsistent with Conservative policy, that invited central government intervention. In particular, there were conflicts between Whitehall's desire to incorporate market rationality into local government services (Loughlin, 1986, p. 167) and local government's traditional role of protecting people from the harshest consequences of market rationality (Gyford *et al.*, 1990, pp. 327–32). This was especially the case with what came to be known as 'local socialism'. Authorities committed to this approach favoured a high level of local expenditure on services, stimulating employment and industrial and commercial development, promoting industrial democracy in various forms, democratic control of the police, and policies for minorities – anti-racism and attention to women's issues (Gyford, 1985). In reacting against local socialism, the government was effectively rejecting pluralism in the political system in favour of centrally-determined policy.

The most drastic of the measures taken to reduce waste, lower the overall expenditure of local authorities and remove centres of opposition to government policy was the abolition in 1986 of the metropolitan counties and the Greater London Council (GLC) (Local Government Act 1965). Some of the functions of the abolished authorities were devolved down to the London boroughs and the metropolitan districts. But some functions were removed from local public or political accountability altogether. Transport was transferred to London Regional Transport, an unelected body (London Regional Transport Act 1984). The London Residuary Body and a number of joint boards were left with responsibility for some of those matters which could not be devolved to the boroughs (Local Government Act 1985). Thus the abolition of the GLC left the capital with no single body responsible for the strategic planning of transport, development and environmental policy, and with many functions under the control of unelected bodies. This step undermined the scope for coherent policy making on major strategic issues, and reduced political and public accountability for public services in the capital.

The community charge

The devices of abolishing a tier of local government, removing functions from politicians, limiting grants and rate-capping did not satisfy Conservative ambitions to cut public expenditure and roll back the local state, and the government turned to other methods, among them the controversial reform of the local taxation system, the rates (see, e.g. the 1981 Green Paper *Alternatives to Domestic Rates*, Cmnd. 8449).

It was widely accepted that the rating system suffered from a number of flaws, but successive attempts to find an acceptable alternative had failed. In 1976, the Layfield Report recommended retaining domestic and business rates and introducing in addition a local income tax. They felt that this would promote accountability, efficiency and flexibility. The local income tax was rejected at the time largely because it would be costly to collect. Henney (1982) rejected an alternative approach, assigned revenues, and preferred a local income tax combined with retaining domestic rates. Yet another alternative which Henney considered was to remove the financing of education from local authorities and transfer it to central government; this would enable local authorities to raise less of their revenue locally, so that whatever the system the rate at which it was set would be lower.

The government's White Paper *Rates* (1983, Cmnd. 9008) rejected a community charge on the grounds that it would be hard to enforce, being expensive and complicated. Yet in 1986, the government produced its plans for the community charge, which was introduced in Scotland in 1989 and came into effect in England and Wales in April 1990 (Local Government Finance Act 1988). Given the fate of the charge, the way in which the policy was adopted provides a good example of the shortcomings of the policy-making system: the government was impervious to warnings that it would be hard to collect and extremely unpopular.

The name 'community charge' implied that it was a charge for services, and the government intended it to be viewed as such. However, because it was payable regardless of whether services were in fact received by the charge payer, and because it was not related to the cost of any services that are received, it would be more appropriately called a 'community rate' (see Grant, 1988). It was a flat rate charge or rate payable by all adults in a local government area. Students and those in receipt of certain benefits were to be able to claim relief, but apart from this there was no relationship between the level of the charge and ability to pay.

The other principal aspect of this local government finance package was the removal of the business rate, determined locally by local authorities, and its replacement by a 'uniform business rate' fixed by central government, the proceeds of which are collected centrally and redistributed between authorities according to a national formula. While this system, being redistributive, is fairer as between authorities than the old business rate, it further reduced the autonomy of local authorities by depriving them of this independent tax base.

One of the advantages claimed by the government for the community charge was fairness, in that it spread the burden of financing that portion of local government expenditure over a wider section of the local population, i.e. all adults, whereas the rates were payable by property owners or 'rateable occupiers', only a proportion of the population. Although it was the case that not all voters were ratepayers, there is evidence that a high proportion of voters thought of themselves as ratepayers (Miller, 1986, p. 105, 1988), so the assumption that voters would vote differently according to whether a system of rates or community charge was in operation is dubious. But the claim that the community charge was in any other respect fairer than the rates did not stand up to scrutiny. While the level of rates was not related to ability to pay, ratepayers did receive rebates according to their means. The provisions for relief from community charge were far more restrictive and inflexible. The community charge introduced disincentives to certain people, notably those who could ill afford to pay the charge, to register as electors, since registration would in practice invite imposition of the community charge. This aspect of the system undermined political citizenship rights (see Chapters 2 and 8). The collection of the tax was expensive and there was a high level of defaulters against whom it was difficult to levy payment. In this respect, the charge was inefficient.

In introducing the system, the government assumed that there would be effective local political pressure on local authorities to keep the level of community charge down. This fitted in with the avowed objective in introducing the charge, to increase the accountability of local government for its expenditure decisions by arming local electors to 'influence the spending of their council through the ballot box. ... Effective local accountability must be the cornerstone of successful local government' (1986, Cmnd. 9714, p. vii).

When the community charge came into operation in England and Wales in April 1990, the government found that almost all local authorities had fixed charges higher than the target figures that had been produced by the government in anticipation of local authority figures. One unavoidable implication of this was that the government's figures were unrealistic; another was that the government had misjudged the effectiveness of the ballot box in providing disincentives to expenditure by local government.

The Secretary of State for the Environment's response was to invoke powers contained in the 1988 Act to 'cap' the charges of 20 authorities who he felt were 'overspending' (see Local Government Finance Act 1988, ss. 95, 100). None of these was under Conservative control, although a number of Conservative authorities had exceeded the government targets by more than capped authorities had done. This invited the accusation that the Secretary of State had been partisan in his decisions (the court rejected this allegation and refused to intervene: *R. v. Secretary of State for the Environment, Ex parte Hammersmith and Fulham Borough Council* [1990] 3 All ER 589).

One assumption of the community charge legislation was that it would impose sufficient restraints on local authorities' expenditure so that it would not be necessary for central government to intervene in these matters as it had done in the previous decade. But the government had clearly foreseen that the system might not deter authorities from spending more than the government wished, since it included charge-capping powers in the Act. The capping of authorities in 1990 amounted to an admission that this rationale of the community charge was flawed.

In practice, the community charge did not increase accountability to local electors, as there was a high level of ignorance about what the charge was spent on. This was contributed to by a lack of transparency in the two-tier local government system which made it difficult for chargepayers to know at which tier expenditure was incurred. The lack of transparency in this respect was contributed to by the uniform business rate, which reduced local government responsibility for raising its finance and increased central government control (Bloch, 1991).

The community charge proved very unpopular with the electorate, and was blamed for the loss by the government to the Liberal Democrats of what had been a safe Conservative seat in the Ribble Valley by-election in March 1991. This pushed the government to hasten the decision of the Local Government Review that had been announced by Michael Heseltine when he became Secretary of State for the Environment in December 1990.

The government faced many problems in deciding what should replace the community charge. Apart from the political embarrassment of a U-turn if a property tax were reintroduced, there was the problem that the share of local government expenditure that was met out of locally raised revenue had increased; even if the rates had been reintroduced, they would have been at a higher level than before their abolition. If parts of local government expenditure, for example education, were removed from that tier and borne by the government, then they would have to be met out of increased central taxation, or by cuts elsewhere.

The government's solution to this point was to increase central government grants so as to reduce the community charge by £140. This additional burden on central government was met by an increase of 2.5 percent on the rate of Value Added Tax. As a result, local government became even more dependent than hitherto on Whitehall for its finances: only 14 percent of its revenue was raised by the community charge, and the government proposed that the new 'Council Tax' should also raise only that proportion of local government revenue.

The government decided to abolish the community charge and to reintroduce a property-based tax (Department of the Environment, 1991a). Under this system, properties would be placed in one of seven (later raised to eight) broad bands of value related to the average value of properties in England, Wales or Scotland. This banding would avoid having each property valued. The tax was presented as to 50 percent as a tax on property, and as to 50 percent as personal contributions to local expenditure by residents. The scheme assumed two adults in a household, but provided for 'discounts' of 25 percent if there was only one adult resident. There were further discounts and rebates for people on low incomes.

Under these proposals, authorities would continue to receive grants from government as under the community charge system. The total amount available for general grant would be distributed so that the authorities in each area could finance spending at a standard level laid down by the government by levying standard amounts fixed by the Secretary of State. In this way, the authorities would be compensated for differences in their expenditure needs, and for variations in their 'taxable capacity' (Department of the Environment, 1991a, para. 6.1). But if they found the sums paid in grant inadequate, or if the standard level laid down by government did not provide sufficient for them to meet their obligations or the commitments they wished to make, they would have to levy council tax at a higher rate. The Secretary of State would, however, have 'capping' powers. The government also proposed to continue the Uniform Business Rate system introduced with the community charge.

The Audit Commission expressed concern about the administrative implications of the new tax; it also felt that the accountability of local government to its electors was undermined by the fact that only 14 percent of local government revenue came from local tax payers; that there was widespread lack of confidence in the appropriateness of the 'standard spending assessments' on which the grant system is founded; and that the very tight 'gearing' on council tax means that a 1 percent increase in spending above standard spending assessments would result in a 7 or 8 percent increase in council tax (Audit Commission, 1991).

The Labour Party proposes to replace the community charge with a system of 'fair rates' under which liability would be related to ability to pay, and to restore local government control over business rates (Labour Party, 1991a, 828; 1991b, p. 7). Of the various possible alternatives to the community charge (see Hollis *et al.*, 1990), the return to a property tax has turned out to be one that is acceptable in principle to both the Conservatives and Labour, although there are differences between the details of the schemes of these two parties. Property taxes have the strong advantage that they are cheap to collect and there is a very low level of non-payment.

An option that was rejected by both Labour and the Conservatives was a local income tax. This is the solution proposed by the Liberal Democrats. Under such a system, each authority would be able to fix a rate of local tax which could be collected through the Inland Revenue and distributed to the authority. An upper limit could be imposed if thought appropriate. It would be possible to transfer some of the cost of local government from Whitehall to local taxpayers by cutting government grants to local authorities, reducing the standard rate of income tax, and allowing local authorities to raise more by local income tax. Such a system would be fair in that the liability to pay would be shared by all those who could afford it in the area, it would be linked to ability to pay, and it would be transparent in that local taxpayers would know what the local income tax rate was and would be able to make comparisons with other authorities and express their judgements in the ballot box. But from the point of view of the Labour and Conservative parties, the transparency of a local income tax is one of its chief disadvantages, since it would result, naturally, in an increase in income tax rates overall – both parties are sensitive to accusations that they are increasing taxes.

The removal of functions from local government

Local authorities are the creatures of Westminster legislation, and under the UK system as it operates at present there are no legal obstacles in the way of a government which wishes to have legislation passed to alter the legal status and powers of local authorities. One of the responses of the Conservative government to the perceived inefficiency, ineffectiveness and unaccountability of local government, has been the statutory transfer of local authority functions to other bodies. Urban development corporations established under the Local

Government, Planning and Land Act 1980 (for example, the London Docklands Development Corporation, LDDC) and development agencies in Scotland and Wales have been given a range of powers that would normally be exercised by local authorities, including responsibility for planning and the infrastructure. The theory behind the transfer of functions to these appointed, unelected bodies was that they would be more effective and efficient than local authorities because they were not politicized. There had been a long period of inability on the part of the affected local authorities to reach decisions about the future development of London's docklands before the LDDC was set up, and development accelerated remarkably once the corporation assumed responsibility for it. There is, however, by no means agreement about whose fault it was – central or local government – that little had been done before the LDDC took over. And the lack of both political and public accountability and regulatory powers in these new corporations produced some chaotic results. The infrastructure, especially the transport system in the London docklands, was severely underfunded. In enterprise zones, under the Local Government, Planning and Land Act 1980, there is not even any planning control for certain types of development.

Examples of the removal of functions from local authorities on the grounds that they are inefficient and unaccountable to their consumers include the shift of responsibilities for the provision of homes for those unable to buy from local authorities to housing associations. The housing role would have been further eroded if council tenants had taken the opportunity to vote, under a biased voting system (see Housing Act 1988, s. 103), for estates to be taken over by some other landlord, whether private or a housing association or Housing Action Trust; however, this policy did not prove popular with tenants.

Schools too may opt out of local authority control and a number (though fewer than the Secretary of State for Education would have wished) has done so. There is also a trend against the provision by local authorities of homes for the elderly; these are increasingly to be provided by the private sector with charges paid for by the Department of Social Security. The granting of corporate status to polytechnics under the Education Reform Act 1988 (part II, ch. II) may be seen in the same light.

The potential for central government to assume increasing control over functions that have been 'hived off' from local authorities, in the fields of education (Meredith, 1989) and housing in particular, raises issues of remoteness and lack of accountability in the provision of these services. And where functions are taken over by unelected, unrepresentative bodies – housing associations, private landlords – there will be no system of public or political accountability at all and in practice no real exit or market mechanism to protect the consumer either.

Another version of the process of removing functions from local authorities is the transformation of their role from that of providing to enabling. In many areas of activity, local authorities now provide the funds with which others supply services, rather than providing them directly. They contract with private sector organizations or with their own direct labour organizations (which are under a competitive tendering regime: Local Government Act 1988) for refuse collection. They finance schools on which governing bodies and the heads have the primary responsibility for the running of the school (Education Reform Act 1988, part I). The objectives are to increase consumer accountability and efficiency.

Many of these devices are as yet in their infancy and it is too early to pass judgement on them. Their effectiveness must depend largely on how they are funded. And there is reason for scepticism about the ability of school governing bodies, with volunteer members often without experience in education (Meredith, 1989) or administration, to perform their functions in relation to the school adequately.

Legal regulation of the political process

It is a characteristic of the UK system of government that the political process in central and local government is relatively unregulated; politicians are, for the most part, politically and publicly – not legally and administratively – accountable for the way in which they reach political (as opposed to administrative or operational) decisions. In the field of local government, however, this position has changed.

Until the early 1970s, local authorities had been relatively unpoliticized. In 1967, the Maud Committee found that only 50 percent of authorities had been under party control. There was relatively little difference between authorities in different parts of the country or of different political complexions as far as the level of spending on services and the approach to their delivery was concerned.

The Widdicombe Committee found that the party system in local government was 'widely accepted' (Widdicombe, 1986, para. 2.43). This process might in principle imply a desirable political pluralism in the sense that some local authorities are controlled by a party other than that in control in Whitehall. However, the 1970s and 1980s saw a steady polarization of politics and with it an intensification of political conflict at local government level (Gyford *et al.*, 1990, chs 1, 9). In practice, this raised a range of problems. As the political parties polarized, and as the New Right gained ground in the Conservative Party and the New Left in the Labour Party, greater diversity entered local government. But this generated conflict within and between the parties and between central and local government.

This intensification of political and conflict undermined the liberal-democratic tradition and the policy of minimal legal or administrative regulation of the political process. Until the 1980s, local authorities enjoyed considerable freedom from legal regulation in their political activity and the principal restraints against abuse of their wide discretions came from constitutional conventions, comity between the parties and respect for liberal-democratic traditions (Gyford *et al.*, 1990). The acceleration and intensification of politicization in local government in the 1980s put strains on the comity between the political parties that had underpinned the codes of behaviour of local councillors.

Some of the old unwritten, non-partisan conventions about the conduct of local government have steadily been eroded. In the 1980s, there were repeated allegations that majority parties were using their positions to promote the interests of the party and party members or to discriminate against opponents. Examples included the dissemination of party political propaganda 'on the rates' (Committee of Inquiry into the Conduct of Local Authority Business, 1985; see *R. v. Inner London Education Authority, Ex parte Westminster City Council* [1986] 1 WLR 28; Local Government Act 1986 as amended by Local Government Act 1988, ss. 27, 28). Other examples were the practice of 'twintracking' (Widdicombe, 1986, paras 6.30–6.34; Local Government and Housing Act 1989, ss. 1–3) and of the employment of politically committed officers in local government (Widdicombe, 1986, paras 6.183–6.203). There were also instances of local authorities blacklisting or excluding organizations, political parties or pressure groups of whom they disapproved from council property and local government contracts (e.g. *Wheeler* v. *Leicester City Council* [1985] AC 1054; *Ettridge* v. *Morrell* (1986) 85 LGR 100; *Webster* v. *Southwark London Borough* [1983] QB 698; *R. v. Barnet London Borough, Ex parte Johnson, Independent* 17 August 1990; *R. v. Derbyshire County Council, Ex parte The Times Supplements, Times* 19 July 1990; *R. v. Ealing London Borough, Ex parte Times Newspapers* (1986) 85 LGR 316).

Some of these allegations surfaced in the courts (see cases noted above; see also *R. v. Waltham Forest LBC, Ex parte Waltham Forest Ratepayers' Action Group* [1987] 3 All ER 671; *R. v. Sheffield City Council, Ex parte Chadwick* (1986) 84 LGR 563; *R. v. Hackney LBC, Ex parte Gamper* [1985] 1 WLR 1229). The judges sought to uphold the principle that councillors owe their duties to all their electors and the public interest, while at the same time acknowledging the political reality that party organizations exist and party political considerations influence councillors. So, for example, in the 'Fare's Fair' case, the House of Lords based one of their objections to the Labour majority's cheap fare policy on the fact that Labour councillors had felt themselves irrevocably committed to the local party's policy formed before their election and had not consulted and carefully considered it once elected (*Bromley London Borough Council* v. *Greater London Council* [1983] AC 768 at 829–831 (per Lord Diplock) and at 853 (per Lord Brandon)). On the other hand, in the Waltham Forest case, Sir John Donaldson, MR, accepted that councillors may take the view that it is in the interests of their constituents for the party to remain in power and vote accordingly, even though they would have voted otherwise if the party consideration had been irrelevant (see *R. v. Waltham Forest LBC, Ex parte Waltham Forest Ratepayers' Action Group* [1987] 3 All ER 671). The judges were not finding it easy to find a middle way between non-partisan liberal-democratic traditions and the reality of partisan politics in local government.

The Widdicombe Report

In response to press and public disquiet (often exaggerated but sometimes well-founded) over the problems of politicization and partisanship in local government, the government set up a Committee of Inquiry into the Conduct of Local Authority Business under the chairmanship of David Widdicombe QC. The committee produced its interim report on *Local Authority Publicity* in 1985, in which it recommended legislation to prohibit local authority publicity of a party political nature. The government responded by securing the passage of the Local Government Act 1986, which prohibited the publication of 'any material which, in whole or in part, appears to be designed to affect public support for a political party' (for a discussion, see Gyford *et al.*, 1990, pp. 284–8). This marked the beginning of a period of increasing legal regulation of the political activity of local government. The fact that the original Act had to be amended by the Local Government Act 1988 to achieve the government's purpose, illustrates the difficulties inevitably experienced in trying to reduce constitutional conventions to the form of statutory rules.

In its main report, the Widdicombe Committee (1985) found many of the allegations about improper politicization in local government to be exaggerated, but recommended nevertheless that steps should be taken to protect the older conventions about non-partisan, neutral local government administration by depoliticizing some aspects of local government activity (for a discussion, see Gyford *et al.*, 1990, esp. ch. 8).

As indicated above, one of the complaints about partisanship related to twintracking. The committee found the practice to be objectionable in only a very few cases: many twintrackers were teachers, who are not bound by the rule that council officers should be and be seen to be politically neutral (Widdicombe, 1986, para. 6.210). The principal objection identified by the committee was that, in some instances, employing councils were allowing their employees an excessive amount of paid leave to allow them to work almost full-time for the councils of which they were elected members, which was a waste of the employing authority's money (Widdicombe, 1986, para. 6.120).

The government's response to Widdicombe

The government accepted some of the Widdicombe Committee's recommendations (see Cm. 433, 1988) and introduced legislation in the 1988–89 session of Parliament to deal with the problems. Under the Local Government and Housing Act 1989, twintracking is limited by a provision enabling the Secretary of State for the Environment to make regulations disqualifying the chief officers and other major officials in local authorities, and other non-clerical employees earning in excess of £19 000 per annum from membership of a local authority, and restricting their political activities (ss. 1, 2; Local Government Officers (Political Restrictions) Regulations 1990, s.1. 851; Local Government (Politically Restricted Positions) (No.2) Regulations 1990, s.1.

1447). The original proposal had been to set the pay level at a much lower figure, but this was dropped in response to complaints that it was an unjustifiable invasion of the civil and political rights of the employees concerned. (The Labour Party is pledged to remove these restrictions: 1991b, p. 15.) The amount of paid leave that may be granted to council employees is limited to a maximum of 208 hours a year (Local Government and Housing Act 1989, s. 10).

The use of patronage for political purposes is stopped by the provision that all appointments are to be made on merit, which implies that it will be unlawful to take account of a person's political activities or affiliations in reaching decisions about appointments (Local Government and Housing Act 1989, s. 7). But an important exception to this general rule, and an acknowledgement of the usefulness of political advisers in local government, is that a maximum of three appointments may be made for the purpose of providing political assistance to members of political groups in the authority, provided that no such appointments may be made unless each of the three largest groups is to have such an adviser (ibid., s. 9; see Local Government (Committees and Political Groups) Regulations 1990, s.1. 1553, part III). Further, council committees are to reflect the political balance on the council (Local Government and Housing Act 1989, ss. 15–17; s.1. 1553, part IV; cf. *R. v. Greenwich London Borough, Ex parte Lovelace* [1991] 1 WLR 506 CA: a council has the right to remove members of a committee who vote against council policy proposals as long as the power is not used maliciously or to punish the member for past conduct). These decisions by government and their implementation through legislation have led to the introduction of rules defining political groups and indicating how they should be constituted, a step in the direction of regulating political parties which is novel in local government law.

In order to prevent the majority party manipulating the council's procedures and its bureaucracy for its own ends, the Secretary of State has the power to issue a National Code of Local Government Practice, a draft of which is to be laid before Parliament (Local Government and Housing Act 1989, s.31; Department of the Environment Circular 1990/8; Welsh Office 1990/23; Scottish Office 1990/11). Each authority is to designate a 'monitoring officer' who must present a report to the council if they consider that the code of practice has been breached, or that there has been maladministration (Local Government and Housing Act 1989, s.5). The Act also provides that appointed, non-elected committee members are not entitled to vote at committee meetings (Local Government and Housing Act 1989, s.1), and that the Secretary of State may make regulations requiring members to register their interests, on pain of criminal penalties (ibid., s.19). A role in policing the political process has thus been committed to officers, where previously it was seen as falling within the functions of the checks and balances in the process itself.

In this field of local government activity, then, a degree of legal and administrative regulation has been introduced in the last decade, most of which has a depoliticizing effect (Ganz, 1990). In many respects, the values which these provisions make explicit are not controversial. They seek to put into legal form the liberal-democratic political tradition. What is controversial is the use of the law to enforce these values. That these values are not easily defined is indicated by the detail which some of these measures have involved. It is likely that politicians will be tempted to concern themselves only with complying with the letter of the law, losing sight of the spirit which informs these measures. The approach has much in common with the financial controls to which local government has increasingly been subjected in the last decade; the reaction of central government to the perceived inefficiencies and lack of accountability of local government has been to subject the political process to greater regulation, and therefore accountability, by the courts and Whitehall. It is to be considered whether or not a better alternative would have been to seek to reform and revitalize the political process, which gives rise to inefficiencies and a lack of accountability, through such measures as electoral reform or a move from the committee system to an executive system in which the opposition parties would have a more clearly defined role in holding the controlling party to account (cf. Widdicombe, 1986, paras 5.19–24, 30–35 and see Department of the Environment, 1991c). The Labour Party proposes annual elections of a proportion of councillors as a means of enhancing their public accountability (Labour Party, 1991, p. 29).

Consumerism in local government

The rationale for some of the reforms of local government services introduced in the 1980s has been to by pass politicians and to devolve power to consumers of public services, thus introducing a form of public accountability (see Chapter 2). In effect, government has been using citizens as consumers to control councils.

To take schools to illustrate the point, the Education Act 1980 provided for the publication of information about schools and admission arrangements and for the expression of parental preferences as to the schools which their children should attend; it set up an appeal procedure for dissatisfied parents (see Education Act 1980, ss. 6,7). The Education Reform Act 1988 requires open admissions to schools so that local education authorities cannot impose artificial limits on the intake of popular schools in order to protect the less popular; this increases parental choice (see Education Reform Act 1988, part I, ch. II, ss. 26–33). The provisions in the Education (Number 2) Act 1986 for school governing bodies on which parents, teachers and other members of the community are represented, is on the face of it consumer-oriented, an introduction of a measure of self-government by or on behalf of the users and consumers of education. The provision for schools to opt out of local authority control and become funded directly by the Secretary of State is another ostensibly consumer-oriented aspect of education policy in the sense that it offers 'exit' (the initial decision rests with the governing body unless the parents of 20 percent of the pupils request a ballot: Education Reform Act 1988, ss. 58,59).

In the field of housing, a 'tenants' charter' was introduced in the Housing Act 1980 which granted tenants not only the 'right to buy' at a large discount

(Housing Act 1980, part I, ch. I) but also security of tenure (Housing Act 1980, part I, ch. II), rights to receive information about secure tenancies (Housing Act 1980, s. 41), rights to be consulted by the authority about matters of housing management (Housing Act 1980, ss. 42,43) and the right to receive information about housing allocation policies (Housing Act 1980, s. 44). Under the Housing Act 1988, tenants are offered 'exit' from local authority control. A private landlord may take over a council estate if the tenants support the proposal, though the tenants' ballot is rigged in favour of the takeover. The transfer will go ahead if more than 50 percent of the tenants vote in the ballot, unless 50 percent of the total number of tenants vote to remain tenants of the authority: Housing Act 1988, s. 103). Alternatively, estates may be taken over by a Housing Action Trust in certain circumstances, but if a majority of tenants responding in the ballot are opposed to the proposal it cannot go ahead (see Housing Act 1988, s. 61(4)). As indicated earlier, tenants have not chosen these exits.

Although the Conservatives have been pioneers in introducing consumerism into local government, the importance of the consumer is recognized in the Labour Party's Policy Review *Meet the Challenge: Make the Change* (1989, p. 4): 'Modern "consumerism" is . . . the expression of people's desire for greater control over the goods and services they use . . .' (for further discussion of the Labour approach to consumerism in public services, see Plant, 1988; see also Labour Party 1991b, pp. 10–11). Labour would not, however, go as far as the Conservatives in allowing 'exit' as a form of consumerism.

Other devices have been employed by both Labour (Labour Party, 1989, p. 44, 1990, p. 24, 1991a p. 29) and Conservative authorities to promote the interests of consumers of local government services; these have included the introduction of 'contracts' by which authorities undertake, for example, how often streets in a given area shall be swept and how often refuse shall be collected. The explicit definition of standards enables the public to pinpoint where standards have fallen short of the authority's promises, and they enable authorities to hold their own workforces or contractors to account for failing to meet the standards set. Labour is committed to extending the use of customer contracts and introducing a Quality Commission, which would incorporate the work of the Audit Commission. The idea here would be to shift the emphasis from value for money and cost-cutting towards improved quality (Labour Party, 1991a, 29b, pp. 12–13); the Conservatives' *Citizen's Charter* proposes use of the 'contract' as a vehicle for quality control.

It is too soon to know whether the introduction of consumerism in local government will result in a genuine improvement in efficiency and effectiveness, and it is difficult to know to what extent shortcomings in services result from underfunding – over which authorities may have little control, as they have lost much of their independent tax base – or bad management. It will also be difficult to balance any improvements against obstacles placed in the way of local authorities planning education or providing homes for the homeless. As long as local authorities retain some discretion as to how their resources should be deployed outside the area of strict statutory obligations, it will also be difficult to assess performance where authorities have made a deliberate commitment to put more resources into one service than another. Nevertheless, the consumerist approach represents a welcome shift towards stressing that the interests of the public in the local government area are paramount over those of political parties, trade unions or employees.

Citizenship and the community in local government

One aspect of citizenship is participation in the local community; political citizenship rights in their active form entail opportunities to participate at local as well as central government level in the political process (see Chapter 2). A number of local authorities have attempted to stimulate community spirit and citizenship through various forms of multipurpose neighbourhood decentralization. The approach was pioneered by Labour in Walsall in the early 1980s (Hambleton, 1988). In Islington, a programme of decentralization was implemented between 1982 and 1986. After winning control in Richmond-on-Thames in 1983, the Liberals on the council introduced area consultation and area housing management committees, on which both councillors and tenants are represented, and mobile council offices. There have been many other initiatives of this kind, taken predominantly by Labour authorities (for further information about decentralization, see Hambleton, 1988; Lansley et al., 1989).

The Liberal Party had a longstanding commitment to community politics, which won them dividends electorally. The objective of this form of politics was rather that the councillor should act as encourager of a measure of direct democracy and the channel of effective participation by the people than that they should win votes from the other parties. Meadowcroft argues that only by raising the political consciousness of the people can 'latent compassion and neighbourliness' be realized (Meadowcroft, 1982, p. 3, quoted by Gyford in Widdicombe, 1986, vol. IV, p. 116). In other words, local political activity can act as a catalyst for promoting citizenship and a sense of community. Here is an important role that local authorities can and should assume in an age where citizenship and a sense of community spirit are agreed by all parties and in many sections of society to be in need of fostering and promoting.

The objectives of the political parties in promoting community politics have varied. Gyford suggests that the priority for Liberals has been to increase the power of the individual in the face of bureaucracy; this contrasts, he argues, with the rationale for community politics in the Labour Party, which has generally been to educate people to understand how local government operates and thus to restore their faith in those institutions. In this respect, it has been an exercise in the legitimation of authority rather than a genuine attempt to substitute self-government for government.

On the other hand, there is a strong 'self-government', 'bottom-up democracy' strain in Labour Party thinking on community politics. David Blunkett (1981, p. 102, quoted in Widdicombe, 1986, vol. IV, pp. 116–17) expresses the need for 'not paternalistically doing things for people but throwing our weight behind them . . . to do what they want to do in their way in their community'. Also 'no-one will easily defend a socialist principle (like for example direct labour) if it is encapsulated in a service (like council housing repairs) which is paternalistic, authoritarian or plain inefficient' (Blunkett and Green, 1984, p. 2). In practice, therefore, the Labour and Liberal approaches to community politics have been in many respects similar save that their ultimate objectives are different, those of Labour often being to establish 'local socialism' and those of the Liberals being to promote individual self-determination and responsive administration.

Devolution in local government

The most radical experiment in decentralization, or more accurately devolution, has been undertaken in the London Borough of Tower Hamlets since 1986. The Liberal Democrat controlled council has created autonomous 'neighbourhood committees' consisting of the councillors elected for their neighbourhood, to which most council functions and decisions, notably in the fields of housing allocation and repair, social services and street cleaning, are devolved. The process may be interpreted as one of empowering local councillors by giving them clear responsibility for their own areas and making lines of responsibility more transparent.

The novelty of this scheme is that it involves political devolution as well as the administrative devolution practised in some other authorities. The neighbourhoods are based on the 'hamlets' or urban villages in the borough. Political control passes to the party with most seats in each neighbourhood. So some of the neighbourhood committees are controlled by parties which are in a minority on the council. Each has its own budget, determined by the council as a whole. The neighbourhoods have set up 'first stop shops' in accessible locations where people can make inquiries, request repairs or social service visits without having to travel across the borough or be referred to a variety of offices. To encourage local participation and consultation, some of the neighbourhoods have arranged for the election by single transferable vote of 'neighbourhood forums' which can make recommendations to the neighbourhood committees.

The experiment is being monitored by the School of Advanced Urban Studies at Bristol University and there is as yet no published detailed assessment of its workings. Among the benefits of this strategy claimed by the Liberal group has been the fostering of the sense of community in each of the neighbourhoods; improvement in the efficiency and effectiveness of services; giving local councillors more power; and ensuring that the councillors and the officers actually know the areas in respect of which they make decisions. Previously, many councillors attending and voting at council meetings at which decisions were made did not know the areas, due to the large size of the borough. It was widely felt that the council was remote and unresponsive. (This account is based on an interview with the deputy leader of the council, Councillor Flounders; see also Tower Hamlets London Borough Council, *Decentralisation: A Change for the Better*, 1988; *The Independent*, 24 August 1989.)

But criticisms are also emerging. It is said that the system is expensive to run since it involves separate administrations in each neighbourhood, and that it creates barriers to access to services between the neighbourhoods – those in one neighbourhood who need to be rehoused may not be accepted for rehousing in another neighbourhood. And there have been allegations that the majority group in each neighbourhood channels resources into those wards where its support is strong and discriminates against those where other parties may have a majority (*The London Programme*, ITV, 8 March 1991).

Judgement on this experiment must await a detailed assessment. The shortcomings may result from the details of the scheme rather than fundamental flaws in it. The information so far available highlights the ways in which accountability and effectiveness can be at odds with one another, and the problems in finding the right balance between the two.

Local government and 'active citizenship'

While the Conservatives see themselves as the party of active citizenship (see Chapter 2), they have been reluctant to cast local government as a channel for encouraging it. This tallies with the Conservative concept of active citizenship as, in essence, a non-political social institution and even to some extent as a substitute for politics and state provision of citizenship rights (see Chapter 2).

As suggested in Chapter 2, an active citizenry, even of a non-political Conservative sort, will not evolve spontaneously in response to government exhortation; it needs encouragement from a variety of organizations in the public, private and voluntary sectors. Local government is well placed to play a role here, and far better placed than central government which is too remote from the communities out of which citizenship develops. But this point should not be taken to imply acceptance of the Conservative view of the non-political active citizen. As indicated in Chapter 2, a modern concept of citizenship must involve political competence too.

If local government is to perform a role as a promoter of citizenship and community effectively, some institutional reorganization is necessary. Local government areas, even district councils, are at present too large to engender any real sense of local community. Smaller sub-units, which could be called neighbourhoods, as in Tower Hamlets (or villages, parishes), would need to be formed. Neighbourhood decentralization should become more widespread, and should be based as far as possible on the natural communities that make up most local government areas.

A scheme of this kind does, however, raise the question of the role of the council itself. It would in effect be responsible for deciding on the budget of each neighbourhood and the level of the local tax. It could also have a role in regulating relations between the neighbourhoods and their duties to one another. These would be important roles and ones that could not realistically be performed by each neighbourhood alone. The council would also represent the neighbourhoods in communications with central government or national and regional assemblies.

The future of local government

We have seen how local government was undermined in the 1980s by a reduction in its financial autonomy, loss of functions and increased legal, political and administrative regulation. These increased the degree to which it was accountable to central government to its officers and to the law, and reduced the range of activities in respect of which it could be accountable and responsive to its own electorate. As we have seen, the reduction of the autonomy of local government goes against opinion in the international community, which regards effective local government as 'one of the main foundations of any democratic regime' (*European Charter of Local Self-Government*, Council of Europe Treaty 122, Preamble). It is also inconsistent with the subsidiarity principle (see Chapter 1). On the other hand, the public accountability of local government has been increased through legislation imposing a greater degree of openness in its operations (see Chapter 10) and its local accountability by the enhancement of the rights of consumers of local services. The changes of the 1980s have not all been detrimental to accountability and effectiveness in local government.

In the climate of the 1990s, it is fruitless to dwell too long on exactly what functions local government should perform and how. A more constructive approach is to look to the future and consider how the efficiency, effectiveness and accountability of local government could be enhanced in the functions that it is given to perform, and what role these authorities might have to play in promoting community and citizenship.

First, there is a need to enhance the accountability of local government to its own electorate. This is particularly important in that it could raise the status of councils' duties to the local public interest. The question is how can electoral accountability be enhanced? Rallings and Thrasher would like to see increased media interest in local government elections, but this is unlikely to occur unless the outcome of such elections is more affected by local party politics and attracts more local controversy and a higher turnout. This cannot be achieved by exhortation or wishful thinking. The introduction of schemes of neighbourhood devolution should stimulate local interest in elections; annual elections of a proportion of councillors would also expose local government to regular public accountability. Labour is committed to this reform (Labour Party, 1991b, pp.8, 14); a more proportional system of voting, i.e. the single transferable vote, would raise the level of political interest in local elections by securing that results are more responsive to shifts in public opinion and making it possible for smaller parties to win seats by concentrating their efforts in winnable areas. Proportional representation would also revitalize the liberal-democratic traditions of the political process and should mitigate the effects of political polarization and partisanship; if this could be achieved, the case for legal regulation of local government would fall. Other options include elected mayors (Department of the Environment, 1991c)

Elections alone do not impose sufficient accountability, and ways to increase accountability to those affected by local government activity could be developed, e.g. contracts, neighbourhood committees and forums, tenant involvement in the management of housing estates, even vouchers for local services. It is being suggested by all three main parties that legal entitlements in respect of local services should be 'enforceable' by consumers whose services fall short of the agreed level, for example by allowing council tenants to have repairs done and then send the bill to the authority, by entitlements to compensation, or by giving people vouchers (Plant, 1988, pp. 12–13, 1990, pp. 29–32; see also Ashdown, 1989, p. 62).

Financial accountability to the local electorate and consumers of services also needs to be enhanced, and some better method than central government limits on local levels of tax found for encouraging efficiency, effectiveness and responsibility in local government expenditure. A local income tax would be far more transparent than the community charge or a property tax could be, it would be related to ability to pay and it would be payable by a larger proportion of the local electorate than a property tax.

There is also criticism of the two-tier system and growing support for replacing this with a single tier of 'most-purpose' authorities. Some would prefer these to be based normally on the district councils, with room for parish councils operating at a local level (see, e.g. Labour Party, 1989, p. 58, 1991a, p. 30; b, pp. 14–15; the Conservative-controlled Association of District Councils has also indicated support for such a measure: *Closer to the People*, 1987). But in some areas the counties could provide the only tier, and in others a new authority would do so. This approach was adopted by the government in its consultation paper on *The Structure of Local Government in England* (Department of the Environment, 1991b).

If a new tier of government were to be introduced for the English regions and Scotland, Wales and Northern Ireland (see Chapter 6), local government would have to be restructured. The consensus is that it would be pointless to retain the two-tier structure of local authorities and that most functions should be devolved down to the lower level of local government, while those that cannot be performed at such a local level should pass to the regional tier. John Macdonald, in his draft constitution in *'"We, The People . . ." – Towards a Written Constitution'* (Liberal Democrats, 1990), envisages single-tier principal authorities below national and regional governments, with the appropriate tier to be decided locally, with community, parish and town councils operating below them. Hence some assemblies might decide on district councils as the principal authorities, whereas others might prefer county councils.

If regional and national assemblies were to be elected on a system of proportional representation, then it would make sense for the same system to be used for local elections, and for constituency boundaries for regional assemblies

to follow those of local authorities, so that a pattern of community representation would develop.

When Michael Heseltine, the new Secretary of State for the Environment,
embarked on a review of local government which was to extend to questions of
finance, structure (including whether a single-tier system should be adopted)
and functions in December 1990, he expressed the hope that a cross-party
consensus could be found that would provide a secure basis for local
government. This was greeted with scepticism by the Labour Party, which saw it
as a ploy for getting the government out of the embarrassing situation into
which it had been pushed by its adoption of the community charge. But be that
as it may, it must surely be right to seek to achieve a sound and secure basis for
local government given its central role in promoting accountability and
effectiveness in the delivery of public services, and a sense of citizenship.

6

Decentralization

The UK constitution is highly centralized. Local government is the only elected tier below Westminster, and as we have seen (Chapter 5) the autonomy of local authorities has been progressively eroded in the last decade or so. There is no legal impediment to the Westminster Parliament legislating to abolish local authorities, or to reduce their freedom of action. Nor are there in practice effective political impediments to such action, since a government at Westminster will almost invariably have a majority that it can use to alter the powers of local government, even though it does not have the support of a majority of the electorate.

The implication of this degree of centralization is that government is accountable to the national public rather than to local publics, and political accountability too is owed to national rather than local political institutions. This in turn means that effectiveness in government is measured in nationwide terms rather than in terms of the effectiveness of policies on, for example, employment, economic development, environmental protection, in solving local problems. The unitary, centralized system also encourages the population to think in one-dimensional terms where senses of citizenship and community are concerned: citizenship is essentially British. There are almost no other political institutions that foster 'multiple citizenship' (Heater, 1990, ch. 9), a sense of belonging to a range of communities – some local, some functional.

Devolution

The centralization of power in the UK started to become a political issue in the late 1960s, and continued to be so throughout the 1970s. It was the growth of nationalism in Scotland and Wales that put the issue on the agenda and, in response to this pressure, the Royal Commission on the Constitution was set up by the Labour government in 1969 to 'examine the present functions of the central legislature and government in relation to the several countries, nations and regions of the United Kingdom' and other related issues (for discussion of the political background to Labour's policies towards Scottish devolution, see Geekie and Levy, 1989). Its report was published in 1973 (Cmnd. 5460).

As we shall see, the report's recommendations for 'devolution' did not bear fruit; but, given the resurgence of interest in decentralization in the 1990s, its findings are instructive. The commission ascribed the rise in interest in decentralization of government to popular dissatisfaction with the remoteness and unresponsiveness of Westminster and Whitehall to the needs of the remoter parts of the country, and the ineffectiveness of government attempts to deal with the problems of those areas (Kilbrandon, 1973, chs 8,9). In Scotland and Wales, the desire for greater participation in the development of policy was bolstered by the fact of nationhood (ibid., ch. 10) but, the commission felt, there was a general demand from people in England too to 'win back power from London' (ibid., paras 1–7). The findings of the Kilbrandon Commission (1973, ch. 1) in effect recognized the importance of the principle of subsidiarity (see Chapter 1; Wilke and Wallace, 1990), although the terms of the debate did not then, and for the most part still do not, conceive of the issues explicitly in those terms.

There were, and are, a limited number of broad options for resolving the problems identified by the Kilbrandon Commission: the two extremes would be separatism for Scotland, even for Wales and England, although there is no pressure for this; or maintaining the status quo. Between these two poles are a range of possibilities for decentralizing government: a federal or quasi-federal solution under which the powers of the Westminster Parliament would be limited and Assemblies in the nations or regions would have some exclusive powers, or what the commission referred to as 'devolution'. Within the option of devolution there is a choice of the transfer of legislative and executive powers to 'Assemblies' below Westminster in the constitutional hierarchy, or the transfer of executive powers only.

Devolution differs from a federal or quasi-federal arrangement in that it would not limit the powers of the Parliament at Westminster and entrench the powers of the national and regional assemblies. It would be 'a delegation of central government powers which would leave overriding control in the hands of Parliament' (Kilbrandon, 1973, para. 543).

There is also a choice to be made between 'decentralization all round', or only to, say, Scotland, Wales or Northern Ireland; and between uniform decentralization on the same model to all the nations and regions; or 'lopsided' decentralization under which some nations or regions would enjoy a range of powers that would be greater or less than the range enjoyed by others.

The Kilbrandon Commission rejected separatism for Scotland and Wales as a solution; it found very little demand for federalism; and it felt that the status quo was unsatisfactory. It recommended instead 'devolution'. But the members of the Kilbrandon Commission were divided about the form that devolution should take. The majority felt that it was not necessary for the same system of devolved government to be applied to all parts of the UK. There was agreement that assemblies should be established for Scotland and Wales, but disagreement about whether this should be legislative and executive or merely executive devolution.

The Scotland and Wales Acts 1978

The government's response to the Kilbrandon Report was to attempt to establish assemblies in Scotland and Wales. After an abortive attempt to secure the passage of a single Scotland and Wales Bill in 1977, Labour opened negotiations with the Liberals for their support for the second attempt to legislate for devolution in 1977–78; this was one of the cornerstones of what came to be called the 'Lib-Lab pact' (Steel, 1980, ch. 8). Separate Scotland and Wales Acts were passed in 1978.

The Scotland Act provided for an elected assembly with legislative and executive powers, whereas the Wales Act provided for an assembly with only executive powers. Neither assembly's powers would be entrenched and protected from encroachment from the Westminster Parliament. Both assemblies were to be financed from block grants from central government calculated on the basis of a formula. They would have had no revenue-raising powers. The government would not lend its support to the Liberals' wish to see elections to the assemblies use a form of proportional representation (see Chapter 8) and nor would they countenance a Bill of Rights to protect the fundamental rights of the Scots and Welsh (see Chapter 9).

The 1978 Acts contained controversial provisions requiring that referendums be held in Scotland and Wales before the legislation could be brought into effect. Unless 40 percent of the electorate voted in favour of devolution, the Acts should be repealed. In the event, the necessary support was not forthcoming in either Scotland or Wales. A majority of those who voted in Scotland supported devolution; but the 'yes' majority represented only 32.9 percent of the electorate and so did not satisfy the 40 percent requirement. In Wales only 20.2 percent of votes cast favoured devolution, some 11.9 percent of the electorate. Both Acts were therefore repealed.

On the face of it, devolution had little support in Wales and large numbers of Scots were either indifferent, since they had not voted, or hostile, since they had voted against devolution. But the referendum result may have reflected rejection not so much of devolution in principle as of the particular package on offer, which did not include taxation powers, proportional representation or reduction to a single tier of local government. Whatever interpretation one puts on the results, after the referendums in Scotland and Wales decentralization ceased to be a major issue for a decade.

The Scottish Constitutional Convention

Political considerations have played an important part in the revival of pressure for the decentralization of power, especially to Scotland, since 1987. In the general election of that year, support for the Conservatives in Scotland fell to a low of 24 percent, adding to resentment of the fact that the country had been governed by the Thatcher administration for nearly a decade, having policies imposed upon it that were rejected by a large majority of Scottish voters. By far the most popular party was Labour, with 42.4 percent of the Scottish vote. The importance of this support to Labour may be seen from the fact that for this 42.4 percent of the votes, it received 70 percent of the Scottish seats, 50 in number. The Scottish Nationalist Party (SNP), with 14 percent of the votes, won 3 seats. The Alliance parties, who were committed to devolution to Scotland in their election manifesto, won 19.2 percent of the vote and 9 seats. The Conservatives had only 10 seats.

There are clear electoral gains to be made by Labour in espousing, as it has done, the cause of a Scottish parliament, and losses to be risked if it does not. The political facts of life were brought home to the Labour Party by their loss of a seat in the Govan by-election of 1989 to Jim Sillars, a SNP candidate. The Labour front bench was then and remains dominated by what has been dubbed a 'Jockocracy' of influential Labour politicians from north of the border, many of them also committed to a Scottish parliament. Hence Labour has been under continued pressure to adopt a pro-decentralization stance despite its historical preference for a strong, central, socialist state. It is not surprising, then, that Labour should have committed itself to decentralization in Scotland.

Pressure for decentralization in Scotland has been channelled through the Campaign for a Scottish Assembly, a cross-party organization formed in the wake of the 1979 referendum on devolution. The campaign had not had a high profile before the 1987 general election. After the election, however, it sprang back into life and set up a committee to produce a report entitled *A Claim of Right for Scotland*, which was launched in July 1988. It recommended that a Constitutional convention should be established to draw up a scheme for a Scottish assembly or parliament. The Scottish Constitutional Convention (the SCC) was set up and held its first meeting on 30 March 1989 in Edinburgh.

The aim of the convention was 'to reach agreement on how Scotland ought to be governed' (SCC, 1989, p. 1). Although it has no official status, its members include 80 percent of Scotland's MPs and MEPs, members from the Regional and Island Councils and most district councils, and representatives from the churches, business, industry, the unions, and from the Labour Party, the Social and Liberal Democrats, the Social Democratic Party, the Green Party and the Communist Party. The Conservatives and Scottish National Party refused to take part.

The SCC has proposed that a parliament should be established for Scotland, with legislative powers (SCC, 1990a,b). The SCC took as its starting point the Claim of Right referred to above which acknowledges 'the sovereign right of the Scottish people to determine the form of government best suited to their needs'. This right is acknowledged in the UN Covenant on Civil and Political Rights, Article One and the International Convenant on Economic, Social and Cultural Rights, Article One (both of which read 'All peoples have the right of self-determination').

The MORI *State of the Nation* poll 1991 found that 51 percent of Scots respondents were in favour of Scotland having a devolved assembly with tax raising and spending powers. Twenty-three percent of Scots were in favour of independence for Scotland within the European Community and 9 percent were in favour of an independent Scotland outside the European Community. Nationally 43 percent of respondents were in favour of a Scottish assembly with taxing and spending powers. Sixteen percent of Scots were in favour of no change; nationally the figure in favour of no change for Scotland was 30 percent (MORI, 1991).

Home rule all round?

The MORI *State of the Nation* poll found that nationally 60 percent of respondents thought that government power in Britain was too centralized, and only 18 percent disagreed. Forty-two percent supported giving greater powers of government to Wales, and 42 percent to Northern Ireland. But opinion on the topic was fairly evenly balanced as far as Wales and Northern Ireland were concerned: 40 and 43 percent respectively were against giving these countries greater powers of government (MORI, 1991).

Tony Benn in his Commonwealth of Britain Bill (Benn, 1991) proposes separate assemblies for England, Scotland and Wales, but this is not the solution most generally proposed by those in favour of decentralization. The more usual suggestion is for regional government for England. Although the pressure for decentralization has come principally from Scotland, both the Labour Party (1990, pp. 42–3) and the Liberal Democrats (1990, ch. 5) have committed themselves to policies of 'home rule all round', with assemblies in Wales and the English regions as well as a parliament in Scotland. Before discussing the implications of these proposals, let us pause briefly to consider what the devolution of powers to a separate English assembly would mean, and why this, together with a parliament for Scotland and an assembly for Wales is not proposed as a solution to the problem of centralization.

The ratio of the populations of England, Scotland and Wales is approximately 85 : 10 : 5. If it were felt that there should be self-determination all round by the nations of the UK, then the system would be very unbalanced. England could swamp the others in relations between the nations. If the different units were represented at Westminster, in a reformed second chamber for instance (see Chapter 3), then the English might feel under-represented in relation to the Scots and Welsh if each nation received equal representation; but if representation were to be according to population, then English representatives would outnumber the Scots and Welsh very substantially.

Recognition of the difficulties caused by this imbalance in population underlies the fact that there is no real demand for decentralization to take the form of separate assemblies for the four countries of the UK. Instead, assemblies in Wales and the English regions and a parliament for Scotland and, in due course, an assembly for Northern Ireland, would make the balance between the different units more stable, since the boundaries of the English regions could be fixed so as to ensure that no region had so great a population that it could swamp the other regions and the national assemblies for Scotland, Wales and Northern Ireland.

Although regional government in England and a Welsh assembly have come onto the political agenda largely as a response to the pressure for a Scottish parliament, the need to achieve a balance between Scotland and the rest of the UK is not the only argument in favour of decentralization all round (Marquand, 1989). In general terms, the case rests on the belief that bringing government closer to the people allows it to be more responsive, accountable, efficient and effective, and enables people to participate as citizens should in decisions that affect their lives.

More specifically, the case rests on the perception of a need to counteract the disparities and inequalities between the nations and regions (Labour Party, 1989, p. 57; Coulson, 1989). The argument is that central government lacks the will or the capacity to remedy these disparities and that only by increasing the powers of the regions to solve their own problems can this inequality be mitigated. David Marquand is concerned that the absence of regionally based political institutions contributes to the concentration of political activity in an unresponsive London. Only by creating political institutions in the regions will pressures emerge to further the interests of the regions (Marquand, 1989).

Regional government should also promote a sense of community and citizenship (Crick, 1988, pp. 67–73; Heater, 1990, pp. 326–7). Given that the UK is too large and diverse a unit for the population to feel themselves to be UK citizens except when major national problems are at issue, it would be desirable for smaller local communities to be promoted with which people can identify and to which they can contribute. At the most local level, this can be done through neighbourhood associations and through local government. But there is a big gap between local government and Westminster, and this gap could be filled by regional and national assemblies through which citizenship could operate.

Despite the fact that, according to the MORI *State of the Nation* poll (MORI, 1991), nationally 60 percent of respondents feel that government in Britain is too centralized, public opinion in England does not at present support giving greater powers of government to English regions. Only 27 percent were in favour of this and 61 percent opposed it. Given the 60 percent who are concerned about centralization this should not be taken to indicate satisfaction with the existing system. Rather it may imply a lack of awareness of the issues and terms of the debate, which would be dispelled if the subject were to move up the political agenda as more public debate is generated.

Another dimension to the 'decentralization all round' debate is European. The SCC in its proposals for a Scottish parliament proposes separate representation for a Scottish parliament in the Community (SCC, 1990a,b). These steps would represent a move towards establishing direct relationships between the Community and sub-national institutions which would presage a regional dimension in Europe. So the 'Europe of the Regions' question (see Chapter 1) is clearly relevant to decentralization in the UK: Daltrop draws attention to a view that national governments are often forced to adopt policies which are effective nationally, but are not in the interests of particular regions; the Community may be better able to appreciate regional needs and to meet them (Daltrop, 1986, ch. 9). But for the Community to perform this role, the regions would need to have their own political institutions separate from those of the member states. However, a 'Europe of the Regions' that reflected these ideas is looking very speculatively into the future, and would be a highly controversial development. We are at present looking through a glass darkly on this subject.

These, then are the arguments in favour of a system of decentralized government. But there are a number of formidable problems. Before turning to consider some of the more detailed problems, let us look at the general objections.

The case against decentralization

The first fear is that decentralization – especially to Scotland and Wales – could contribute to a problem of 'balkanization' if in due course the smaller nations of Europe were to seek and obtain independence. Heater has expressed the fear that 'multiple citizenship' (the sense of belonging to a multiplicity of political communities such as Scotland, the UK, the European Community) 'could not, naturally, be achieved if present nation-states disintegrated into their smaller component parts'. But he speculates that an alternative, more desirable development than balkanization would be a reduction in the powers of governments of member states in the Community, with some of that power being devolved downwards to provincial administrations and some transferred upwards to the supranational community (Heater, 1990, pp. 326–7). This expresses neatly another aspect of what a 'Europe of the Regions' could involve (see also Daltrop, 1986, ch. 9; Layton, 1990; Coulson, 1990, p. 24).

A second concern is money. The ability of national and regional assemblies to respond to local needs would inevitably depend upon their financial resources. If they were entirely dependent upon Whitehall, their room for manoeuvre would be restricted as would the scope for local people to make choices about expenditure. This consideration suggests the need for assemblies to have their own tax-raising powers. This subject can best be considered in relation to proposals for Scotland (see next section).

Thirdly, relations with the centre are a cause for concern. Again, the effectiveness of national and regional governments in furthering interests must depend on the clout they carry in London. As Coulson (1989, p. 3) puts it: 'The main argument for regional government is that an elected regional Assembly will be able to ensure that its region gets a fair share of the resources available.' But the writings on this subject pay very little attention to how the required clout can be contrived. The mechanisms for extracting money from central government (or from the European Community) would need to be effective, for the less prosperous regions would not be able to bring their standards up without equalization schemes of some kind. A simple, apparently non-political formula that awarded grants on a per capita of the population basis would not necessarily be sensitive to the differing conditions of the nations and regions.

On this point, the Spanish model is instructive. Decentralization to the 'autonomous communities' is progressive. There is a special Council for the Fiscal and Financial Policy of the Autonomous Communities composed of the finance ministers from the communities together with the state finance minister and the minister for public administration. This consultative body looks at co-ordination of policy in regard to public investment, costs of services, the distribution of resources to the regions, etc. There is also elaborate provision for the regions to retain a greater share of revenue as their responsibilities increase and for an Inter-regional Compensation Fund to ensure adequate finances for the disparate regions. The rights of regional assemblies to control their own budgets and the responsibilities of their finance departments are also provided for (Donaghy and Newton, 1987, pp. 105–16).

A way of giving the regions and nations clout at Whitehall and Westminster would be through their representation in the second chamber (see Chapter 3). Labour has linked the question of decentralization to Scotland and to Wales and the English regions to the reform of the second chamber; their rather vague proposal is that 'members of the new second chamber should particularly reflect the interests and aspirations of the regions and nations of Britain' (Labour Party, 1989, p. 55; see also Chapter 3). Although the SCC envisages the second chamber performing a role in representing the nations and regions, they do not see this in terms of 'clout' (SCC, 1989, para. 18.13; see also Holme, 1987, p. 138).

An arrangement by which a second chamber, containing representatives sitting for the nations and regions (see Chapter 3), had a role in scrutinizing and possibly delaying legislation would give them some leverage in dealing with central government over policy towards the assemblies, particularly on financial questions. It is suggested that without some arrangement which put the nations and regions in a strong negotiating position in relation to Westminster and Whitehall, the centre could dominate the national and regional tier and frustrate the objective of redressing the balance in favour of the nations and regions.

In brief, then, these are the arguments about decentralization in principle. In practice, it could raise a number of very complex problems about the relationships between the different tiers and the institutions in each tier. These may be best illustrated by considering fairly concrete proposals for decentraliz-ation to Scotland, and examining their implications both for Scotland itself and for the rest of the UK.

'Key elements of proposals for Scottish parliament'

The SCC produced a lengthy discussion paper in October 1989 (*Towards a Scottish Parliament*) and in September 1990 they produced a short document entitled *Key Elements of Proposals for Scottish Parliament* and in November 1990 their report *Towards Scotland's Parliament* was published. The central proposal is for a directly elected Scottish parliament (this term is preferred to 'assembly': SCC, 1989, paras 12.1–3) with legislative powers having 'a defined range of powers and responsibilities which would encompass sole or shared responsibility for all functions except those retained to the United Kingdom Parliament'. The Westminster Parliament would have responsibility for defence, foreign affairs, central economic and fiscal policy, and other UK matters. The powers of the Scottish parliament and executive should not be altered by the Westminster Parliament without the consent of the Scottish Parliament, in order to prevent unilateral amendment by the Westminster Parliament of the Scottish parliament's powers. Thus the system would be partially federal – only partially because of the lopsidedness of the arrangement.

There would also be a right to have a representative office in Brussels, and a right to be represented in UK ministerial delegations to the Council of Ministers of the European Economic Community. Local government, probably a single-tier structure, would be determined by Scotland's parliament. Special arrangements would have to be made for the Islands. There would be a Charter of Rights 'encompassing and improving upon' the European Convention on Human Rights (1990b, p. 8). These proposals also envisage some form of proportional representation for elections to the Scottish parliament; assigned revenues for Scotland, in the form of a right to receive all income tax raised in Scotland and a sum equivalent to the VAT raised in Scotland. Equalization payments should continue 'on the basis of needs assessment, starting from the present formula base'. Some of these proposals are vague, but they provide a convenient starting point for discussion. The consensus among those Scots who favour decentralization is that a parliament should have legislative powers over a wide range of domestic policy areas and this is also the approach of Labour and the Liberal Democrats. These proposals would cause legal and political problems both for the Scottish parliament and for the rest of the UK.

The West Lothian question

During the devolution debates in the 1970s Tam Dalyell, the Member of Parliament for West Lothian, repeatedly asked what came to be known as 'the West Lothian question' (SCC, 1989, paras 2.2, 8.6–8), i.e. whether or not Scottish MPs at Westminster should have the right to vote on English legislation in subject areas which were devolved to Scotland. It would seem anomalous and unfair that Scotland should have the right to determine its own laws and policies and also to influence decisions about policy in those subject areas for the rest of the UK, especially if, as the SCC envisages, Scotland continued to have the same number of MPs at Westminster as at present (SCC, 1989, para. 13.1–2). This lopsided aspect of the scheme of decentralization to Scotland would be offensive to the tidy minds of some and the sense of justice of others. And yet the same problem would arise if Labour's plans for 'decentralization all round' were implemented, since they propose that English regional assemblies and assemblies for Wales and Northern Ireland should have executive powers only (Labour Party, 1989, pp. 56–7). On the other hand, countries with devolved systems, e.g. Spain, do not always give the same powers to each devolved unit (Donaghy and Newton, 1987, pp. 105–107; SCC, 1990, paras 8.8–12).

These arrangements could stimulate pressure from the regions and from Wales for additional powers to put them on a par with Scotland, and so lead to what may be called 'rolling decentralization' (see SCC, 1989, paras 8.9–12). with additional powers devolved as and when they were required. This was also the basis on which the Northern Ireland assembly was to be set up in 1982. It would have had consultative powers and scrutiny functions to start with, but further powers would have been devolved as and when the members of the assembly reached agreement on devolution (Cmnd. 8541, 1982). The plans were frustrated by the boycotting of the assembly by the SDLP, and it was dissolved in 1986 (McCrudden, 1989).

Clearly, the failure to resolve the West Lothian question, for example by preventing Scottish MPs at Westminster from voting on matters not affecting Scotland, would leave scope for conflict and allegations of abuse of power in future. And yet it would be a constitutional novelty to legislate to limit the voting and speaking rights of certain classes of MPs at Westminster (under the Scotland Act there was to be a 14-day 'cooling off period' between two divisions on the second reading of a Bill whenever the votes of Scottish MPs made a decisive difference in a Commons division: S. 66). If the matter were not dealt with by legislation but left to convention, then it might be hoped that a convention would grow up to the effect that Scottish MPs would not vote on matters affecting only the rest of the UK. But it is difficult to imagine, for example, a Labour government with a majority of 40 in the House of Commons, including 50 Scottish MPs, accepting the defeat of a measure affecting England and Wales when it could call upon its Scottish supporters to push it through. Without legislation regulating the right of the Scottish MPs to vote in the Commons, the risk of deteriorating relations between Scotland and the rest of the UK would be high.

A possible answer to the West Lothian question would be to endow the House of Commons with a dual personality, symbolized perhaps by the presence of a different mace or a different Speaker presiding. In one personality it would be the House of Commons for the UK, dealing with matters of defence, foreign policy, central economic and fiscal policies and other UK matters. All MPs would be eligible to participate. Its other personality would be as House of Commons for those parts of the UK that did not have a separate parliament, and in those sessions MPs sitting for areas with a separate parliament (Scotland and any other nations and regions) would not be eligible to participate. The members of the government of the UK could also, where appropriate, hold office as ministers of the government of those parts of the country that decentralization had not reached. There could be separate ministers as well.

Entrenchment and the allocation of functions

A difficult question is on what basis powers should be devolved to a Scottish parliament or to assemblies in Wales and the English regions, and what powers should rest with central government and the Westminster Parliament (for discussion, see SCC, 1989, paras 10.1–3). Should devolution take the form of an allocation of defined functions to the assemblies, all other powers being reserved to the UK, or a general transfer of power to assemblies subject to specific reservations of limited functions such as defence, foreign relations and macro-economic policy to the centre?

Tony Benn's Commonwealth of Britain Bill (Benn, 1981) proposes that while the national parliaments should have power to legislate on all matters except defence, foreign affairs and finance the Westminster Parliament should have power to legislate so as to override laws passed by the national parliaments.

The SCC proposes that Scotland's parliament would have a 'defined range of powers and responsibilities which would encompass sole or shared responsibility for *all* (emphasis added) functions except those retained to the United Kingdom Parliament'. It then goes on to list functions that would be 'included' in the powers of the parliament. These range through administration of social security, education, health, housing, planning, transport, water supply, and many aspects of economic and industrial policy.

It is not clear from this whether what is intended is the transfer of general powers to legislate for the 'peace, order and good government' of the inhabitants of Scotland subject to specific reservations to Westminster. That was the basis of the powers devolved to the Northern Ireland Assembly at Stormont under the Government of Ireland Act 1920. These general powers were made subject to specific matters being reserved to the Westminster Parliament, including the power to levy certain taxes, and responsibility for the armed forces, relations with foreign countries and external trade.

However, the SCC proposals differ from the Stormont set up in important respects. The SCC, as we have seen, envisages the entrenchment of the powers of the Scottish parliament in the sense that its legislation could not be overridden without its consent. By contrast, despite the devolution of general powers to Stormont, the Westminster Parliament retained the power to legislate on all matters for Northern Ireland. However, this power was seldom exercised: during the life of the Parliament at Stormont from 1921 until its dissolution in 1972, a convention developed that the Westminster Parliament would not legislate for Northern Ireland on matters devolved to Stormont (see Bogdanor, 1979, p. 50; Jennings, 1959, p. 158).

A similar convention could develop in relation to a Scottish parliament if its powers were not entrenched; but the SCC is not prepared to risk it and, as indicated above, proposes entrenchment of the Scottish parliament's powers. This would introduce a degree of entrenched subsidiarity into the UK constitution.

The method of entrenchment envisaged by the SCC, that the powers of the

Scottish parliament should be unalterable save with the consent of that parliament, raises interesting issues about methods of entrenchment (see Chapters 9 and 11; see also SCC, 1989, paras 5.1–11). There are a range of possibilities, of which the SCC proposals are only one. The method of protection favoured by Labour in its policy review involves the reformed second chamber having new delaying powers over measures affecting fundamental rights: 'It will possess the power to delay repeal of legislation affecting fundamental rights for the whole life of a Parliament, thus providing an opportunity for the electorate to determine whether or not the government which proposes such measures should remain in office.' The extra delaying power would apply to all items of legislation specifically designated as concerning fundamental rights and all legislation establishing the national and regional assemblies (SCC, 1989, p. 56).

To return for a moment to the precedent set by the Northern Ireland system in 1920, it is worth noting that the policy of non-intervention in the province by Westminster was one of the reasons for the failure of that constitution; the system allowed for one-party rule throughout the period and the Protestant majority used its power to keep the Catholic minority out of positions of power, thus generating intercommunal ill-will and a well-founded sense of injustice (McCrudden, 1989; Bogdanor, 1979, pp. 48–55). One lesson to be drawn from the Stormont experience, then, is that non-intervention in devolved government by Westminster will not always be beneficial. The design of institutions based on the principle of subsidiarity is crucial – it would be wrong to assume that any form of subsidiarity is better than none. Much must depend upon factors such as the legal protection of minority rights, the working of the electoral system and the distribution of support for the political parties. Let us now turn to these matters.

A Bill of Rights for Scotland?

The SCC has opted for a Charter of Rights based on the European Convention on Human Rights (ECHR) (see Chapter 9; SCC, 1989, paras 7.1–10; 1990b, p. 8). This ought to secure minorities against majoritarian government, and keep the political process in Scotland open through the exercise of free speech, freedom of association and the like. Perhaps the most significant aspect of this commitment, should it be implemented, is that the concession of the need for a Bill of Rights for Scotland by, for example, a Labour government, would be a major step in the campaign for a Bill of Rights for the UK. At present, Labour has made no express commitments on this issue. But it would be hard for the party, committed as it currently is to the transfer of legislative powers to Scotland, to resist what appears to be the wish of the Scots for a Bill of Rights, while at the same time continuing with its objections to a Bill of Rights for the UK as a whole or for assemblies in England and Wales.

If the SCC proposals were implemented, the Scots would enjoy better legal protection of their civil and political citizenship rights in relation to devolved matters than citizens of the rest of the UK. But in relation to UK matters, the Scots would not be protected. This would be highly anomalous, and it is to be expected that it would add fuel to the pressure for a UK Bill of Rights.

Proportional representation in Scotland?

The SCC has also committed itself to a form of proportional representation, although it has not decided which system should be adopted (SCC, 1989, paras 11.1–2, app. 2; 1990b, p. 17). Its criteria include the need for proportionality between the parties, the need to encourage equal representation of men and women, and fair representation of ethnic and other minority groups; the preservation of a link between the member and the constituency; simplicity; and adequate representation of less populous areas (see Chapter 8). Again, Labour may find its position on proportional representation for the House of Commons compromised by its commitment to a Scottish parliament (see Chapter 8).

The interrelationships between various possible measures of constitutional reform are central to any discussion of the subject, and this is particularly the case in relation to decentralization. In Chapter 9, for example, the point is stressed that the introduction of a Bill of Rights should not be seen as a panacea. So too with decentralization and proportional representation. If a system of proportional representation were not introduced in a Scottish parliament, it is possible that there could be prolonged periods of one-party rule (Labour has for years been by far the strongest party in Scotland). No partisan point is intended in the suggestion that one-party rule would be likely, in Scotland as elsewhere (in Northern Ireland from 1920 to 1972, for example), to produce unresponsive government. This might, incidentally, giver rise to plausible claims that the Westminster Parliament ought to intervene: if the Scottish parliament's powers were entrenched it would be unable to do so.

But proportional representation alone might not provide sufficient safeguards against abuse of power by a Scottish parliament. Even under proportional representation, there could be long periods of single-party government or a coalition with one party dominant. Hence measures such as the introduction of a Bill of Rights in Scotland and public rights of access to official information would also be desirable. We see here an example of the subtle balance that should be achieved in the constitution between different checks and balances and different forms of accountability.

Both the Liberal Democrats and the Scottish Labour Party accept the case for a form of proportional representation for a Scottish parliament, but the British Labour Party is uncommitted on this issue and has until recently been resolutely opposed to proportional representation for the House of Commons. At its party conference in 1990, Labour set up a working party to consider what electoral system there should be for national and regional assemblies and for the second chamber, but they also required the system for the House of Commons to be considered, a sign of flexibility on this point (see Chapter 8). The interim report of the working party was non-committal (Plant, 1991).

Financing a Scottish parliament

A major difficulty arises over the financing of a Scottish parliament and indeed of any devolved assembly. Although the following discussion focuses on Scotland, the same issues arise in relation to decentralization to Wales, English regions and Northern Ireland. There are in principle three broad options. At one extreme, the Scottish assembly could be left to rely entirely on revenue raised by itself. If this were adopted, it might also be given the function of raising the Scottish share of UK expenditure on such matters as defence and remitting it to Westminster. However, it would not be possible for Scotland to finance solely from its own revenue expenditure to the level it enjoys under the present system without raising the rates of taxation. It is doubtful whether increases in tax rates or reductions in the level of services would be acceptable to the Scots, and so there is bound to be a demand for subsidy from the UK. The Scottish self-financing option, then, is seen to be unrealistic.

At the other extreme, a Scottish assembly would have no revenue-raising power of its own and would rely entirely on a block grant from Whitehall. This was the plan under the Scotland Act 1978 (Bogdanor, 1979). A major disadvantage in the financing of national or regional government solely out of block grants from Whitehall rather than from any taxing power, is that it separates responsibility for raising the money from responsibility for spending it and results, therefore, in limited accountability to the local electorate (Ancram, n.d. ch. 1) but increased accountability to Whitehall. A further shortcoming is that without some financial independence, a devolved assembly's ability to develop its own pattern of public services in response to the wishes and needs of the people is limited. This was the experience of the Stormont government (Bogdanor, 1979, pp. 55–62).

The middle option is partial funding from Westminster through grants supplemented by assigned revenues or revenue raised by the parliament in Scotland. This is in fact the option favoured by the SCC, which proposes that the Scottish parliament should have assigned to it all Scottish income tax and either all Scottish VAT or a sum equivalent. The parliament should have power to vary the income tax rate, but within a defined range. Equalization, it suggests vaguely, should continue, starting from the present formula basis. The SCC accepts that a Scottish parliament must be responsible to some degree for both raising and spending money – without that there is power without responsibility (SCC, 1989, pp. 69–84; 1990b p. 16).

This middle option was also favoured by the Labour Party in its policy review, which promises an assembly with legislative and tax-raising powers in the form of the right to vary income tax rates in Scotland. The objective in this solution is to:

> make sure the financial powers are effective and allow real room for discretion. If Scotland's elected representatives want higher public investment they must raise the cash and answer for what they do at the ballot box. It is an essential discipline for any democratic arm of government (Labour Party, 1989, p. 57).

The party seems therefore to be going for a narrow range of revenue-raising powers.

There are, however, problems with this option also. Whenever services were seen to be inadequate, the blame would be placed on the UK Government rather than the Scottish parliament. Ancram (n.d., p. 3) draws a parallel with local government which has blamed its need to raise the level of rates (and community charge) on what it sees as the inadequacy of central government grant. He fears that the assemblies would pass the buck to Whitehall and evade responsibility for high national or regional taxes.

It is far from easy to know whether and to what extent Scotland is presently a net beneficiary of equalization schemes and of its membership of the UK, but it seems that overall it is a substantial beneficiary (SCC, 1989, pp. 69–72, 82–3). Kellas (1990, p. 430) suggests that spending on devolved services from the UK Government is some 30% higher in Scotland than in England. The government calculates that public expenditure per head in 1989–90 was below average in England on a wide range of functions (trade and industry, housing, education, health, social security, roads and transport and others), and above average on each of those functions in Scotland and indeed, on most of those functions, in Wales (Official Report 1990–91, sixth series, vol. 182, written answers 13 Dec. 1990, cols. 449–60). If a system of devolution were introduced, it would be important for relations between Scotland and Westminster to remain cordial. The relationship between a Scottish parliament even partly dependent on Westminster for its finances and the government at Whitehall would inevitably be delicate if, as could well happen, the relationship came to be perceived as essentially one between Scotland and England. This is another respect in which the Scottish question is different from the question of regional government for England. In a system of general devolution, the regions of England along with Scottish and Welsh parliaments would be regarded by the English or the British as sub-units of the UK: there need be no greater degree of resentment on the part of the rest of the country contributing to the poorer regions under such a system than there is at present. But if the Scots persisted in the view that Scotland was a separate country but that it should be subsidized by the rest of the UK, the English could well come to question whether there was any good reason why they should subsidize Scotland, especially since England too has its poorer regions who do badly under the current system.

Another referendum?

An important question must be whether referendums should be held in Scotland, Wales and England as a prelude to decentralization, and whether a simple majority or a specified proportion of electors should suffice to bring decentralization into effect. If referendums were held, the MORI State of the Nation poll suggests that the chances of even a majority of voters supporting national government in Wales and regional government in England are less than even, although in Scotland they appear to be higher. So if referendums were required, the result could well be lopsided decentralization with all the political problems that that entails both for Scotland and for the UK as a whole. If however, the commitment were to 'decentralization all round' on the grounds that this would enhance accountability, effectiveness and citizenship, referendums would not be necessary. It is only if decentralization is conceived as a response to the wishes of the people of Scotland and Wales for self-determination that a referendum, designed to see whether the people do indeed assert a right to self-determination, is called for.

If it were felt that referendums ought to be held, the outcome would depend crucially on the stage at which this was done. The answer in a referendum held at the end of a lengthy period of political debate and administrative decentralization, such as that stretched over 6 years or so envisaged in the Liberal Democrat paper *"We, the People . . ."* (see Chapter 11), could well be different from the result if a referendum were held at the beginning of such a process; very few members of the public, in England in particular, have given serious thought to these matters, and most would tend to vote for the status quo without such a debate.

Legal problems

There would also be legal problems in decentralization. Those arising from any attempt to entrench the powers of parliaments or assemblies and to limit the power of the Westminster Parliament to legislate on matters transferred to national and regional assemblies are considered in Chapter 11. There would also be problems in deciding questions about the vires of legislation and actions by the assemblies and these would have to be determined by the courts. One question is whether such issues should fall to be determined by the ordinary courts or whether they should be referred to a constitutional court (for consideration of this issue in relation to Scotland, see SCC, 1989, paras 6.1–6.4). For reasons explained in Chapters 9 and 11, my preference is for these issues to be determined as and when they arise in the ordinary courts. The SCC (1989, paras 6.3–6.4) also seems to favour this solution.

Conclusions

The various proposals for national and regional government that we have considered have in effect been based on acceptance of the principle of subsidiarity, although like M. Jourdain's prose, we may not be very aware of that fact. The strongest arguments for systematic decentralization all round are that it would make government more effective and more accountable to its publics, that it would reduce overload at Whitehall and thus make central government more effective and that it would be tidier than lopsided, piecemeal decentralization would. It would foster a sense of community and thus contribute to citizenship. If it gave a boost to the campaign for a Bill of Rights, electoral reform and reform of the second chamber, then that would be an added bonus.

Lopsided decentralization, on the other hand, could create ill-will between the different parts of the country and in the House of Commons if, say, Scottish MPs were entitled to vote on matters not affecting Scotland. Whether the benefits of any measures of decentralization would outweigh the problems must of course be a matter of speculation and opinion.

Behind the arguments about decentralization are larger issues about the future structure of government in the European Community, in particular the operation of the principle of subsidiarity in relations between the Community and the smaller nations and regions within the Community. If, as is widely accepted, functions should not be performed at Community level if they can be more effectively performed at the level of the member states, it is difficult to see why the same argument in favour of subsidiarity should not be extended to nations and regions within member states (for a fuller discussion of the various ways in which the principle of subsidiarity may be formulated, see Kapteyn, 1990, ch. 1).

Let us indulge briefly in speculation again. Ultimately, we may see the emergence of a 'Europe of the Regions'. This dimension of relations in the Community could in the long run serve to undermine the nation state as a dominant political unit, and this is highly controversial (de Rougemont, 1983). Unless the problem of the 'democratic deficit' in Europe is solved, we could be jumping out of a British chip pan onto a European barbecue. But it raises a possible scenario for a solution of the Northern Ireland problem, which has hitherto eluded us. If a 'Europe of the Regions' were to develop as another dimension of the Community, Northern Ireland's relations with the Community could assume greater and more direct importance and its relations with the UK or the Republic of Ireland, which are at present the source of much of the communal ill-will in the Province, could come to be less important and therefore less irksome to the communities in Northern Ireland. That in turn could serve to defuse those relationships. Regional governments in the European Community could provide the basis for the building of a new set of relationships between regions in the Community and between them and the member states and the Community institutions themselves (Layton, 1990).

7

The system of justice

'The system of justice' embraces a range of institutions and functions: the courts, their relationships with other state institutions, and the placing of constitutional responsibility for matters such as law and order, legal aid and the protection of citizens' rights. The effective operation of the system is crucial in any democracy. The law is a valuable resource for government, since it is through judicially enforceable legislation that much government policy is put into effect (Rose, 1986). But the legal system is not only the servant of the government in this sense; the courts have an important role in holding government to account for its actions, and citizens look to the courts to assert their rights against the state (see in particular the discussion of citizenship in Chapter 2 and of civil and political rights in Chapter 9).

In this chapter, we shall primarily be concerned with the role of the courts in these matters, but we must not lose sight of the other important functions, in upholding the rule of law, in resolving private disputes in a just and orderly way and protecting citizens in their private lives. The need for an effective system of justice in these areas is no less crucial than in imposing legal accountability on the government.

The courts and the legal accountability of government: Judicial review

As indicated in Chapter 2, legal accountability is one of a number of mechanisms that form part of the complex system of constitutional checks and balances in the UK constitution. Judicial proceedings impose 'explanatory accountability' by requiring public bodies to justify their actions in legal terms; since judicial remedies are enforceable, they also impose amendatory accountability.

The courts exercise this power to impose legal accountability through what has come to be known as 'judicial review'. The subject is extremely complex and no attempt will be made to consider it in any detail here – the issues can only be sketched in (for a discussion of the grounds for judicial review, see Wade, 1988; Justice-All Souls Review, 1988; Jowell and Oliver, 1988; Jowell and Lester, 1987). An important feature of the jurisdiction is that the criteria according to which the courts judge the actions of public bodies are not only legal in a narrow sense. Apart from technical issues of legality, the courts require procedural propriety (e.g. compliance with the rules of natural justice and fairness) and 'rationality' on the part of decision makers. These three grounds for review – legality, procedural propriety and rationality – were expounded by Lord Diplock in *Council of Civil Service Unions* v. *Minister for the Civil Service* [1985] AC 374. He added a possible ground of proportionality, but the courts have been unwilling to regard this as a ground apart from rationality (see also the discussion in Chapter 9). Examples of what is required of administrators and ministers making decisions that affect individuals and organizations will serve to illustrate the importance of the jurisdiction. They include giving individuals a right to be heard in their own defence before a decision is made that affects them adversely; acting without personal bias; keeping an open mind and not feeling oneself bound by policy that has not been put into the form of specific legal rules; not being influenced by irrelevant considerations; not turning a blind eye to relevant considerations; and generally acting consistently and not unreasonably.

Each of these requirements that the courts impose on the decision-making process should enhance the quality of the decision that is ultimately made. Bearing in mind Sir Douglas Wass' criteria of what he called efficiency (discussed in Chapter 2), i.e. that actions and decisions should be taken in a rational and systematic way, that internal conflicts and inconsistencies are brought to the surface and resolved, and that objectives are defined and optimal means employed to secure them, judicial review should promote, although it cannot guarantee, effectiveness in public administration. The Master of the Rolls has articulated this role for judicial review on the basis that there is now 'a new relationship between the courts and the administration . . . a partnership based on the common aim, namely the maintenance of the highest standards of public administration' (*R.* v. *Lancashire County Council, Ex parte Huddlestone* [1986] 1 All ER 941, at 945).

But the grounds for judicial review have no basis in statute, having been developed on a case-by-case basis by the judiciary. In certain respects, the grounds may be criticized for being too narrow. There is, for example, no general requirement that reasons be given for an administrative decision, and this means that the courts are not in a position to discover whether a decision was taken in a rational way and whether internal conflicts and inconsistencies were resolved or objectives defined – this limits accountability. There is a strong case for subjecting decision makers to a duty to give reasons on request, subject to exceptions where for example considerations of national security or confidentiality arise (Justice-All Souls Review, 1988, pp. 157–8). Another criticism is that the courts have been too willing to accept pleas of 'public interest immunity', which means that government documents need not be disclosed to applicants for judicial review if sensitive issues of national security are in issue (see Chapter 10); this too operates to limit the effectiveness of judicial review in promoting good government through accountability.

The grounds for judicial review of administrative action are also criticized, however, for being too broad; in particular, the courts' willingness to quash decisions for irrationality, for example because a decision maker was influenced by a matter which the judges consider to be irrelevant (*Associated Provincial Picture Houses* v. *Wednesbury Coporation* [1948] 1 KB 223), attracts the accusation that judges are substituting their own opinions on matters of public policy for those of ministers or local authorities. Some commentators approve of activism in these matters on the part of the judiciary (see, e.g. Jowell and Lester, 1987), whereas others argue that since the judges are ill-qualified to interfere in administrative matters, they should leave the checking of government action to political channels (Griffith, 1979).

There is a risk not only that judges may interfere inadvisedly in administration, but that government may react by legislating to oust the jurisdiction of the courts altogether, and such a step would undermine the rule of law. However, the view that complaints about government action are better dealt with through political channels than by the courts, is not persuasive for so long as political channels remain, as they are at present, ineffective. In any event, it is difficult to envisage political channels ever offering redress to all aggrieved citizens.

A range of solutions has been advanced to these problems. One would be to improve court procedures in judicial review cases so that the impact of a decision on public policy and administration could be ventilated in court and taken into account when a decision is made (Griffith, 1985a; Woolf, 1990, ch. 4). Another approach would be to provide judges dealing with public law cases with some form of training or experience of public administration; judges could benefit from discussions with administrators, visits to government departments and interest groups (Woolf, 1990, pp. 115–20). But improvements in procedure and judicial training would not resolve the most fundamental problems posed by the system for imposing legal accountability on government: the substantive content of administrative law, including judicial review, needs to become more sophisticated. It has been suggested, for example, that the grounds for judicial review should be clarified and codified by statute so as to make clear to administrators what is expected of them, as has been done in Australia (Australian Administrative Decisions (Judicial Review) Act 1977, s. 5; see also Justice-All Souls Review, 1988, pp. 157–8) and to legitimate that judicial review jurisdiction. The requirements of good administration embodied in the grounds for judicial review could be 'internalized' through the formulation of principles of good administration, issued as guidelines in government departments (Justice-All Souls Review, 1988, ch. 2; Woolf, 1990, pp. 122–3) so they would know what was expected of them and be able to avoid judicial review and other forms of complaint by complying with the rules. Supplementary and alternative methods of dealing with 'irrationality' on the part of government should also be devised, through administrative mechanisms such as improved grievance procedures, openness and other measures. Legal and administrative forms of accountability (see Chapters 2 and 4) are closely linked and need to be developed together to provide redress and to enhance accountability. Such steps would contribute to a developed system of administrative law, the need for which was brought out in the discussion of executive agencies in Chapter 4.

The independence of the judiciary

Let us turn now from our all too brief consideration of the role of the courts in promoting accountability and effectiveness in government to the constitutional status of the courts and their relationships with other state institutions. Central considerations here are the independence and impartiality of the judiciary, recognized as a fundamental constitutional principle in the United Nations' *Basic Principles on the Independence of the Judiciary* (General Assembly resolutions 40/32 and 40/149, 1985). Independence is not the same as impartiality, but the two are clearly closely related.

'Impartiality' means that judges should so far as possible be neutral between different groups of litigants and between religions and ideologies, and that they should not be influenced by personal considerations in their treatment of individual litigants. Without impartiality, the legal process would come into disrepute and lose its legitimacy and certain laws could become unenforceable in practice.

'Independence' involves both the collective independence of the judiciary and the individual independence of each judge from outside pressures, particularly from government and parliament; to put it another way, the bench, unlike other state bodies, is not to be subjected to political forms of accountability. This in turn requires security of judicial tenure, financial security and institutional independence with respect to the administration of the courts (*Valente* v. *The Queen* (1986) 24 DLR 4th 161 (Supreme Court of Canada); Green, 1985; Patchett, 1975; Shetreet, 1976, pp. 17–19; Bell, 1983, p. 4), but as we shall see it does not necessarily preclude other forms of accountability, particularly administrative processes.

Since responsibility for the courts lies primarily with the Lord Chancellor, and to a lesser extent with the Home Secretary, both members of the Cabinet, the institutional independence of the courts is secured only by convention, not by a strict separation. There have been expressions of concern about this position not only here but in other Westminster-based or common law systems (Green, 1985; Browne-Wilkinson, 1988). This has given rise to consideration of how the independence of the system might be improved. While there is no evidence to suggest that the judges are in practice influenced by government and other political pressures, there is ground for concern that at some future date they may be so influenced, or that their legitimacy may be undermined by public loss of confidence in them.

In recent years, notably during the miners' strike of 1984–85, public confidence in the independence of the courts from the government fell. A Gallup poll in February 1985 found that 43 percent of respondents believed that judges are influenced by government, whereas 46 percent thought they were completely independent. By contrast, in a similar poll in 1969, 67 percent thought the judges were completely independent and only 19 percent thought they were influenced by the government. The same poll in 1985 disclosed public concern about the neutrality and impartiality of the courts: in answer to the question 'Do the courts in this country dispense justice impartially or do they favour the rich and influential?' only 42 percent thought that they were impartial and 50 percent thought that they favoured the rich (Oliver, 1986, p. 13). Concern about the public's loss of confidence in judicial independence from government is one of the arguments in favour of transferring responsibility for judicial appointments, promotions and dismissal to a non-political administrative body.

Judicial appointments

There is no formal system for applying for appointment to the High Court (the procedure for lower appointments is more formal), although the Lord Chancellor has published a booklet entitled *Judicial Appointments* (Lord Chancellor's Department, 1986; extracts are published in Brazier, 1990, pp. 548–65) in which he sets out the criteria for appointments. The posts are not advertised. The system of selection involves the informal and confidential 'sounding out' of various people including senior members of the judiciary about possible appointments. Reasons why certain eligible persons are not appointed are not necessarily disclosed to them (though they may be asked to clarify doubts: Shetreet, 1976, p. 400) and so they may have no opportunity to correct the record should non-appointment be attributable to inaccurate information in the hands of the department.

There are other respects, too, in which recruitment to the bench needs to be improved. The judiciary is predominantly male and there are very few members from the ethnic minorities. Recent Lord Chancellors have expressed their concern to increase the numbers of women and members of these minorities on the bench, so that its composition should more fairly reflect the balance within the population; but these efforts are hampered by the fact that the bar itself is predominantly white and male. As solicitors become eligible for the bench under the Courts and Legal Services Act 1990, the wider catchment for appointments should result in a slightly more representative bench. But it is likely to be many years before the legal profession from which judges are appointed is more representative of the population at large.

The present system of judicial appointments has been defended by successive Lord Chancellors. Shetreet (1976, pp. 393–404), after a careful consideration of the system, found many of the criticisms of the system to be groundless and concluded that it worked well. But there are powerful arguments based on both principle and practicality for reforming and formalizing the appointment of judges: the closed nature of the system undermines its legitimacy in the eyes of the public; as the catchment area extends to the solicitors' profession, the present highly personalized system will not be able to cope; and under the present system there can be no guarantee that ministers responsible for the judiciary will not allow political considerations to influence them.

A Judicial Services Commission?

There are a range of ways in which judicial appointments can be made and the necessary protections provided (for a summary of systems in 18 different jurisdictions, see Skordali, 1991). Tony Benn's Commonwealth of Britain Bill (Benn, 1991) proposed that county court judges and magistrates be elected. This would, however, expose judges to partisan public opinion pressure which could undermine the legitimacy of the courts. Nevertheless the MORI *State of the Nation* poll in 1991 found that 60 percent of the public would favour the election of magistrates, a surprising figure which implies considerable public concern about the present system of appointment or the standard of the magistracy. Benn also proposes that High Court judges be appointed by the President (he proposes a President to exercise many of the powers of the Monarch) subject to approval by a House of Commons select committee. This would leave room for party political considerations to influence judicial appointments. An alternative approach that would secure the process against political interference, open it up and make it more accountable would be to give the function of appointment, or making recommendations for appointments, to independent commissions. The commissions could be made to account to a select committee (see below), so that there was a degree of political accountability in the system, but not to the government.

The Labour Party (1989, p. 31, 1990, p. 61) and the Liberal Democrats both propose independent judicial commissions on these lines having responsibility for the appointment of judges. But these ideas are as yet undeveloped. The draft constitution in the Liberal Democrats' Green Paper *"We, The People . . ."* (1990, Article 69) provides for a judicial services commission 'established by Parliament approved by a resolution of both the House of Commons [*sic*] and appointed by Her Majesty . . .'.

Academics in the UK have put forward more detailed proposals. Brazier, having considered a range of options, rules out the appointment of judges by ministerial nomination or by election (which is provided for in relation to some judges in the USA but is falling out of favour). He proposes instead a Judicial Service Commission based on 'judicial self-perpetuation' (Brazier, 1989, pp. 88–9) and composed of representatives of the senior judges but with some lay membership which would offset professional insularity and thus widen the pool of potential judicial candidates. This commission would be responsible for the higher-level appointments. Officials of a Department of Law (or Ministry of Justice) could provide a link on an informal basis with the minister. Brazier would not rule out informal soundings such as take place under the present system, but he does wish the process adopted by the commission to be generally more open than at present. As far as appointments to the circuit bench and of stipendiary magistrates and recorders are concerned, Brazier suggests that the commission should establish circuit judicial committees in the six circuits to advise on the appointment of persons to those posts. That committee could also play a role in the appointment of the lay magistracy, and in dealing with complaints.

Provisions for the dismissal of judges are as important as the procedures for appointment. Judges of the High Court, the Court of Appeal and the House of Lords enjoy very considerable security from dismissal (Supreme Court Act 1981, s. 11), but Recorders are appointed only for a 3-year period and they have no right to be reappointed. Magistrates may be removed by the Lord Chancellor at any time (Brazier, 1988, ch. 11). These judges then, are in a sense politically accountable, though constitutional conventions about the exercise of power by the Lord Chancellor are supposed to prevent the accountability being tainted by party political considerations.

To meet these problems, the Judicial Services Commission could be given functions in relation to the renewal of appointments or removal of members of the lower judiciary: these should be subject to procedural requirements, limited grounds and safeguards such as a duty to report to Parliament; such arrangements would impose administrative rather than political accountability on judges when any question of non-renewal or removal arises. This, it is suggested, would be preferable to the present arrangement which is open to political abuse (although there are few suggestions that it is in practice abused in that way).

Under the present arrangements, insulation of the judiciary from politics goes beyond the system for appointment and dismissal. There are strict parliamentary rules about the criticizing of a judge's conduct or of judges generally, which is only permitted on a debate on a substantive motion calling for dismissal. Comments may be made by backbench MPs about a decision or a sentence once it has been delivered, but the *sub judice* rule requires that no comments be made about a case in the Commons until after the decision has been made (for a summary of the position, see Brazier, 1988, pp. 234–40). There is therefore virtually no scope for parliamentary supervision of judges. In principle, it is suggested, this approach is a wise one. Some commentators have expressed the view that the rules about comments by MPs on cases and judges are unduly restrictive and that judges sitting without juries would not be influenced by comments made in Parliament. But there would be a risk that parties to cases and members of the public might believe that judges had been so influenced and this in my view justifies the strictness of the present rules.

The administration of the courts

So far we have been discussing the independence of the judges, but it is necessary also that court administration be insulated from improper political interference. There has been a 'very substantial shift' (Browne-Wilkinson, 1988, p. 46) in the control of the administration of the courts from the judges to civil servants in the Lord Chancellor's Department since the reorganization of the court system in 1971; this has given rise to tensions between judges and the administrators, since the latter are answerable to their superiors in the department, not to the judges.

This issue formed the subject of a public lecture by the Vice-Chancellor (the President of the Chancery Division of the High Court), Sir Nicolas Browne-Wilkinson, in 1988. His concern was that the executive's control of finance and administration posed a threat to the independence of the judiciary as a collective body, and to the independence of the legal system (Browne-Wilkinson, 1988, p. 44). The other contributory factor in eroding the independence of the system is Treasury control, which has increased under the Financial Management Initiative: this goes beyond fixing the amount a department receives from public funds and extends to supervising and monitoring how each department spends its money in order to secure 'value for money'. The objection to this approach put by the Vice-Chancellor was that justice cannot be measured in terms of value for money, and to the extent that the exercise involves setting the policy objectives of the courts, this should not be a matter for the executive alone.

The Vice-Chancellor's principal complaint was that the judges were not being consulted in these decisions. By way of example, he gave the debate about rights of audience in the courts which were to be reformed by the Courts and Legal Services Bill: 'The whole question has been raised and discussed not on the basis "what is in the best interests of justice?" but on the basis "what will be cheaper?"' He felt that insufficient regard had been paid to considerations such as the impact of the changes on the length of trials, the need to secure that litigants' cases were properly deployed, the role and resources of the judge, and the place of oral as opposed to written submissions in trials. His point was not about the merits of the decision, but about the process by which and the persons by whom it was taken, and he felt that this should be a matter where the judges were at least consulted. He also complained about the lack of consultation between the Lord Chancellor's Department and the judges about other matters of policy such as the decentralization of court work to provincial centres based on the county courts, on which the judges, as experienced experts, would have much to contribute.

There is considerable force in these complaints. In a number of common law jurisdictions (Australia, Canada and the USA), this problem of control of the administration of the courts has been addressed and court administration has been placed under the direction of the judiciary (Green, 1985; MacKay, 1991). The Vice-Chancellor proposed that the British system should move in that direction. The fixing of the total budget for court administration should remain a political matter for the government, but the judges should be involved in preparing the estimates; they should also be involved in the allocation of the budget among the various functions of the legal system so as to secure that the administration of justice remains under independent control.

A Collegiate Body of Judges?

To facilitate judicial involvement in these matters, the Vice-Chancellor felt that a collegiate body of judges should be established. It would be charged with responsibility for taking policy decisions on behalf of the judges, and would be responsible for the management of certain functions of court administration, with the assistance of an administrative staff answerable directly to the collegiate body. The body would be accountable to the Lord Chancellor for the efficient use of its funds.

At present, there is no collegiate body of the kind envisaged by the Vice-Chancellor, and the absence of such an organization that can represent the judiciary causes a number of problems. In 1988, the Lord Chief Justice, Lord Lane, established a Judges' Council, consisting of himself, the Master of the Rolls, the President of the Family Division, the Vice-Chancellor, the Senior Presiding Judge and two Puisne (High Court) judges. But the council is informal (though it is supported by a small staff provided by the Lord Chancellor's Department): it discusses a range of matters of concern but has no powers (Scott, 1989) and it is not representative of the judiciary as a whole.

If a formal representative judicial collegiate body were to be set up and given responsibility for a large labour force and budget, there would be a number of problems. It is unlikely that judges as members of the collegiate body would relish the prospect of appearing before a select committee to give an account of their management of the courts. In any event, the members may not have the time to undertake responsibility for court administration and financial management as well as judicial duties. And they would be exposed to political pressures that could undermine the independence of the system (Mackay, 1991).

Decisions about the size of the overall budget for the courts and the allocation of resources within a budget are intensely political and often technical. It would be unwise for judges to seek a formal, responsible status in this process. The only reason why judges might wish to be involved is that the allocation of resources could be used as a method for interfering with the integrity of the judicial process, for example by withholding the necessary resources and back-up from judges for political reasons, or altering court procedures in order to save money, possibly at the expense of the interests of justice. A good example would be a government decision to abolish the right to silence in order to encourage pleas of guilty in order to save money on trials. It is suggested that other measures could provide better safeguards against such actions than transferring responsibility to a collegiate body, e.g. the setting up of a Ministry of Justice, giving the judges a right to be consulted and the introduction of a Bill of Rights (see Chapter 9).

In reality, despite the unease expressed by the Vice-Chancellor about the relationship between the judges and court administration, there is no evidence that the judiciary really wants or feels itself qualified to take on formal responsibility for court administration. In pressing for a greater say in these matters, judges are expressing their anxieties about government encroachment on their professionalism and independence (I am grateful to Cyril Glasser for this point).

These problems deserve serious consideration, even if the Vice-Chancellor's tentative solutions are open to criticism. The difficulties derive from the politicization of legal issues and public expenditure policies because of economic pressures that are unlikely to disappear; they indicate a need to alter the balance between the judiciary and the executive in order to protect the system of justice, but not in such a way as to expose the judiciary to greater political pressures than under the present system, where the Lord Chancellor's Department operates as a protective buffer between the judges and the executive (Mackay, 1991).

Although the case for giving judges responsibility for court administration is flawed, there is indeed a problem over the independence of the legal system and a risk that politicians may either seek to subvert it deliberately (which the Vice-Chancellor did not suggest was happening) or that it might happen, as he put it 'unperceived and unappreciated' (Browne-Wilkinson, 1988, p. 51).

The nub of the complaint of the Vice-Chancellor is the lack of consultation with and involvement of the judges in decisions in these areas. An approach to solving these tensions and concerns about the integrity of the system of justice that would not mean making the judges formally responsible and politically accountable for court administration, would be to increase the level of judicial involvement and participation in decisions about administration and to introduce other reforming measures such as a Ministry of Justice and a Commons Select Committee for Legal Affairs.

If judges are to be involved in decisions, a collegiate body would have to be established, which should include in its membership representatives from all ranks of the judiciary. Such a body should have the right to be consulted on the needs of the court system, the distribution of resources, reforms of procedure and other matters to do with the running of the system on which the judges have expertise and a legitimate interest to be consulted.

The administration of the courts could be immunized from party politics and at the same time put under pressure to increase efficiency and effectiveness if it were transformed into a *Next Steps* executive agency (see Chapter 4). The judges could have an input into the agency if a collegiate body or advisory committee of judges were established with a right to be consulted and to offer advice to the chief executive of the agency. And the chief executive would be accountable to the House of Commons for the efficiency and effectiveness of the service and its fulfilment of the framework document with the relevant minister. The minister would be accountable for the terms of the agreement and the resources given to the system. This would be a better solution than to make the judges themselves responsible for administration.

Accountability and the judges

As we have seen, the judiciary is insulated from political and other external pressures in order to maintain its independence and impartiality. The possible reforms of methods of appointment and dismissal referred to above are put forward in order to enhance this independence. But it does not follow that the judges should not be accountable in any way for their activities, only that they should not be politically accountable (save to the extent that they may be dismissed on an address from both Houses of Parliament: Supreme Court Act 1981, s. 11).

In fact there is a degree of public and legal accountability under the system as it operates at present. The courts sit in public and their proceedings can be reported (Green, 1985). The provisions for appeals up the court hierarchy impose legal accountability. However, the effectiveness of these mechanisms of accountability was called into question by events such as the series of convictions of suspected terrorists in the 'Guildford Four', the 'Maguire Seven' and the 'Birmingham Six' cases, which were set aside many years later as having been unsound for reasons connected with the trial process. The Royal Commission set up after the Birmingham Six decision will no doubt consider not only matters of criminal procedure but the institutional arrangements for dealing with cases where miscarriages of justice are suspected to have taken place (for discussion of possible reforms, see JUSTICE, 1989; Report of the Home Affairs Committee, HC 421, 1981–82; Labour Party, 1990, p. 41).

'Maladministration' in the courts

Suggestions have been made from time to time that some formal procedure should be set up to deal with complaints about 'maladministration' in the courts and about aspects of judicial behaviour which cannot be the subject of appeal. The Courts and Legal Services Act 1990 extends the jurisdiction of the PCA to the administrative acts of court staff. But under this new provision, the PCA is still prevented from investigating acts done on the direction or authority of a judge. The purpose of this exclusion is to preserve the independence of the judiciary. There is by no means consensus about the need for additional provision for the investigation of complaints about the judiciary. Shetreet found in the course of interviews about the issue that the general opinion was against a Complaints Tribunal. He was uncommitted on the matter, though he concluded that 'some features of the informal checks need improvement' (Shetreet, 1976, p. 414). But the JUSTICE conclusion in its report on *The Administration of the Courts* in 1986 was that 'It seemed to us that people who should complain do not do so, and that where complaints are made they sometimes achieve nothing, so that there is some lack of confidence in the present system' (JUSTICE, 1986, para. 3).

The JUSTICE report recommended that these matters should be brought within the jurisdiction of the PCA, rejecting fears that this could 'encourage MPs to pry into the affairs of the judiciary'. They noted that in Sweden the Judicial Ombudsman, and in France the Conseil Supérieur de la Magistrature, deal with complaints about the judiciary (other countries that have ombudsmen or equivalent officers to investigate complaints include Denmark, Norway, Australia, New Zealand and some states of the USA; see JUSTICE, 1986, app. C for a summary of complaints systems overseas). Although neither country is directly comparable with the jurisdictions in the UK, since each has a career judiciary with particular problems arising from the presence on the benches of young inexperienced judges, they nevertheless manage to maintain the independence of the judiciary even though judicial behaviour is subject to this kind of investigation.

An alternative for those who fear that investigation by the PCA could lead to damaging parliamentary interference with the independence of the judiciary would be to give this function to the judicial services commissions if they were established. However, if the commissions were largely composed of judges this would not inspire confidence in the impartiality of their investigations.

It is suggested that fears about parliamentary 'prying' would not in practice be a danger if the PCA had jurisdiction in these matters, since he or she would act as a 'buffer' between MPs and the judges. In any event, MPs generally appreciate the importance of judicial independence – the risk of improper interference comes more from members of the government than from a select committee of the Commons.

Ministerial responsibility for the system of justice

We have been concerned so far in this chapter primarily with matters to do with the courts, but the system of justice extends beyond these. Responsibilities for the system are shared between a range of government departments, particularly the Lord Chancellor's Department and the Home Office. The Lord Chancellor's Department, as we have seen, has responsibilities for appointments to most judicial offices, magistrates and members of tribunals; it is also charged with the administration of courts other than magistrates' courts, including civil procedure, the state of the civil law, and legal aid and advice (for a summary of the powers of the Lord Chancellor, see Mackay, 1991).

The Home Office is responsible for public order, including the police service, national security, the treatment of offenders including the administration of prisons; these functions rest uncomfortably with its 'system of justice' responsibilities for civil rights, some aspects of magistrates' court administration and criminal law reform. The Home Secretary also has other important functions which contribute to a problem of overload in the department – public safety, public morals, immigration, nationality and naturalization, passports, elections, broadcasting and other matters.

The Law Officers too have responsibilities for some aspects of the system of justice, for giving legal advice to the government, for government litigation, for the Director of Public Prosecutions, the Crown Prosecution Service, the Treasury Solicitor's Department and the Government Legal Service, and to answer in the Commons for the Lord Chancellor. The Prime Minister has responsibility for certain judicial appointments, the determination of judicial salaries, and for the Office of the Parliamentary Counsel. And the various government departments have responsibility for law reform in the areas covered by their portfolios (for a list of the principal ministerial responsibilities for the law in England and Wales, see Brazier, 1989, pp. 93–4).

Of the two principal ministers operating in this area, the Lord Chancellor is not accountable to the elected chamber. The Home Secretary is charged with a range of functions, some of which are incompatible with his or her justice functions and which mean that the system of justice cannot have a high priority in claiming his or her attention. One of the effects of this division of responsibility is that various aspects of the system have been neglected over the years. Law reform has had a low priority on the political agenda. Legal research has often been neglected (Legal Aid Advisory Committee, 1984, para. 169) but a research officer was appointed by the Lord Chancellor in 1985 and a first research programme was announced in 1985–86. Civil rights have been left unprotected in important respects (see Chapter 9), largely because they are formally the responsibility of the Home Secretary whose preoccupation is likely to be more with police policy and maintaining law and order than with protecting civil rights. Public concern about miscarriages of justice and the need to reform aspects of criminal procedure that drew criticism as contributing to wrongful convictions was ignored for many years until the release of the Birmingham Six in March 1991, when the Home Secretary belatedly announced a Royal Commission into the question.

A Select Committee for the system of justice?

When the new select committee system was set up in 1979 (see Chapter 3) a deliberate decision was made that no committee should monitor the Lord Chancellor's Department or the Law Officers for fear that this might lead to political interference with the independence of the judiciary.

The reasons for this decision were dismissed as 'ludicrous' by one commentator (Drewry, 1987a, p. 358). In a Report of the Select Committee on Procedure in 1990 (HC 19–i, 1989–90), a number of the chairmen of select committees commented on the lacuna in coverage of the system of justice functions. The Home Affairs Committee chairman regarded the exclusion as 'quite unjustifiable', particularly since the Home Affairs Committee had resolved not to look into individual cases and had been scrupulous to avoid comment on matters currently before the courts (HC 19–I, 1989–90, Memorandum 4 submitted by the chairman of the Home Affairs Committee, para. 18). The study of Parliament Group also expressed the view that the omission of the Lord Chancellor's Department was 'indefensible' (HC 19-i, 1989–90, Memorandum 17 submitted by Professor Gavin Drewry, p. lviii).

The chairman of the Liaison Committee stated that 'ideally the Law Departments should have their own committee' (HC 19-i, 1989–90, Memorandum 29 from the chairman of the Liaison Committee, para. 8). In practice, the Home Affairs Committee has sought to fill the vacuum in select committee activity in its inquiries and has found the Lord Chancellor's Department willing to cooperate with it. The Lord Chancellor has given evidence to the committee on a number of occasions.

In the absence of any new committee being established, it was suggested that the terms of reference of the Home Affairs Committee should be extended to include the Lord Chancellor's Department and the Law Officers (HC 19-I, 1989–90, Memorandum, para. 290; 1989–90, HC 19-i; Memorandum 4 from the Chairman of the Home Affairs Committee, para. 19; Memorandum 17 from the Study of Parliament Group, p. lviii). This would give explicit recognition to the right of the committee to carry out work on which it has already embarked. In a lecture in March 1991, the Lord Chancellor expressed the view that 'It may be that the time is now right for such an extension, subject to the exclusion of, for example, examination of individual cases' (Mackay, 1991). And finally the government conceded this point in its response to the Procedure Committee (Cm. 1532, p. 19). The Home Affairs Committee will be given power to monitor the policy, administration and expenditure of the Lord Chancellor's Department, including the work of staff provided for the administrative work of the courts and tribunals, but excluding consideration of individual cases and appointments. Scrutiny of the Attorney-General's Office, the Treasury Solicitor's Department, the Crown Prosecution Service and the Serious Fraud Office will also exclude individual cases and appointments, and advice given within government by the Law Officers. In addition the policy of the Law Officers would not be included in the orders or reference of the Home Affairs Committee, because of the 'delicate constitutional position' concerning prosecution policy and the independence of the Crown Prosecution Service, the Director of Public Prosecutions, and the Serious Fraud Office (the Procurator Fiscal Service in Scotland) in relation to prosecution policy. However, the new order of reference would not exclude consideration by the select committee of systems of appointment. This represents a welcome step forward in increasing accountability for the system of justice, and is something of a victory for the select committees, and a vote of confidence in them by the government and the Lord Chancellor's Department.

A Ministry of Justice?

A number of commentators has proposed that the problems arising from the absence of a minister in the House of Commons with responsibility for all 'system of justice' functions should be overcome through the establishment of a Ministry of Justice, with a minister in the House of Commons and a select committee charged with monitoring the performance of its functions (Brazier, 1988, ch. 11, 1989). These proposals would probably result in the end of the office of Lord Chancellor, although it would be possible for the Lord Chancellor to survive as a minister in the second chamber with special responsibility for such matters as judicial appointments and the administration of the courts. This could meet some of the objections put by more conservative commentators, including Lord Chancellor Mackay (1991).

The suggestion for a Ministry of Justice goes back to the Haldane Report (1918) on the 'Machinery of Government' (see Drewry, 1983) and even before then – Bentham was in favour of a Ministry of Justice – but ideas about the form that such a ministry should take have changed over the years. The main issues are how the independence of the judiciary could be protected, what functions the ministry should be responsible for, whether the ministry should have a minister in the House of Commons, whether there should be a select committee monitoring such a ministry, and whether the post of Lord Chancellor would survive such a reform.

The Conservative government has shown no interest in the argument for a Ministry of Justice, largely because of fears expressed by successive Conservative Lord Chancellors about implications for the independence of the judiciary (Mackay, 1991). Lord Chancellor Mackay sees positive merit in the fact that the Lord Chancellor, the minister with responsibility for the courts, is a judge and a member of the executive and the legislature: 'the office of Lord Chancellor provides a link, which our long history of gradual development has produced, between the judiciary, the executive and the legislature that is broken at our peril' (Mackay, 1991). He has also counselled against measures that might load even more work onto an already overloaded department (see Mackay, 1991, for the arguments against change). However, as suggested above, it would be possible to retain the office of Lord Chancellor even within a Ministry of Justice with a minister in the House of Commons.

The opposition parties are considering these issues and a number of proposals for a Ministry of Justice have come from them in recent years. In 1990, the Labour Party was committed to establish 'a Department of Legal Administration responsible for all courts and tribunals and accountable to the House of Commons', and an independent commission having responsibility for judicial appointments (Labour Party, 1990, p. 40). The Liberal Democrats are moving towards a commitment to a Ministry of Justice responsible for the protection of human rights and the administration of the legal system, the courts and legal aid, including responsibility for the legal profession. An independent commission would be responsible for the appointment of judges. The Attorney General would retain responsibility for the prosecution of criminal offences, including the Crown Prosecution Service (Social and Liberal Democrats, 1989). The Liberal Democrats' Federal Green Paper No. 13 *"We, The People . . ."* (1990, p. 32) endorses these proposals. The party is not explicit about what would become of the office of Lord Chancellor, or about whether the Secretary of State would be a member of the House of Commons.

Academic writers have paid more attention to the implications of introducing a Ministry of Justice (Brazier, 1988, ch. 11, 1989; Drewry, 1987b). Out of this writing there emerges a fairly coherent idea of the basic ingredients of a Ministry of Justice or a Department of Legal Affairs – Brazier prefers 'Department of Law' (1989, p. 83), or 'Department of Justice' (1988, p. 257). There is general agreement that if such a department were formed, the functions connected with the appointment of judges should be given to independent commissions on the lines discussed earlier in order to overcome fears about the independence of the judiciary. The Secretary of State for Legal Affairs should be a member of the House of Commons and should have responsibility for funding the system, the legal aid scheme, the availability of legal services, relations with the legal professions, the state of the law including the compatibility of English law with international law obligations and with European law, civil and criminal procedure, the needs for substantive law reform and civil rights.

As indicated above, the purpose of creating a department with a Secretary of State in the House of Commons would be to increase the political accountability of the responsible minister, and this would be an argument for having a separate select committee to monitor the activities of the department. While the maintenance of judicial independence is indeed of central importance, this consideration need not preclude a select committee having responsibility for other 'system of justice' functions. The objections to establishing such a committee when the new departmentally related select committees were set up in 1979 were based on fear for the independence of the judiciary; these objections would not apply to the functions referred to above, so the arguments for creating a separate select committee for legal affairs would be compelling.

Conclusions

The debates about a Ministry of Justice and other reforms to the system of justice have been clouded by muddled thinking about the independence of the judiciary and unfounded fears that the setting up of a ministry would interfere with that independence. As a result of the lack of a minister in the Commons with responsibility for the system of justice, it has been neglected over the years.

The independence of the judiciary is indeed a vital element in the system, but it could be protected, indeed enhanced, if independent commissions were given responsibility for judicial appointments and related matters. The integrity of court administration could be protected and its efficiency enhanced if it were made into a *Next Steps* agency, and if judges were entitled to be consulted through a collegiate body over policy relating to the financing of the courts, law reform and other matters on which they have expertise. If reforms along these lines were introduced, judicial independence would be secure against encroachment by government or Parliament. A Minister of Justice would be in a position to deal with areas currently neglected – civil and political rights, court procedure, legal services. The whole system of justice would benefit from such reforms, accountability, efficiency and effectiveness would be enhanced, and with a minister of its own the status of citizenship would move closer to centre-stage in constitutional debate.

PART III

The political process

8

The electoral system

The electoral system is central to our themes of accountability, effectiveness and citizenship. The rights to vote and to stand for election were identified by Marshall (1950) as the crucial political elements in his citizenship of entitlement (see Chapter 2). It is through the operation of an electoral system that these rights can give the citizen a real role in the political process. Elected representatives are a central channel through which government is both held to account to the public and put under pressure to operate effectively and efficiently.

Discussion in this chapter will focus on elections to the Commons and local government. At present, there is no electoral process for the House of Lords, but should the second chamber be reformed, the powers and method of elections of its members could be crucial, as there would be little point in having the same system of election for two chambers unless their powers were significantly different. There would be problems of conflict between the two chambers if they both enjoyed the same degree of democratic legitimacy. If assemblies were to be established for Scotland, Wales, Northern Ireland and the English regions, as promised by the Labour Party (1990, pp. 56–8), then the system of election to those assemblies would also have a major impact on their operation. These problems are discussed in Chapters 3 and 6, and the question of elections to a reformed second chamber will only be considered in passing in this chapter.

Reform of the electoral system has been a subject of discussion among political scientists and constitutional lawyers since the early 1970s (e.g. Lakeman, 1974; Finer, 1975; Hansard Society, 1976; Bogdanor, 1981; Joint Liberal/SDP Alliance Commission on Constitutional Reform, 1982). But it was not until the 1980s that practising politicians began to voice criticisms of the first past the post system as it operated for elections to the House of Commons and in local government. Suggestions began to surface for the adoption of a form of proportional representation.

Interest in the topic grew with the resurgence of support for the Liberals in the

1970s, since this support was not reflected in the number of seats they held in the House of Commons. It was further stimulated during the Labour administration of 1974–79, which was elected on 37.1 percent of the vote in February 1974 and confirmed on 39.2 percent of the vote in October of that year. With a turnout of 72.8 percent in the October election, the actual proportion of the electorate that had voted for Labour candidates was only some 28 percent. The government used its Commons majority to pursue a number of controversial policies in the face of strong opposition, sometimes from within the party and often from the public at large, for example: support for the closed shop; the social contract which represented a bargain between the government and trade unions under which government adopted policies on matters such as rent and tax levels in exchange for unenforceable and often broken 'solemn and binding under-takings' from the unions to moderate pay claims; nationalization of the aircraft and shipbuilding industries; the imposition of comprehensive education on local education authorities; the 'blacklist' policy which sought to enforce pay policy on public contractors and to punish those who failed to comply; cuts in public expenditure to comply with IMF conditions for financial support. The question of the accountability of government to the public through Parliament under this system came to be debated in terms of elective dictatorship (Hailsham, 1976) and contributed not only to discussion of electoral reform, but also to the climate in which the reformed select committee system was introduced in the House of Commons in 1979 (see Chapter 3).

Public opinion is moving in favour of proportional representation: the MORI *State of the Nation* poll found that 50 percent of the respondents supported changing the electoral system to a system of proportional representation. Only 23 percent opposed such a change (MORI, 1991).

First past the post

In order to appreciate the reasons why electoral reform has come onto the political agenda, it is important to know how the present first past the post (otherwise known as 'relative majority') system operates in practice.

First past the post secures that the House of Commons consists entirely of MPs sitting for single member constituencies: this is something that no other electoral system can do. There being no requirement that an MP should have won over 50 percent of the votes cast, the candidate with more votes than any others in a constituency is declared elected. Individual MPs are commonly elected on less than 50 percent of the vote; and so over 50 percent of votes in many constituencies are 'ineffective' in the sense that they do not produce a member for whom the elector has voted.

The national election results generally give an overall majority in the House of Commons to one party, but it will have won the support of fewer than 50 percent of the voters. In every election since the war, a single-party government has been formed by a party that received less than 50 percent of the vote. The closest to a majority was the Conservative victory on 49.7 percent of the vote in

1955. On two occasions, the largest party has received fewer votes than the runner up: in 1951, the Conservatives won with 26 more seats than Labour, having received 230 000 fewer votes; in February 1974, Labour won 4 more seats than the Conservatives with 230 000 fewer votes.

Under this system, smaller parties with support fairly evenly distributed geographically have very little chance of winning seats. Labour, the Conservatives, the Scottish Nationalists and Plaid Cymru tend to have their voters concentrated in particular areas and they have an advantage over parties with more widely distributed supporters. The Liberal Party and the Social Democrats were unable to win seats in anything like due proportion to the level of their electoral support in elections in 1983 and 1987; this is inevitable under first past the post. They won 23 and 22 seats (3.5 and 3.4 percent of the total in the Commons) on 25.4 and 22.6 percent of the votes cast in 1983 and 1987 respectively. The Greens would suffer the same disadvantages.

Electors and the two-party system

If the turnout in elections is anything to go by, for much of the post-war period the electorate appeared to be broadly satisfied with the first past the post system: turnout reached a peak of 84 percent in 1950 and was 82.5 percent in 1951. Of those who voted, some 96.8 percent supported Labour or the Conservatives in 1951, indicating support for the two-party system. But the turnout dropped to a low of 72 percent in 1970 and did not reach 80 percent again until 1987.

As turnout dropped, so support for other parties rose. The two main parties' share of the vote dropped to a post-war low of 70 percent in the 1983 election, when support for the Alliance reached 25.4 percent. Despite a loss of support for the two main parties, the system nevertheless makes it almost inevitable that one of those parties will win a majority at an election and that no other party can do so. It is important, therefore, to consider why the two main parties lost support, and more particularly whether the operation of the electoral system is responsive to changes in society which ought to influence government if it is to be accountable and effective.

This point about the ability of the political system to respond to social change is central to the effectiveness of the constitution. David Marquand (1988) has argued that we suffer from an institutional inability to adjust to the new demands created by the changes in the world economy. The arguments for intra-party democracy in the Labour Party have been based in part on the need to make the party more responsive to changing needs as articulated by party activists (on intra-party democracy generally, see Ware, 1979). But these changes – election of the party leader by a conference dominated by the trade unions, reselection of candidates through a process dominated by party activists – would not increase the accountability of the party to the public; nor would they produce a government better able to adjust to needs not perceived by party activists. But the increased consciousness of the unadaptability of the British political system in these proposals is significant. It is suggested that the need for adjustability can be better met by opening up the political process to new ideas and securing that it can provide a channel through which the needs for change can be articulated and then met.

To return to the reasons for the fall in support for Labour and the Conservatives in the 1970s and 1980s, a number of conflicting explanations has been advanced. One is that it was partly to do with the fact that Labour is traditionally seen as representing the working class, and this class had shrunk. The internal organization of the party, dominated by the trade unions and party activists, who do not reflect the views of ordinary Labour voters, prevented it from responding to these changes by producing policies acceptable to a wider range of voters. But this does not explain the fall in support for the Conservatives, who would have been expected to benefit more than they have done from the shrinking of the working class.

Heath *et al.* demonstrated that in the 1983 election there was substantial electoral support for policies that crossed the conventional two-party divide. In a survey of electoral attitudes of Alliance voters, they found that on economic issues they were towards what may be conveniently called the centre or right of the political spectrum, whereas on non-economic issues, such as defence, the welfare state and civil liberties, they tended to be much closer to Labour than to the Conservatives. This was a large tract of effectively unrepresented ground in British politics. Their conclusion was that there was a much more distinctive ideological profile to the Alliance voters than had commonly been realized, and neither of the two main parties accommodated that particular set of views (Heath *et al.*, 1985, 1986). Nor could the electoral system do so.

Electoral support for Labour since the 1970s

The loss of electoral support for the two main parties in the 1970s and 1980s was largely Labour's. Their share of the vote declined from a post-war peak of 48.8 percent in 1951 to a low of 27.6 percent in 1983 (by contrast, the Conservatives' post-war peak was 49.7 percent in 1955 and its post-war low was 35.8 percent in October 1974). As suggested earlier, Labour's loss seems to have been partly due to changes in the social structure (Franklin, 1985); this has been influenced in turn by increased prosperity and economic and technological developments. Not only has manufacturing industry in the UK – a natural home for Labour voters – declined dramatically, but the trend away from 'Fordist' methods of mass production (Aglietta, 1979) and the development of production methods using flexible specialization and advanced technology mean that workers in those industries have not inherited the Socialist tradition of class and worker solidarity that had been fostered by low pay and work on assembly lines. Workers earn more and have greater control over their work as self-management at work is gradually replacing hierarchical employment relationships. With prosperity has come owner-occupation, share ownership (encouraged by the Conservative government in its privatization of industries), ownership of consumer durables, access to foreign holidays and the like. These workers tend either to regard themselves as middle class or not to think of themselves as belonging to any particular class (Norton, 1985, ch. V); they do not identify as strongly as their forebears did with the Labour Party and so Labour has lost part of its natural constituency (Lash and Urry, 1987; Gamble, 1988). But many of these voters did not feel at home in the Conservative Party either in the 1980s.

At the same time as Labour was losing working-class support in the 1970s and 1980s, it found a new constituency. Throughout the post-war period, there had been a growth in the number of workers employed in central and local government, the NHS (the largest employer in the UK) and the nationalized industries. Many of them were not employed in traditional working-class manual work where Labour support had been strongest. But these workers had a vested interest in high public expenditure on the provision of public services, and would therefore naturally tend to give their support to high-spending Labour administrations rather than to Conservatives with policies of low taxation and privatization.

But in the late 1970s, Labour alienated many of these new supporters by its policy of public expenditure cuts and pay restraint, imposed by the IMF as a condition of its support in the financial crises of the mid-1970s. This led to the radicalization of parts of the Labour Party and contributed to the political polarization that took place in the 1970s and 1980s (see Chapter 1). The Campaign for Labour Party Democracy sought to counter the influence of the business and commercial establishment on which it blamed the policy of cuts by increasing the influence of activists in the Labour Party. Some of these new radicals formed the militant left-wing of the party, but they were often out of sympathy with more traditional working-class Labour supporters and contributed to the defection of numbers of the latter to the Alliance or to the Conservatives in elections after 1979.

Most dramatically in the 1983 by-election in Bermondsey, a very traditional working-class constituency and a deprived inner city area, the seat was won by the Liberal candidate Simon Hughes against a candidate associated in the public mind with militant left-wingers in the party. The Liberals won largely on their longstanding commitment to community politics, which in this constituency provided a sharp contrast both to the way in which the old Labour Party that had controlled the local authority and provided the MP had treated its constituents, and to the practices of new party activists which deterred ordinary members from involvement in the party (Seyd, 1987, ch. 3). Hence the new constituency that Labour had gained among the public sector white-collar workers in some respects exacerbated its electoral problems.

Part of the problem, then, is that in the 1980s the electoral system which discriminates in favour of Labour and the Conservatives excluded from representation in the House of Commons a large body of political opinion which was not comfortable with the two main political parties or indeed with a two-party system. This in turn has meant that government was not under public pressure to respond to social developments and produce effective policies to deal with them.

Pendulum politics

There are other criticisms of the first past the post system; the first is that it encourages 'pendulum swing' politics. The fact that the electoral system favours the two main parties, even at a time when they are polarizing and each would seek to reverse the policies of the other if elected to government, as was the case in the 1970s and 1980s, means that there is a risk of repeated policy U-turns: this must be damaging to the economy (Finer, 1975; Bogdanor, 1981; Caldecote, 1980; Hansard Society, 1979).

The pendulum problem has arisen mainly in the economic area. The most dramatic example has been the steel industry, which has undergone nationalization, denationalization, renationalization and privatization. But it has been suggested that these swings are caused as much by the need to deal with crises and stress as by the two-party system and the fact that changes of government bring changes of policy (Debnam, 1989). The pendulum swing effect has not been such a problem in other areas of policy and nor is it an inevitable aspect of the electoral system. It was not operating in the 1950s when there was little to choose between the parties and the talk was of 'Butskellism', implying that it was difficult to distinguish between the policies of Labour's Hugh Gaitskell and the Conservatives' R. A. Butler. Indeed, there is a case for the argument that in the 1960s there was a 'directionless consensus' which made it impossible for governments of any complexion to tackle the country's problems (Rose, 1976). The pendulum swing argument in favour of electoral reform can therefore be exaggerated (Norton, 1981, pp. 223–4).

The North–South divide

The operation of the voting system also means that divisions and splits within the electorate are encouraged, indeed exaggerated. A sharp north–south divide has developed in the electoral landscape (as in the economy) in mainland Britain in recent years (Curtice and Steed, 1982; Johnston, 1985; Johnston *et al.*, 1988). After the 1987 election, there were only 108 Conservative MPs but 142 Labour MPs in Wales and the north and north-west of England. There were only 10 Conservative MPs in Scotland, compared to 50 Labour MPs. There were a mere 37 Labour MPs in the south and east of England, and those were concentrated in Greater London (23), as compared with 259 Conservative MPs. In effect, Labour was reduced by the electoral system to a regional party, despite the fact that it had substantial support in constituencies in the south and south-east (Johnston *et al.*, 1988, p. 19, table 1.3).

The electoral system reflects to a degree a real north-south divide, but it also exaggerates it, and this, as Bogdanor (1981, part IV) argues, is damaging to the economy and to the sense of national community, which is essential to citizenship (see Chapter 2, see also Finer, 1975). Among other detrimental side-effects of this aspect of the working of the electoral system, is the effect on the regional policies adopted by governments. Labour and Conservative governments have by turns shifted the distribution of resources and grants to local government towards those areas where their support is strong or they have a chance of winning seats from their opponents (Bogdanor, 1981, part IV). The resulting instability of policy is damaging to the local economies and to industry, which cannot make long-term plans and invest with sufficient security.

Fairness to the parties?

This brings us to the question whether it is legitimate for an electoral system to discriminate against certain political parties, especially those with small or widely distributed support? A number of justifications in terms of our themes of accountability, effectiveness and citizenship could be advanced for discrimination against small parties. First, there is the argument that they are often extremist and extremism should be discouraged. In West Germany, there is a 5 percent threshold for parties seeking certain seats in the *Bundestag*, and this is designed to discourage and exclude from the parliament very small, possibly 'extremist' parties. But not all small parties are extremist, and some large parties are. It would be a radical departure from the liberal-democratic tradition to ban or discriminate explicitly against 'extremist' parties as such. Extremism, if it involves incitement to violence or racial hatred, can be dealt with by the criminal law, and it is suggested that this approach is preferable to proscribing or discriminating against parties. Yet the first past the post system clearly does discriminate against some parties that have substantial support.

Coalition or single-party government?

A justification that is sometimes advanced for discriminating against small parties in the election process is that it reduces the chances of coalition government. Coalitions are said to have a number of disadvantages as compared with single-party governments. With members drawn from a wide range of parties, a government might take time to hammer out a programme after the election and this could be damaging to the country. (One must suppress the unworthy thought that there might be something to be said for having a rest from being governed for a while after an election while the politicians argue about a programme.)

The problems caused by a delay in forming a new coalition government after an election are real – under the present system, a new Prime Minister is appointed generally within hours of the election result. But many countries live with transitional arrangements and caretaker governments – these problems are not insuperable or conclusive of the argument.

Coalition governments might be weak and unstable. Such has been the experience of Italy and the Netherlands in recent years. (On the other hand, Italy's economy has been relatively successful despite her political problems.)

It is clear that there are advantages in a system that encourages stable government by discouraging a proliferation and fragmentation of parties. But there are other ways of doing so apart from the choice of voting system, including, for example, the requirement (which is part of the present system) for candidates to pay deposits which are forfeit if a specified proportion of votes is not won. The Representation of the People Act 1985 (s. 13(a)) requires parliamentary candidates to pay deposits of £500 which are forfeit if candidates fail to win 5 percent of the vote (for a further discussion see, Rawlings, 1988, pp. 122–4). An alternative discouragement to candidates with a low level of support would be a requirement of a large number of subscribers to the nomination as a precondition to the candidacy, for example 200 subscribers per candidate in each parliamentary constituency. In any event, the formation of coalition governments is by no means the inevitable result of a proliferation of small parties.

Nevertheless, there is of course a possibility that coalition governments would have to be formed if the present discrimination against small parties in our electoral system were to end, whether naturally by a surge in support for those parties in particular areas, or by the introduction of another electoral system. But it is far from obvious that coalitions are to be avoided. It depends upon the coalition, especially its stability.

Let us consider, then, the arguments against coalitions. The first is that the voters end up with a government for which they did not vote and a programme cobbled together by the coalition partners that was not put to them. This need not be the case. In what was the Federal Republic of Germany, for example, coalitions have been formed for most of the period since 1949 consisting of one or other of the main parties (the SPD or the CDU/CSU) and the FDP, the small 'centre party'. But before each election, the FDP has indicated which of the other parties it would be prepared to join in a coalition and voters therefore have known in advance what they were voting for or against. If the smaller parties in the UK announced before the election with which party they would be prepared to join in a coalition (or, alternatively, on what terms they would join in a coalition with either of the main parties), or if the main parties were to indicate whether and on what terms they would be prepared to include the smaller parties in a coalition, then the electors would know what they were voting for (or against) when casting their votes.

As far as the objection to the programme 'cobbled together' by a coalition is concerned, the point is weaker than it seems. It implies that voters endorse the manifesto of the party they vote for so that it would be unfair to lumber them with another programme. But research has shown that in practice voters do not by any means intend approval of every item in the manifesto of the party they vote for; and in some elections, they have approved of very few of their own party's pledges and a substantial number of the pledges in the manifesto of the opposing party (Oliver, 1989, pp. 126–9; Rose, 1976, pp. 305–309, 1984, pp. 34–42).

The view that coalition government is undesirable or, more accurately, more undesirable than single-party government, is often based on the argument that single-party governments are good because they are 'strong and effective', whereas coalitions are bad because they are weak and indecisive (Maude and Szemerey, 1982). Again these assumptions need to be examined. A single-party government will not necessarily be either strong or effective. The Labour administrations from 1974–79 did not succeed in beating inflation and revitalizing the economy; to this extent, their policies were ineffective. And if 'strong' government means decisive government, that administration was not strong either, for it changed policies quite drastically during the period, particularly in the late 1970s when, at the behest of the IMF, it reversed its policies of high public expenditure and embarked on a series of cuts. Equally, it is very debatable whether the Conservative government in the 1980s was effective: it managed to get most of its legislation through Parliament and if that is the measure of effectiveness then it succeeded. On the other hand, there are wide divergences of opinion as to whether its policies to beat inflation, to modernize the economy and make the state machine more efficient and effective were successful except in the short term. And if the Conservative governments under Mrs Thatcher are to be regarded as having been strong and decisive, there would by no means be agreement that this was an unmitigated blessing. The difference between good strong decisive government and stubborn, intransigent government is difficult to define and highly subjective.

In truth, the argument that single-party government is 'effective' is bedevilled with the ambiguity of that term used in that context. And if strong government means determined government that does not give in to pressure or respond to criticism, it is not necessarily a desirable quality: it can come close to authoritarianism and a lack of accountability. 'Effectiveness' and 'strong government' are good if one approves of the policies in question, and bad if one does not.

Nor is it necessarily the case that coalitions are 'weak' and 'ineffective'. Like single-party governments, some coalitions are strong and effective and others are not, and either way the government may be good or bad. In the Federal Republic of Germany, governments have been formed of coalitions for most of the period since the post-war constitution was implemented in 1949, and on most criteria they have been successful. Hence the argument that single-party governments are to be preferred to coalitions because the former are strong and effective whereas the latter are not needs to be analysed carefully and in terms of the actual political balance in the country in question. In the UK, the probable result of introducing a more proportional electoral system would be to boost the representation of the Liberal Democrats, and any coalition or pact would be likely to include them. This would resemble the experience in the Federal Republic of Germany.

Even if it were the case that single-party governments can be counted on to be strong and effective, this can only be regarded as advantageous if the single-party government is also responsive and accountable. No-one would seriously suggest that a strong, effective tyrant was a good thing. But the present system does not promote responsive accountable government. Where a government has a safe majority, there is very little to make it responsive to pressure from inside Parliament. Its own backbenchers may be able to exert some influence over its activities (see Chapter 3) and a government may succumb to such pressure in order to avoid the embarrassment of a backbench revolt, but these pressures will not generally do more than secure minor adjustments to government policy. They were not sufficient to deflect the Conservative government from introducing the community charge, privatizing the water industry and implementing other unpopular legislation in the late 1980s. The events of November 1990, which led to the replacement of Mrs Thatcher as Prime Minister by John Major were unusual: they reflected concern both in cabinet and among Conservative backbenchers about the party's ability to win the next election, rather than a desire to improve the day-to-day accountability of the government to the House of Commons.

The Lib–Lab pact

A taste of the effect of coalition government on ministerial responsiveness was had in the period of the Lib–Lab pact from 1977 to 1978. The Labour government had to pay heed to the wishes of the Liberals, who sustained the government in power by agreement until 1978 and thereafter on an *ad hoc* basis (Steel, 1980, chs 4, 5, 6; Marsh, 1990). The fact that the government had to placate backbenchers of other parties during this period enhanced the influence of the House of Commons and hence the accountability and responsiveness of the government.

   Marsh (1990) has concluded that an arrangement such as the pact 'needs to be buttressed by an enlarged framework of institutional and procedural changes' including stronger Commons committees. But, as we saw in Chapter 3, stronger Commons committees are unlikely to emerge in the absence of political change. One could add that better access to information and more resources for parliamentary parties are needed to improve their contributions to the policy process (these are considered in Chapters 3, 4 and 10). Electoral reform alone would not solve the problems. But lessons could be learned from the Lib–Lab pact when the possibility of coalitions and pacts between parties as a result of electoral reform is under consideration.

Parliamentary majorities and electoral minorities

Under the system as it operates at present, with government generally enjoying an overall majority in Parliament, the principal pressure on a government to be responsive to public opinion is the real possibility of loss of office at the next general election; the system did not offer this through the 1980s, despite the fact that electoral support for the Conservatives was well below 50 percent for most of that period, largely because the anti-Conservative or non-Conservative vote was split. In such a climate, there is little real pressure on a government to be responsive between elections.

In other respects, too, coalitions may be positively beneficial. Hirst (1989) has argued, for instance, that Labour should embrace the cause of proportional representation in order to secure the election of a coalition government that would allow a wide range of interests to participate in government and thus ensure that it had the legitimacy and authority to implement a radical programme.

Another disadvantage of the present system of election is that it makes it difficult for women and members of the ethnic minorities to be adopted as candidates in winnable constituencies and thus to win seats. Each constituency party can only select one candidate. Most parties are dominated by white men. Generally, white male candidates are regarded as 'safe' and, for this and other reasons such as the unwillingness of women to put themselves forward, there are few women candidates or candidates from the minorities (especially in winnable seats) and shockingly few women or ethnic minority MPs (Hansard Society Commission, 1990). Thus the political citizenship rights of these groups are in practice of little use to them.

Proportional representation

It does not of course follow from the arguments considered above to the effect that the first past the post system is defective that any other system would be better. Indeed, some of the systems on offer around the world would be a good deal worse if adopted for the UK.

The various alternative election systems are commonly referred to as systems of 'proportional representation', indicating that their purpose is to secure that the parties win a proportion of seats in Parliament which corresponds closely with the level of their support. This expression will be used for the sake of brevity in this chapter, but it is more accurate to distinguish two groups of system, those based on preferential voting and those designed to secure proportional representation. In practice, both can secure a high degree of proportionality between the parties, but the principal objective of preferential voting systems is to give the voter a choice between candidates and to improve the level of the effective vote (i.e. the number of voters who are represented by a candidate for whom they voted), whereas the purpose of proportional systems is to do justice between the parties. In any system, it is suggested, voters should come before parties. Important though the parties obviously are, we should not lose sight of the importance of the entitlements of citizenship, including equal and real rights to participate in and influence politics, by slipping into discussing the electoral system in terms of *parties* rather than *voters*.

One system of preferential voting that does not produce remotely satisfactory proportionality is the alternative vote or a variant on it, the double ballot. Under these systems, only one candidate can be elected; voters express their preferences in order and if the first preference is for an unpopular candidate, then that preference will be disregarded and the second preference counted instead. Under the double ballot system, used for example for presidential elections in France, all but two candidates are eliminated in the first ballot and the second ballot is a run-off between the two front runners. These systems work well where only one candidate can be elected, as in presidential elections; they have the advantage of overcoming the reluctance of voters to vote with their hearts for unpopular candidates, and the second vote can take account of other appeals that other candidates may have. But they cannot produce proportionality in parliamentary elections and thus produce a parliament which fairly reflects the support for the parties in the electorate. These systems, then, continue to make it difficult for supporters of smaller parties to elect their candidates.

Many Western European countries use party lists for their elections. These are true 'proportional representation' systems, since they secure proportionality between the parties. Party lists involve dividing the country into large regions instead of constituencies (Israel is an exception: the lists cover the whole country). Each region is allotted a certain number of seats and the parties put up lists for the electorate to vote for. These systems do not allow for the close relationship that British MPs have with their constituencies, and which they regard as very important. They also give the party organizations that select the names of candidates for the lists considerable patronage and power, and in effect this imposes a form of political accountability as candidates are accountable to their party organizations (Maude and Szemerey, 1982). The use of pure lists has not had any support in the UK, presumably for these reasons (cf. Hirst, 1989).

The German system

A major contender for the UK is the German 'Additional Member' system, one of the proportional representation systems which uses lists. This was introduced into the Federal Republic by the Allies in 1949. Briefly, half of the members of the *Bundestag* are elected in large single-member constituencies by first past the post as in the UK. The other half of the seats are awarded from party lists in sufficient numbers to compensate the parties for the disproportionate results produced by the constituency votes. No seats are awarded to those on party lists unless the party obtained 5 percent of the vote. This 'threshold' is designed to keep small, possibly extremist parties out of the *Bundestag*. The outcome is almost perfect proportionality between the support for the parties as indicated by their share of list votes and the number of seats they hold in the Bundestag (Holme, n.d.; Bogdanor, 1981, part V; Rogaly, 1976, ch. 8).

There are major differences between the German political system and the British system which make the Additional Member formula problematic for the UK. Germany has a regional tier of government – the *Länder* – below the national Parliament. Hence the constituency responsibilities of members of the *Bundestag* are fewer than those of Westminster MPs. The large size of German constituencies does not therefore produce real problems in this respect. In the UK, by contrast, MPs have an important role as channels for the redress of individual grievances and it would be difficult for them to continue with this if their constituencies were doubled in size, as they would have to be if the system were introduced here and the House of Commons were to have the same number of MPs as now. On the other hand, if assemblies were established in Scotland, Northern Ireland, Wales and the English regions, this aspect of the Westminster MP's work would diminish in importance and volume (see Chapter 6). Alternatively, the MPs' role in the redress of grievance could be transferred to the Parliamentary Commissioner for Administration (the Ombudsman) if their power and staffing were increased; but Westminster MPs seem very attached to this aspect of their work. It is in the present climate unlikely that they would be willing to surrender this function to the PCA.

Another problem with the German system arises from the seats awarded to those on the party lists. These seats are awarded to candidates on the list in the order in which their names appear. It is the party organizations that are responsible for drawing up these lists and determining in what order the names should appear.

In Germany, the risk of this considerable political patronage being abused by party activists is reduced by the constitutional requirement that the parties be democratically organized. Article 21 of the Constitution provides that: 'Their internal organisation must conform to democratic principles.' Details are to be regulated by federal laws, currently the Federal Electoral Law of 1956 as amended and the Political Party Law of 1967. By section 22 of the 1956 Law, constituency candidates are nominated in a secret ballot by party members or their delegates. Candidates for state lists are nominated by the state representatives' conferences prescribed by that Law, but in practice this function is usually carried out by the state delegates' conferences or party conferences on the basis of lists prepared by the party executives or special commissions. In the present political climate in the UK, it is again highly unlikely that regulation of political parties would be introduced. So a list system in the UK would be open to abuse by the parties.

In theory, an alternative to a list system under which candidates take seats in the order in which their names appear on the list would be for candidates' names to be entered on the lists in random or alphabetical order, and for voters to be given the right to mark their preferences in order. But with large lists of 20 or so names, it would not be easy for voters to express their preferences (if they know enough about the candidates to have any) with any accuracy, and the temptation would be for the party organizations to recommend 'slates' which could defeat the object of the exercise.

The German system could not be used for local government elections in the UK – the areas would be too small to justify having a mixture of first past the post and party list members, especially if, as seems possible, the county councils were abolished and district councils were the only tier below regional and national assemblies. So if the German system were adopted for House of Commons and possibly assembly elections, a different electoral system would have to be used for local government. This could be first past the post, but this would perpetuate the problems referred to earlier. If another system such as the single transferable vote were adopted for local government, the electorate would be faced with a confusing array of different voting systems for different elections.

The chief advantage of the German system, then, is that it produces a high degree of proportionality between the parties and thus avoids the discrimination against smaller parties that is a characteristic of the first past the post system, and it retains the constituency MP. One of its disadvantages is the low effective vote in the first past the post part of the election. But a way round this was being mooted by Robin Cook MP in May 1990, a Labour frontbench spokesman who favours proportional representation: constituency Members should be elected on a preferential voting system, thus securing that the person elected to such a seat had at least 50 percent of the vote. The party lists would compensate for the disproportionality of these results.

Other disadvantages of the German system include the size of constituencies, the increased power of the political parties which raises issues about their legal regulation, and its unsuitability for local government elections. On balance, it is suggested, these disadvantages outweigh its advantages, especially since the alternative system, the single transferable vote achieves good proportionality and overcomes most of the other disadvantages of both the first past the post system and the German system.

The single transferable vote

The single transferable vote (STV) is used for local government elections in Northern Ireland, a significant acknowledgement by both Labour and the Conservatives of its suitability for at least part of the UK. The use of first past the post had given rise to partisan one-party rule in the Province, a major factor in the feeling of alienation of the Catholic population which led to the troubles of the last 20 years – a story that vividly brings home the dangers of an electoral system that does not promote public accountability and responsiveness in government (Bogdanor, 1979, ch. 3; McCrudden, 1989). STV is also used for elections to the Dail in the Republic of Ireland, and in Australian Senate elections. It is familiar to many organizations in the UK, including some trade unions and the Liberal Democrats who use it for internal elections.

Although the system for returning officers counting votes under STV is complicated, for voters the system is simple. The effective vote is high (i.e. a large proportion of voters have an MP for whom they vote) and proportionality between the parties is good. Briefly, each constituency returns several members, five being the optimum number as a rule because it achieves a high effective vote (83.3 percent). On the other hand, the system is flexible so that the number of members per constituency can vary according to local conditions: in thinly populated rural areas, only one or two members might be returned in order to avoid imposing too great a burden of travel on representatives or their constituents. Also, in cities and other areas where there is a strong local sense of community, it would be possible to have a single constituency with the appropriate number of members for the size of the electorate – a better means of fostering community spirit than under the present system which often divides natural communities into separate single-member constituencies. STV can of course also be used in local government elections – and for elections to national and regional assemblies – and so adoption of this system would have the advantage over the German system that it could be used for all elections, which would reduce the element of confusion for electors that would flow from using different systems for different elections.

As far as local government elections are concerned, STV would work well if a scheme for neighbourhood decentralization along the lines adopted in Tower Hamlets, discussed in Chapter 5, were introduced, since each neighbourhood could be a multi-member constituency whose councillors would form the neighbourhood committee. STV can represent natural communities and this is one of the bases on which it was adopted as policy by the Alliance parties in 1983 (Joint Liberal/SDP Alliance Commission on Constitutional Reform, 1982).

The ballot paper in an STV election contains the names of the candidates in alphabetical order with a note of which party they stand for, if any. Each party may put up as many candidates as it wishes, but in practice they will put up as many candidates as they expect to win and possibly one more for luck. The voters mark the candidates they support in order of preference. When the count takes place, the first-preference votes are counted first and any candidate with sufficient support to win a seat is declared elected at this stage. Then the votes of the least popular candidates are transferred to the second choices of those electors (in the first past the post system these votes are wasted). The surplus votes of any winning candidates are also transferred at a fraction of their value to the second-choice candidate. Then the votes are counted again and any candidate with sufficient votes is declared elected. This process of transferring votes continues until all the seats are filled (Rogaly, 1976, ch. 9, 10; Bogdanor, 1981, part V).

No electoral system is perfect and it has to be acknowledged that the single transferable vote has a number of disadvantages as against first past the post and the German system. The principal problem is that the multi-member constituencies under STV are large and this affects the ability of MPs to discharge their functions in the redress of grievances which, as mentioned above, is jealously guarded by Westminster MPs. On the other hand, these responsibilities would diminish if regional and national assemblies were established.

However, there are a number of compensating advantages in STV. The effective vote is high – about 83 percent of voters in five-member constituencies will be represented by at least one MP for whom they have voted, as compared with well under 50 percent in most UK constituencies at present and in German constituencies. Proportionality under STV is also high; parties normally win seats proportionate within about 3 percent to their support judged by first preferences. The contrast with first past the post is stark. There would not be the problems about party patronage and the possible legal regulation of the parties that arise in list systems. The system also gives incentives to the party organizations responsible for candidate selection to be responsive to the wishes of their supporters by putting up candidates whose views reflect those of local people. Also, unlike first past the post, there would be added incentives to include candidates from ethnic minorities in areas with substantial ethnic populations, and women candidates. (This is also true of systems that use party lists.) And STV could be used for all UK elections, to Westminster, to assemblies and to local government.

Electoral reform and political change

As we have seen in Chapter 3, many critics of the constitution, especially of Parliament, are convinced that the political climate needs to change if government is to become more accountable and effective and a sense of community and citizenship is to be encouraged. Mere procedural reforms will not suffice to achieve this (Crick, 1989, p. 396); it is necessary to redress the balance of power in favour of the public and Parliament, especially back-benchers; the attitudes of MPs must alter (Norton, 1981, pp. 219–35).

Proportional representation would do more than any other reform to achieve a change in politics and attitudes in Parliament. By reducing a government's chance of an overall majority or making pacts or coalitions more likely, it would increase backbench influence over government and so make it more accountable to the House of Commons. It would also be more accountable to the public at election time. This should have the effect of making governments responsive to changing social conditions by producing policies designed to meet and solve them; in this respect, proportional representation could promote greater effectiveness.

By reducing the present north–south divide (i.e. producing members from all parties from all parts of the country), proportional representation should promote a sense of national unity and community. A reformed system should also make it easier for women and members of the ethnic minorities to win seats, which would improve their sense of 'belonging' to the system and enhance the political element of citizenship.

The choice of electoral system is important and of the systems on offer the single transferable vote seems best suited to the UK. The disadvantages of list systems outweigh the advantages they have to offer, which are primarily advantages for the parties rather than for the voters.

Whether the political climate will change so as to make electoral reform possible will depend largely on the Labour Party. Labour has less to fear from proportional representation than the Conservatives. In 1987, Labour would have won 27 fewer seats under proportional representation (202 instead of 229), whereas the Conservatives would have won 96 fewer (279 instead of 375). The Alliance would have won 149 instead of 22. So Labour may have something to gain if (another irrelevant and unworthy thought) proportional represen-tation was the only way in which the in-built advantages enjoyed by the

Conservatives could be countered. The Conservatives have no incentive to contemplate reform. If Labour feared that it would not be likely to secure a majority at yet another election, it would be in its interests to enlist the support of the Liberal Democrats and possibly the Scottish and Welsh Nationalists and negotiate pacts as to which party would put up candidates to stand against the Conservatives in an election and what programme they should support. The Liberal Democrats would be likely to lay down as a condition of their support for this arrangement that the programme should include a commitment to electoral reform. But what is really needed is a commitment to electoral reform, not simply in order to avoid prolonged periods of unaccountable government (important though that is) but to improve the quality and stability of policy and the political rights of citizens.

Elections, of course, cannot fulfil the tasks of improving accountability, effectiveness and citizenship unaided. The mechanisms for the promotion of citizenship, accountability and effectiveness in the UK's political system are many and varied and some of them are discussed in other chapters in this volume. But reforms of the electoral system through the introduction of the single transferable vote in elections to the House of Commons and local government would revitalize the operation of political processes and make a major contribution to the development of a more accountable, effective system and a more influential citizenry.

9

A Bill of Rights for the United Kingdom?

Bills of Rights form part of the constitutions of many Western democracies. It is in the Bill of Rights that the essence of the civil and political elements of citizenship in those countries is to be found. But the UK, unlike many of its political allies, has no such constitutional instrument. This is largely due to the accident of history (or more appropriately in this context, the relatively accident-free history of the UK, which has escaped the upheavals such as defeat in war, invasion, federation or political revolution that precipitated the adoption of Bills of Rights by many other countries).

Traditionally, the UK has prided itself on the extent of civil liberties enjoyed by Her Majesty's subjects. The use of the term 'subject' (see Chapter 2) is deliberate, since individuals in the UK have no rights, as citizens do, only residual liberties. But in the last quarter of a century, concern has been increasingly expressed at the ease with which civil and political liberties can be eroded or interfered with, and this, together with the international climate of opinion on human rights, has produced a movement in favour of the adoption by this country of a Bill of Rights (for a history of the Bill of Rights debate, see Zander, 1985, ch. 1).

A Bill of Rights sets out the rights of individuals in their private lives and as citizens, and gives them a special status. Such bills generally cover civil and political, rather than economic, social or even environmental rights. There are difficulties in protecting social and economic rights by legislation which, as Bills of Rights normally are, is protected against repeal and enforceable in the courts (Lester *et al.*, 1990, pp. 7–8; see also Chapter 2). A right to 'decent housing' or 'a basic income', for example, are not readily enforceable through the courts. Alternative possible safeguards in the constitutional system for these rights could include international instruments, such as the European Social Charter (Spencer, 1990, ch. 5; Wedderburn, 1990). The Institute of Public Policy Research Constitution (Institute of Public Policy Research, 1991) seeks to protect social and economic rights by requiring Parliament and assemblies to be guided by the principles contained in international covenants and charters to which the UK is signatory, but does not make this obligation justiciable, or enforceable in the courts. Desmond King (1987, pp. 174–7) has commented that there is ideological and institutional support for the welfare state in the UK, and that these are not easily undermined.

The rationales for rights

The underlying rationales for civil and political rights need to be appreciated if the arguments for and against a Bill of Rights are to be properly balanced (on the need to identify rationales or 'tele' for rights, see Benn, 1978; on dignity, autonomy and respect as rationales for rights, see Rawls, 1972; Finnis, 1980; Dworkin, 1987; Donnelly, 1985; Benn, 1978). These may be analysed in various ways. The Articles of the European Convention on Human Rights (ECHR; see Appendix) will be used to illustrate the point.

Some rights, for example the right to marry and found a family (Article 12 of the Convention), the right to respect for private and family life, home and correspondence (Article 8) and the right not to be subjected to torture or inhuman or degrading treatment or punishment (Article 3) are primarily concerned to preserve the dignity and autonomy of individuals in their private lives. As indicated in Chapter 2, it is essential that some areas of an individual's life are preserved from state interference and the demands of citizenship, and provisions along these lines can help to preserve the dividing line between the private individual and the public citizen.

Some civil and political rights are crucial in promoting accountability in government through the activities of a mature citizenry. The rights to freedom of expression (Article 10) and freedom of peaceful assembly and association (Article 11) operate to institutionalize the citizens' rights to discuss the actions of government and public policy and so to expose government (and private interests) to public accountability. The freedom of citizens to form pressure groups, associations, charities and political parties enables them to become active, effective citizens, able both to contribute to the political process and the life of the community and to protect themselves against abuse of power by public or private bodies. In this respect, civil and political rights may be seen as one means by which the weaker members of society are protected against the stronger members and organizations, whether state institutions or private bodies. In redressing the balance of power, these rights or freedoms open the way for achievement of a greater degree of democracy, equality and justice in the system. Citizenship and accountability are closely related in this area.

As we saw in Chapter 2, citizenship is also about social cohesion and a sense of national identity. Provisions which outlaw discrimination on grounds of sex, race and political opinion (Article 14) serve to promote cohesion by ensuring that minority groups (or even majority groups such as women) can participate as full citizens in the community. This in turn promotes the sense of national identity which is politically vital in any democracy.

Why a Bill of Rights?

It does not of course follow from the position that civil and political rights are essential to accountability and citizenship and need to be legally protected that this country actually needs the additional protection for civil and political 'rights' (or more accurately liberties) that a Bill of Rights would offer. These 'rights' are already protected to a considerable extent by the ordinary law of the land. And there are processes which secure, in the absence of a Bill of Rights, continued protection – the strongly liberal political tradition, the jurisdiction of the courts in judicial review and habeas corpus, and international pressures through the United Nations and the Council of Europe. Why, then, is there debate about the need for a British Bill of Rights?

A major and often-cited legal weakness in the protection of civil and political rights in the UK is that the Westminster Parliament, being sovereign and subject to no legal restrictions on the subject matter over which it may legislate (*Cheney* v. *Conn* [1968] 1 WLR 242; for further discussion, see Chapter 11), has the power to pass legislation detracting from individual liberties. In doing so, it is not subject to any special procedural requirements, such as a two-thirds majority in Parliament; such legislation is passed in the same way as legislation to alter the speed limit.

Some legislative restrictions on civil liberties may be perfectly legitimate, and many of the existing restrictions are well within the provisos to measures such as the ECHR and the UN Covenant on Civil and Political Rights, on the grounds, for example, that limitation is necessary in a democratic society in the interests of national security, public morals, public safety, public order, or the protection of the rights of others. The *Handyside case* (1979) 1 EHRR 737, for example, upheld the Obscene Publications Acts restrictions on possessing obscene articles for gain. The UK Parliament is not, however, limited by those exceptions. Some measures on the statute book have gone well beyond what is necessary to protect national security or public morals, etc. The Official Secrets Act 1911, for example, criminalized all unauthorized disclosures of official information, however trivial or, more to the point, important.

In practice, Parliament's ability to legislate in derogation of civil liberties has not often posed a major threat to those liberties, since there is a strong liberal tradition on these issues in both Houses of Parliament. Few of the ECHR decisions against the UK have raised issues about express provisions in statutes limiting civil and political rights. However, exceptions include *East African Asians* v. *United Kingdom* (1981) 3 EHRR 76; and *Abdulaziz, Cabales and Balkandali* v. *The United Kingdom* (1985) 7 EHRR 471, in which the Immigration Act, which discriminated between husbands bringing their wives into the country and wives bringing in their husbands, was found to be in breach of Article 8 (respect for family life) and Article 14 (sex discrimination) taken together. In *Brogan* v. *The United Kingdom* (1989) 11 EHRR 117, the European Court of Human Rights found the Prevention of Terrorism Act 1984 provisions for detention for 4 days without bringing the suspect before a judge to be in breach of Article 5(3). The UK sought to derogate (see Finnie, 1991) but the European Commission on Human Rights has decided that the derogation is unlawful. If the European Court of Human Rights confirms the Commission's finding the UK government will be obliged under the Convention to amend the detention provisions.

The UK Government is generally careful when introducing new legislation to check that the provisions will not breach our international obligations. Nevertheless, a number of statutory measures has had to be amended as a result of adverse findings by the European Court of Human Rights, e.g. in the areas of child care law and parental participation in decisions about children in care, and access to them (see *W., R., O., and H. v. United Kingdom* (1988) 10 EHRR 29).

It cannot by any means be assumed that Parliament will not pass legislation that is incompatible with the protection of civil and political rights, or with our international obligations in this area. Under pressure of terrorism, governments have been panicked into unnecessarily illiberal measures which, incidentally, alienate sections of the population and damage the sense of social cohesion. This has been part of the problem in Northern Ireland, where the operation of the Prevention of Terrorism Act has led to a sense of injustice for many. There are also fears that in periods of polarized politics and divided opposition to government, Parliament may be more easily persuaded to legislate in breach of civil and political rights, particularly if a government desires to avoid the accountability that civil and political rights promote.

Civil and political rights and discretionary powers

A more widespread, though often less dramatic, threat to civil liberties than that offered by Parliament is posed by the exercise of political or administrative discretionary powers by ministers, local authorities and public officials. Statutes regularly give wide discretionary powers to public bodies that go beyond the normal powers of the individual – compulsory purchase and taxation powers, powers to make or refuse grants, or to give or withhold planning permission, and police powers to enter property to search for stolen goods are obvious examples. At common law public officials are often free in principle to act in any way that is not forbidden by law (*Malone v. Metropolitan Police Commissioner* [1980] QB 49). This leaves a great deal of scope for public bodies to seek to regulate or to interfere, e.g. through applying pressure and withholding benefits, with the free exercise of civil and political rights by individuals or private institutions.

The point may be illustrated by examples (see also Dworkin, 1990, pp. 1–9). First, in the area of the right to receive and impart information (which forms part of the right to freedom of expression in Article 10 of the ECHR), there have been repeated instances of attempts by government ministers to pressurize the BBC and Independent Broadcasting Authority (IBA) not to broadcast programmes of which the government disapproves, e.g. the Zircon Affair, 'Real Lives' (eventually transmitted in October 1985) and 'My country, right or wrong' (eventually broadcast on Radio 4, commencing on 27 June 1988) (see Thornton, 1989, ch. 2; Buchan and Sumner, 1989, chs 2, 3). The 'Spycatcher' litigation, and the prosecution of Clive Ponting for disclosing embarrassing information are further instances of government-inspired interference with freedom of expression (Thornton, 1989, ch. 3; Buchan and Sumner, 1989, chs 2, 3, 8, 11, 12, 13). In 1988, the Home Secretary made an order banning the transmission of interviews with members of certain terrorist organizations in Ireland and this was in due course upheld by the House of Lords (*Brind* v. *Secretary of State for the Home Department* [1991] 1 All ER 720).

Certain councils have boycotted local newspapers which make critical comments about council policy, in attempts to influence editorial content, an example of non-coercive but oppressive interference with the freedom of the press with a view to stifling criticism, one of the rationales of press freedom (see the examples given in Goodson-Wickes, 1984). A number of local authorities has discriminated against candidates of political parties of which they disapprove and refused them rooms for election meetings (*Webster* v. *Southwark London Borough Council* [1983] QB 698; *Ettridge* v. *Morrell* (1986) LGR 100). And in a case which reached the House of Lords (*Wheeler* v. *Leicester City Council* [1985] AC 1054), a local authority had demanded that a rugby football club committee express views that it did not hold in order to influence club members not to participate in a rugby football tour of South Africa, thus attempting to interfere with freedom of expression, association and movement. Some councils have attempted to suppress political activity, for example by refusing to allow Amnesty International, Friends of the Earth or the Campaign for Nuclear Disarmament (CND) to set up stalls at a community festival, thus denying a public forum for unwelcome views. This action was taken by Barnet Council against the organizers of the East Finchley Community Festival (*R.* v. *Barnet London Borough Council, Ex parte Johnson Independent* 17 August 1990). The National Council for Civil Liberties (NCCL) has reports of a number of such actions taken by local authorities against pressure groups.

Moving from freedom of expression to the vital interests of individuals to freedom from restraint and imprisonment, during the period of the Gulf war numbers of Iraqi nationals and Palestinians were detained under the royal prerogative on suspicion that they posed a threat to national security, but the government was not required by law to establish grounds for their detention in a court and the detainees were not given full reasons for their detention. Amnesty International (1991) has expressed grave concern about this and other aspects of human rights law in the UK.

It is not only politicians in central and local government who have disregarded the civil and political rights of citizens. There has been growing concern in recent years about the arbitrary powers of the police, security services and officials in the Inland Revenue and other government organs with coercive powers. There is no express right to protection from invasions of privacy and interferences with liberty by these bodies. In a number of cases, the judges have upheld broad discretionary powers. Police constables are allowed very wide discretion in exercising their powers of arrest and search (see, e.g. *Piddington* v. *Bates* [1961] 1 WLR 162; *Wills* v. *Bowley* [1983] AC 57). In the *Rossminster* case (*R.* v. *Inland Revenue Commissioners, Ex parte Rossminster* [1980] AC 952), the House of Lords upheld powers of search by the Inland Revenue under a broadly worded general warrant which did not specify what offence was suspected nor limit what papers should be seized.

In Canada, the Charter of Rights and Freedoms sets out certain fundamental civil and political rights and limits the grounds on which they may be lawfully overridden. It provides, for example, that 'Everyone has the right to be secure against unreasonable search or seizure' (s. 8). There is no equivalent provision in English law. In the case of *Hunter* v. *Southam* (1984) 11 DLR (4th) 641, the Canadian Supreme Court was faced with a similar broad power of search to that in *Rossminster*. Relying on the provision of the Canadian Charter giving protection against unreasonable search and seizure, the Supreme Court found the search unlawful (see Alexander, 1989). The ECHR Article 8 protection for private and family life, home and correspondence could be similarly invoked to restrict wide and imprecisely worded powers of search if it formed part of the domestic law of the UK. But lacking such a prohibition, English courts do not approach these problems from a starting point that civil and political rights should only be infringed in strictly limited circumstances. Some of the proposals for a Bill of Rights have been inspired by this weakness of the common law in protecting civil and political rights (see, e.g. Scarman, 1974, p. 8).

Part of the problem is that the English courts do not have any set of guiding principles or priorities where civil and political rights clash with public interests. Despite the popular belief that the courts represent the bulwark between the individual and the state, and despite the pride expressed by judges from time to time in their role as guardians of individual liberty, the recent record of the courts in these matters has been inconsistent and on occasions distinctly illiberal (see Griffith, 1991). In particular, the courts have tended to side with the forces of law and order and national security against individuals exercising civil and political rights such as freedom of expression and association.

The 1984–85 miners' strike cases illustrate the dilemma in which the UK courts may find themselves when faced with a conflict between public interest considerations and competing civil and political rights. In *Moss* v. *McLachlan* [1985] IRLR 76, for example, the police had stopped a convoy of striking miners travelling by car from Yorkshire to working mines in Nottinghamshire, which they wished to picket. The convoy was stopped at a motorway exit a few miles from their destination. The Divisional Court upheld the police action in cases where the constable has 'a fear that a person or persons he is dealing with may cause a breach of the peace, even if he cannot precisely pinpoint when and where'. The police need not have any reason to believe the particular person will cause a breach of the peace (Austin, 1986). This represents a substantial inroad into freedom of movement, association and speech.

There have been cases in other subject areas where the courts have shown a willingness to restrict civil and political freedoms unnecessarily in order to protect other values, moulding the law for this purpose. In the *Sunday Times* (Thalidomide) case, the common law of contempt of court was invoked to prevent publication of comment on the Thalidomide tragedy pending litigation (*Attorney-General* v. *Times Newspapers* [1974] AC 273): this decision was found to be in breach of the European Convention, since the restriction was disproportionate to the public interest in the protection of the judicial process (*The Sunday Times* v. *United Kingdom* (1980) 2 EHRR 245). In *Home Office* v. *Harman* [1983] 1 AC 280, the House of Lords found a contempt of court where material that had been revealed in open court was disclosed to a journalist, who used it to write an article critical of the Home Office. This case was taken to the European Commission on Human Rights, but a 'friendly settlement' was reached between Miss Harman and the government, who proposed to meet the criticism by amendments to the Rules of the Supreme Court. A major problem in such cases is that the burden is on individuals challenging government action to prove their 'rights', whereas under a Bill of Rights, the right is presumed and the burden would be on the state to bring its actions within an express legal exception.

Some of the 'rights' that are protected by international agreements and the Bills of Rights in other countries are not protected in the UK at all. For example, English law does not recognize a right to privacy as such against either state or private interference (the ECHR does protect privacy: see Article 8; *Malone* v. *United Kingdom* (1985) 7 EHRR 14; *Gaskin* v. *United Kingdom* (1990) 12 EHRR 36). The protection for privacy is 'patchy, capricious and, often, uncertain' (Markesinis, 1990, p. 805).

There are then severe defects in the protection of civil and political rights in the UK which, in other countries, are protected by home-grown bills of rights or through international instruments such as the ECHR, which are enforceable in the domestic courts of most Western European states. It is recognition of these defects that has produced pressure for the adoption of a Bill of Rights for the UK.

Pressure for a Bill of Rights does not come only from specialists in the field. The MORI *State of the Nation* poll found that 72 percent of respondents were in favour of a Bill of Rights and only 11 percent were opposed. Thirty-eight percent felt that individual citizens' rights were less well protected in Britain than in the rest of the European Community, while 24 percent did not. Fifty-four percent felt that the British government could change individual citizens' rights too easily, while 22 percent did not. Public opinion is running strongly in favour of a Bill of Rights (MORI, 1991).

The form and content of a Bill of Rights

The question of 'whether a Bill of Rights' is inseparable from the question 'what form and content' should a Bill of Rights have? In recent years, a consensus of a sort has developed, even among those who are sceptics about Bills of Rights or opposed to them in principle, to the effect that the ECHR should provide the model for any British Bill, and that if we were to take the step of enacting our own Bill of Rights this should be achieved by incorporating the Convention into English law with such alterations as are necessary to take account of the fact that it would have domestic effect. For example, in the *Report of the Select Committee on a Bill of Rights* (House of Lords Paper 176 (1977–8)), the members of the committee were not in agreement over whether a Bill of Rights was desirable but agreed unanimously that the ECHR should be the basis of a Bill of Rights if one were to be enacted (see also Wallington and McBride, 1976; Dworkin, 1990; Vibert, 1991; Haseler, 1991).

It would be a mistake to assume that this consensus about the ECHR is complete. Jaconelli (1980, 1988), for example, argues that while a Bill of Rights ought to be enacted, the ECHR is not suitable for a number of reasons (discussed below) and suggests a 'tailor-made' Bill of Rights instead. And others have suggested putting together the best parts of the ECHR and the International Covenant on Civil and Political Rights (the IC; see Lester *et al.*, 1990).

The status of the European Convention on Human Rights

The present status of the European Convention on Human Rights is that it is binding on the UK in international law but it is not directly enforceable in our courts. It is taken into account by the European Court of Justice when dealing with questions of Community law, but these for the most part impinge on commercial matters rather than civil and political rights (Spencer, 1990, ch. 6). Through the direct applicability of European law in the courts of the UK, then, the ECHR may have an indirect impact on our own law relating to civil and political rights, but this is so far of relatively little importance. Our judges do, however, take account of the provisions of the ECHR, and in cases of ambiguity they sometimes attempt to construe English statutes consistently with its provisions. But the courts have vacillated over their attitude to the ECHR and the extent to which it is relevant in public decision making (contrast, for example, *R. v. Secretary of State for the Home Department, Ex parte Zamir* [1980] AC 930 with *R. v. Secretary of State for the Home Department, Ex parte Khawaja* [1984] AC 74; see Jowell and Lester, 1987). However, if English statutes are not ambiguous, the courts will not permit the Convention to be used in deciding, for example, whether statutory discretions have been exercised lawfully. Thus in the *Brind* case (*Brind* v. *Secretary of State for the Home Department* [1991] 1 All ER 720), the power of the Home Secretary to ban the broadcasting of live interviews with those who support terrorism was in issue. The Act gave a wide discretion to the Home Secretary and the applicant alleged that in deciding whether and how to exercise the discretion the Secretary of State should take into account the ECHR, in particular the protection of freedom of speech in Article 10, and should exercise the power only within the limits permitted by the Convention. The House of Lords held that it could not accede to this argument and that since the Secretary of State's action was not unreasonable in what is known as 'the Wednesbury sense' of perversity (he had taken into account the importance of freedom of expression), his decision should be upheld. On this approach, the Convention will be irrelevant in many cases, the government may well be breaching its provisions, but the individual will have no recourse in UK courts.

Any individual wishing to complain that English law does not meet the requirements of the Convention has a right of individual petition to the Commission and the Court of Human Rights at Strasbourg and the UK Government is obliged under the Convention to give effect to the decisions of the Court. There are clear disadvantages in this system, not the least being the delay and expense involved in pursuing a case in Strasbourg.

Incorporation of the ECHR?

The reasons most commonly advanced for taking the European Convention as the model for a British Bill of Rights are, first, that its terms are sufficiently broad to command general acceptance, since it includes all the standard civil and political rights (rights to personal liberty, to freedom of thought, conscience, religion, expression, association and movement, and freedom from discrimination in the enjoyment of Convention rights). In addition, there are the basic procedural rights to an effective remedy for breach of a right and to a fair trial.

The Convention allows for exceptions on a number of grounds, including the public interest in various guises – health, morals, national security. It does not, therefore, create the problems experienced with the US Bill of Rights, which admits of no express exceptions; or the Canadian Charter, which has one 'blanket' exception – 'the Canadian Charter of Rights and Freedoms guarantees the rights and freedoms set out in it subject only to such reasonable limits prescribed by law as can be demonstrably justified in a free and democratic society' (Constitution Act 1982, Part I *Canadian Charter of Rights and Freedoms*, s. 1).

Both major parties in the UK have operated under the terms of the ECHR and given their support to it. Objections to its provisions from the political parties either on matters of principle or detail would therefore carry little conviction. There is already a jurisprudence which establishes a willingness on the part of the ECHR and the Commission to strike down clear breaches of its provisions, and at the same time allows a 'margin of appreciation' to governments, thus offering certain benefits to both sides of the debate. The Convention is sensitive to the rationales for civil and political rights and this has enabled it to be applied realistically and not, for example, so as to protect commercial interests as if they were those of individual citizens, or strike down social legislation. It would not be easy to achieve consensus about any home-drawn Bill of Rights. 'Back to the drawing board' in a system with a multiplicity of political parties and campaigning groups each with its own set of priorities is not a recipe for progress in drafting and agreeing upon a Bill of Rights.

If the ECHR were incorporated, this would be a step in the direction of recognizing that citizenship is no longer based primarily on 'nationality' (see Chapter 2; see also Gardner, 1990, p. 68), but also has a European dimension, what Gardner (1990, pp. 70–71) has called 'new citizenship' (see also Spencer, 1990, ch. 2). Also in favour of the Convention is the well-rehearsed 'dirty washing' argument to the effect that it is better that any defects in this country's protection of civil and political rights be exposed in our own courts rather than in the glare of international publicity. Given that it is virtually unthinkable that this country should cut itself off from the Council of Europe and the machinery of the Convention, the government is irrevocably committed in international law to comply with its requirements, and this is less embarrassingly done by giving it domestic effect.

Criticisms of the ECHR

There are, however, a number of criticisms of the ECHR, over and above the more general objections to Bills of Rights. The ECHR contains no general prohibition of discrimination on grounds of sex, race and other irrelevant criteria; the proscription of discrimination relates only to the rights protected by the Convention. English law, by contrast, extends the protection from discrimination to employment, the provision of services and other important areas where discrimination may operate. The present anti-discrimination laws would, however, remain in force if the Convention were incorporated into English law, although they would not have the stronger status and therefore protection against repeal that would be enjoyed by rights protected by the ECHR.

A number of the Convention's Articles are seen as objectionable by one or other of the two main political parties. The First Protocol establishes a right to education with a duty on the state to respect the religious and philosophical convictions of parents, which means that private education could not be prohibited under the Convention. This would be unacceptable to some on the political left. The Sixth Protocol provides for the abolition of the death penalty, and this is objectionable in the eyes of some on the political right.

Many of the provisions of the Convention are imprecise (Jaconelli, 1980, pp. 266–7). What do 'inhuman or degrading treatment' in Article 3 and 'private and family life' in Article 8 cover? The wording of certain articles, notably Article 4 ('No one shall be held in slavery or servitude') and Article 12 on the right to marry 'seem very strange in a British social setting' and 'would not seem to fall within the category of human rights which are most at risk in the United Kingdom today' (Jaconelli, 1980, p. 277). Article 12 does not impose any limit on the scope of laws which qualify the right to marry. And, thirdly, 'many provisions of the Convention appear to mark no advance at all on the present state of English law' (Jaconelli, 1980, p. 278). This last is in effect an argument that legislation is not necessary in some areas, rather than that the text of the ECHR is objectionable.

Some of these criticisms could be overcome by careful drafting of the statute incorporating the ECHR (Jaconelli, 1980, pp. 258–77). But it is true that the wording of the ECHR is in the European tradition of broadly phrased general principles, not in the modern English tradition of detailed, precise legislation. However, the current English style of drafting is relatively recent: the Bill of Rights of 1689 and other pre-twentieth century legislation adopted a more open-textured, 'broad brush' approach, and has proved remarkably durable. Inevitably, the English system will be absorbing much of the European legislative tradition as the Community and its laws have wider and deeper impact on many aspects of English law, and there can be little doubt that the common law tradition will have to be adapted to meet these new ways. As for the point that protection of some rights is not needed because it is already provided under existing laws, this ignores the fact that the case for a Bill of Rights rests largely on fears for the future state of English law, the future temptations to which politicians, administrators and powerful private interests may yield, to act without respect for civil and political rights. These risks are increased in a system lacking effective opposition and one where authoritarian attitudes to the exercise of state power are proliferating (see discussion in Chapter 1).

Some take the view that the exceptions for national security, public morals and so on in the ECHR are too broadly drawn, leaving the judges with too much discretion, unchecked by political accountability, to make possibly illiberal or unrealistically over-liberal or politically biased decisions (see, e.g. Lee, 1987). Some of the decisions of the Commission and the Court of Human Rights are indeed open to criticism by advocates of a Bill of Rights as being illiberal. The Court has upheld the dismissal of a schoolteacher because of her expression of support for the Communist Party in the Federal Republic of Germany, on the ground that the Convention does not give a right of access to public service (*Glasenapp* v. *Germany* (1987) 9 EHRR 25). It has also upheld the dismissal of a university teacher (a civil servant in Germany) because of his membership of an extremist party, the National Democratic Party (*Kosiek* v. *Germany* (1987) 9 EHRR 328). The *Handyside case* (1979) 1 EHRR 737 decided that the applicant's conviction under the Obscene Publications Act for having possession for gain of obscene articles, namely copies of the 'Little Red School Book', containing information about masturbation, intercourse, homosexuality and abortion was justified by an exception under article 2(2) 'for the protection of morals'.

Other decisions of the European Court and Commission are regarded by some commentators as politically partisan, for example:

1. In *preferring individual to collective interests*. In the closed shop case, it was found that imposition of a closed shop amounted to an interference with freedom of association (*Young, James and Webster* v. *United Kingdom* (1983) 5 EHRR 201), but in *Cheall* v. *United Kingdom* (1986) 8 EHRR 74, the Commission found against a union member complaining about his expulsion from a union.
2. In *preferring public to private interests*. In the GCHQ case (*Council of Civil Service Unions* v. *United Kingdom* (1988) 10 EHRR 269), the Commission

upheld the government's action terminating union membership rights for employees at General Communication Headquarters as being within the Article 11(2) exception to freedom of association 'in the interests of national security'. And in the *Lithgow* case (*Lithgow* v. *United Kingdom* (1986) 8 EHRR 329), where it was alleged that inadequate compensation had been paid to shareholders in companies nationalized under the Aircraft and Shipbuilding Industries Act 1977, the Court allowed a generous 'margin of appreciation' to the UK Government in calculating compensation to owners of the company.

The European Commission and Court have also experienced difficulties where commercial organizations, pressure groups and voluntary institutions have claimed the protection of the convention. The sort of questions raised include whether companies are entitled to the protection of Article 10 (freedom of expression). The Court has found ways of protecting freedom of expression without elevating commercial promotion to the same level as the civil, non-commercial element of rights (see *Markt Intern and Beerman* v. *Germany* (1990) 12 EHRR 61; *Autronic AG* v. *Switzerland* (1990) 12 EHRR 485; cf. *Groppera Radio* v. *Switzerland*, judgment 28 March 1990).

It is not possible for all shades of broadly liberal opinion to be satisfied by all decisions under any Bill of Rights and many of the cases simply illustrate the difficulties inherent in protecting civil and political rights and the fact that judges cannot please all of the people all of the time. Nor can politicians and administrators. Generally, however, it is suggested the decisions under the Convention have been liberal, humane and realistic. Improvements in the rights of prisoners have been achieved largely in response to the decisions of the European Court and Commission. The common law powers of the Crown in relation to telephone tapping and of the courts in relation to contempt have been put on a formal and more liberal basis because of Convention decisions; and the rights of children and families in care proceedings have been enhanced.

Also, a major benefit of the Convention – even *the* major benefit – is that by imposing clear legal accountability it requires those administering it to approach problems from a principled starting point, to support their decisions with evidence, and to allow exceptions only if they are covered by specific provisos. The Convention therefore broadly meets the shortcomings of the present system by which judges protect civil and political rights. It supplies principles and priorities and fills gaps.

However, an alternative to incorporation of the European Convention would be to combine parts of the Convention and the International Covenant on Civil and Political Rights (the IC). This has been the solution in the Institute of Public Policy Research (IPPR) draft of a British Bill of Rights (Lester *et al.*, 1990; IPPR, 1991). The two are very similar in many respects, but the IC is wider and stricter than the Convention on some issues. For example, the IC provides for equality before the law and a right to the equal protection of the law (Article 26), which is not part of the Convention; the IC forbids discrimination on a wider range of grounds (Article 26) than the Convention; and the IC forbids advocacy of national, social or religious hatred (Article 20), which again are not covered by the Convention.

Protecting a Bill of Rights against repeal

If the ECHR were to be incorporated into English law, the question would arise whether it should be protected against repeal or entrenched in any way. Would attempts to entrench such a measure be undemocratic (Dworkin, 1990, pp. 32–8), or legally ineffective as being in breach of parliamentary sovereignty? And if a Bill of Rights cannot be entrenched, is there any point in passing it?

As has been suggested, an important rationale of many of the rights protected by a Bill of Rights such as the European Convention (especially freedom of expression and association) is to keep the democratic process open: it is difficult to see how the protection of those measures against repeal can be regarded as undemocratic. Indeed, any attempt to restrict them in such a way as to frustrate processes of accountability and the status of citizenship would itself be undemocratic. The argument that any attempt to protect a Bill of Rights from repeal is undemocratic is illogical (see discussion in Chapter 11).

Another issue relates to parliamentary sovereignty. It is suggested from time to time that a Bill of Rights ought to override existing law and be protected from repeal by a future Parliament either absolutely or by procedural safeguards, such as a requirement that any measure repealing or overriding a Bill of Rights must have the support of at least two-thirds of the members of each House of Parliament (this issue is considered in Chapter 11).

As far as absolute protection against repeal is concerned, this could pose problems for the doctrine of parliamentary sovereignty (see discussion in Chapter 11). It could also serve to impose undue rigidity in the law. For example, there are legal provisions imposing restrictions on expenditure by candidates and their supporters in local election campaigns in order to secure a 'level playing field'. Such restrictions should, on some views, be extended to the campaigns of central parties (see Ewing, 1987, ch. 8). But restrictions of this kind could be contrary to the protection of freedom of expression in a Bill of Rights. In the USA and Canada, the courts have struck down legislation that controls or limits such expenditure (see *Buckley* v. *Valeo* 424 US 1 (1976); *National Citizens Coalition Inc.* v. *Attorney General for Canada* (1985) 11 DLR (4th) 481; see also Ewing, 1987, ch. 8). The *absolute* protection of a Bill of Rights against repeal or inconsistent legislation could make measures of this kind legally impossible.

A 'notwithstanding clause'?

When attempts have been made by private members' bills to incorporate the ECHR into UK law in recent years, various devices have been adopted to protect it from repeal, including a presumption of interpretation that subsequently passed legislation is compatible with the Bill of Rights, and the use of a 'notwithstanding clause'. Such a clause provides that if a subsequent Act is inconsistent with the provisions of the Bill of Rights, that later provision should be legally ineffective unless the later Act contains a provision that the incompatible provision is to take effect notwithstanding its incompatibility with the Bill of Rights (Blackburn, 1989). The use of a requirement that subsequent legislation be interpreted consistently with the Bill of Rights if at all possible – the device adopted in two private members bills, the Human Rights Bill 1986, introduced by Sir Edward Gardiner, and the Human Rights Bill 1990, introduced by Graham Allen MP – is weak and could not prevent a government securing the passage of legislation that was clearly in breach of the Bill of Rights. It would hardly be worth the candle. So do any steps need to be taken to protect a Bill of Rights from repeal?

If a Bill of Rights were to incorporate the ECHR it would, it is suggested, be sufficiently protected by the addition of a 'notwithstanding clause' together with a provision along the lines of section 2 of the European Communities Act 1972, which incorporated European Community law into the legal systems of the UK. This section provides:

(1) All such rights, powers, liabilities, obligations and restrictions from time to time created or arising by or under the Treaties (of the European Community), and all such remedies and procedures from time to time provided for . . . as in accordance with the Treaties are without further enactment to be given legal effect or used in the United Kingdom shall be recognised and available in law, and be enforced, allowed and followed accordingly . . .

(4) . . . any enactment [of the British Parliament] passed or to be passed . . . shall be construed and have effect subject to the foregoing provisions of this section . . .

The Act incorporating the ECHR should provide expressly that all existing statutes, statutory instruments and other rules of law are to be applied in accordance with the terms of the Bill of Rights, which is to override any rules of law which are incompatible with its provisions. This approach would not pose any challenge to the doctrine of parliamentary sovereignty. Secondly, as far as legislation passed subsequently to the coming in to force of the Bill of Rights is concerned, a 'notwithstanding clause' should be used.

A 'notwithstanding clause' was included in two attempts to incorporate the ECHR into English law: see clause 4(2) of the European Human Rights Convention Bill 1983/4, introduced into the House of Commons by Robert MacLennan MP and clause 4(2) of the Human Rights and Fundamental Freedoms Bill 1985/6, introduced into the House of Lords by Lord Broxbourne (see also Dworkin, 1990, pp. 24–9). The Canadian Charter of Freedoms contains such a clause in section 33, permitting derogation from the Charter freedoms only if there is an express declaration in a later Act that it is to operate notwithstanding a provision in the Charter. This method of protection from repeal should not pose problems for the English doctrine of parliamentary sovereignty (but compare with the House of Lords Select Committee Report (1977–78) HL 176, which was of the view that such a clause would be legally ineffective: pp. 22–6). Such a clause works in Canada (see *R.* v. *Drybones* [1970] 9 DLR (3rd) 473; *Re Singh and Minister of Employment and Immigration* [1985] 17 DLR (4th) 422, discussed in Marshall, 1987). This arrangement would permit 'level playing field' legislation on election campaigns, and other measures which might seem necessary and not against the spirit of the Convention.

Experience with the European Communities Act 1972 (s. 2), shows that our courts are able to operate such a system of protection from repeal effectively. The UK courts have consistently either interpreted UK legislation so as to be compatible with Community law, or held European Community law to prevail over incompatible UK legislation, whether passed before or after our membership of the EEC (Collins, 1990; on the interpretation point, see *Garland* v. *British Rail Engineering* [1983] 2 AC 751; on the point that Community law prevails over incompatible UK legislation, see *R.* v. *Secretary of State for Transport, Ex parte Factortame* [1990] 2 AC 85; *R.* v. *Secretary of State for Transport, Ex parte Factortame (No. 2)* [1990] 3 WLR 856; *Stoke on Trent City Council* v. *B & Q plc* [1991] 2 WLR 42). The only possible exception to effective protection from repeal would be where the UK Act included an express provision to the effect that it was to prevail over Community law (or, by analogy, the ECHR) notwithstanding any incompatibility (see obiter per Lord Denning in *Macarthys* v. *Smith* [1979] 3 All ER 325, pp. 328–9).

But would a notwithstanding clause work in practice? Governments might wish to include such a clause in legislation as a matter of course: would this therefore be an ineffective method of protecting a Bill of Rights from repeal? It is suggested that it would not.

First, such a clause creates strong political inhibitions for a government contemplating legislation in breach of any Bill of Rights (see Jaconelli, 1980, p. 271). The inhibition is stronger than under the interpretation clause referred to above because the notwithstanding clause would involve the government expressly acknowledging that its legislation was or might be (since the question will not always have a certain answer) in breach of the Bill of Rights.

Secondly, if the ECHR or a combination of the ECHR and the IC were incorporated and legislation later passed with a notwithstanding clause to cover possible incompatibilities with the Bill of Rights, government would be acknowledging explicitly that its legislation was or might be in breach not only of the Bill of Rights, but also of its international obligations. So international pressures would militate against breach if it were contrary to the spirit of international law.

Thirdly, a Bill of Rights based on the ECHR or a combination of the ECHR and the IC would be protected from repeal by the legal presumption that 'Parliament does not intend to act in breach of international law, including . . . specific treaty obligations; and if one of the meanings which can reasonably be ascribed to the legislation is consonant with the treaty obligations and the others are not, the meaning which is consonant is to be preferred' (per Diplock L. J. in *Salomon* v. *Commissioners of Customs and Excise* [1967] 2 QB 116, p. 143; see also *Garland* v. *British Rail Engineering* [1983] 2 AC 751; discussion in Jaconelli, 1980, pp. 270–72). Hence only in the case of clear inconsistency between the Act and the Bill of Rights coupled with a notwithstanding clause could the courts give effect to an Act that departs from the provisions of the Bill of Rights. These are important respects in which a Bill of Rights in the form of the ECHR or a combination of the ECHR and the IC incorporated into English law would be better protected from derogation than a home-grown Bill of Rights could be.

In conclusion on this issue, it is important that any Bill of Rights should have effective protection, whether it be legal, political, international, or all three, against repeal. The incorporation of the ECHR or a Bill based on the Convention and the Covenant into English law, protected by provisions on the lines of the European Communities Act 1972 and section 33 of the Canadian Charter of Freedoms would not be inconsistent with the doctrine of the legal sovereignty of Parliament, and it would provide strong protection against legislative encroachment on civil and political rights. Procedural entrenchment of the kind used in the US Constitution and many others is unnecessary given the effectiveness of other pressures against repeal that would result from incorporation of the ECHR (for further discussion of entrenchment, see Chapter 11).

The judiciary and a Bill of Rights

One of the arguments commonly advanced against a Bill of Rights is that the judiciary cannot be trusted to administer it in an acceptable way: 'The harsh reality is that we need to be protected by Parliament from the courts, as much as we need to be protected from the abuse of executive power' (Ewing and Gearty, 1990, pp. 270–71). This objection comes principally from the political left. Professor J. A. G. Griffith (1985, p. 582) is mistrustful of the judges' attitude to a Bill of Rights, in particular when they have to decide whether the public interest in, for example, national security, outweighs the interests of the individual. Griffith (1979, p. 19) prefers these decisions to be in the hands of politicians than of judges:

> [An] advantage in treating what others call rights as political claims is that their acceptance or rejection will be in the hands of politicians rather than judges and the advantage of *that* is not that politicians are more likely to come up with the right answer but that ... they are so much more vulnerable than judges and can be dismissed or at least made to suffer in their reputation. [I am] very strongly of the opinion that, in the United Kingdom, political decisions should be taken by politicians.

Here issues of the interrelationships of constitutional reform arise. The implication that existing political checks make politicians vulnerable in any real sense save in quite exceptional circumstances is unconvincing. It might be otherwise if the electoral system operated differently, or if government were less centralized, or if backbenchers could find a way of exerting more influence over ministers. But, it is suggested, experience of the willingness of politicians in central and local government to interfere with civil and political rights leaves little ground for complacency about their political vulnerability. And even if Parliament (and local government) were reformed and made more publicly and politically accountable, aggrieved citizens could not be sure of receiving redress or a fair hearing of their complaints if they were denied access to the courts on the grounds that politicians were better qualified to deal with their grievances.

Mistrust of the judiciary arises from the record of judges over the years in making findings against trade unions, strikers and others, some of which were discussed above. The miscarriage of justice cases in the 1980s and 1990s have increased public disquiet about the criminal justice system and the higher judiciary's attitude to civil liberties. But here we need to recognize that part of the problem is the law of criminal procedure and that this, it is hoped, will be radically reformed once the Royal Commission appointed after the release of the Birmingham Six in March 1991 has reported. The judges do not have a strong record of upholding the spirit of Bills of Rights when issues about civil and political rights have been raised in court. In deciding in cases where the ECHR has been alleged to be relevant, the courts have been inconsistent. Sometimes they have used the Convention to protect freedoms from governmental incursions, and sometimes they have used it to protect government actions (Ewing and Gearty, 1990, pp. 273–4). The record of UK judges hearing appeals to the Judicial Committee of the Privy Council from Commonwealth countries with written constitutions has been mixed (Ewing and Gearty, 1990, pp. 271–3; cf. Lester *et al.*, 1990, pp. 11–13), with some liberal and some illiberal judgments and generally a narrow legalistic approach rather than a willingness to give effect to the spirit of a Bill of Rights.

Because of its reservations about the judges, Labour proposes instead of a Bill of Rights what they call a Charter of Rights, a series of Acts of Parliament containing detailed, specific rights to freedom of information, a free press and privacy and protections against discrimination, telephone tapping and other interferences with the rights of individuals (Labour Party, 1991c). There could be considerable benefit from detailed legislation on these subjects, but they hardly add up to anything as comprehensive as the term 'Charter of Rights' suggests. There is no commitment, e.g. to general rights of free speech, or freedom of association and assembly. Nor would measures of this kind preclude a Bill of Rights – they could serve to fill out the details. But the major objection to the Labour approach as a substitute for a Bill of Rights is that you would not be able to see the wood for the trees – the broad, vitally important principles behind the protection of civil and political rights would be liable to disappear in a welter of detailed and technical drafting. In June 1991, however, Roy Hattersley, the Labour spokesman on constitutional affairs, indicated that he was changing his mind about an enforceable Bill of Rights, as long as it did not impinge on specific legislation. Here, as in other areas of constitutional policy, Labour may be moving towards reform.

To an extent, concerns about the judges could be met by detailed legislation elaborating the Bill of Rights as Labour's proposed charter would do, or the adoption of a Bill of Rights with tightly defined exceptions. One of the objections to the ECHR, as we have seen, is that its exceptions are not so defined. But there would be acute difficulties in achieving consensus about the terms of these tightly defined exceptions. Some of these problems could be overcome, while retaining the advantages of the ECHR, by combining provisions of the Convention and the IC, as the IPPR proposal does (Lester *et al.*, 1990).

Reservations about giving the judges the power to deal with what would often be highly controversial and party political issues are also expressed on the political right on the grounds that this activity would expose the judges to political pressure and might ultimately politicize them in the sense of bringing political considerations into the process of appointing judges. But this has not been the experience in Canada whose Charter was adopted in 1982, and there is no evidence that the credibility of the Canadian Supreme Court will be undermined by the new duties of interpretation that the Charter has placed upon it (see J. Roberts, a former minister in the Canadian Government from 1976 to 1979 and 1980 to 1984 and closely involved in the negotiations leading to the Canadian Charter of Rights: *The Independent*, 11 May 1989). And a reformed system for the appointment of judges could preclude political considerations (see Chapter 7).

A Bill of Rights as the solution to the 'ethical aimlessness' of the common law?

The difficulties experienced by the judiciary under our present system in weighing up the competing claims to individual liberty on the one hand and the needs of national security, law and order and collective interests on the other, and the fact that they do not have a good track record in upholding civil and political rights in some fields of the law do not strengthen the argument that a court-enforced Bill of Rights is needed. But it is suggested that these difficulties do not imply that the British judiciary is inherently incapable of administering a Bill of Rights in the spirit in which it is drafted. It reflects rather an aspect of the British constitutional system that has attracted growing criticism in the last 20 years or so, namely the lack of a sense of direction or of any order of priority for these often competing values (a similar lack of any real sense of direction and priorities may be found in politics; see Marquand, 1988; Rose, 1976; for further discussion, see Chapter 1). The directionless consensus in the politics of the 1960s and 1970s is mirrored by the directionless development or 'ethical aimlessness' of the common law in constitutional matters (Lester and Bindman, 1972, p. 70; see also Lester, 1984). By way of example, Lord Diplock in the GCHQ case spoke of 'accepted moral values' and suggested that the courts could strike down actions which were in breach of these, but there is no document setting out what these values are and no consensus in the courts on this matter. As we have seen, the Court of Appeal and the House of Lords have recently in the *Brind* case (*Brind* v. *Secretary of State for the Home Department* [1991] 1 All ER 720) rejected an argument that the ECHR sets out these values and the courts are entitled to take it into account in dealing with wide discretionary powers granted to government. If a set of priorities for the resolution of competing values were introduced into the legal system in a Bill of Rights, there is no reason to assume that the judges could not operate it in the spirit in which it was enacted.

The system also suffers from a scarcely developed legal concept of proportionality, a concept that is important in the jurisprudence of the European Convention, and in the administrative law of the European Community, and of France and Germany (Jowell and Lester, 1988). Broadly, it requires that if state activity interferes with the rights and expectations of individuals and other bodies, then the interference should be proportionate to the public benefit being promoted, and should not be excessive or inappropriate (see Jowell and Lester, 1988; Lester *et al.*, 1990, p. 15). English public law has little to say on this subject and, in recent cases of judicial review, the courts have expressed hostility to proportionality as a separate ground for review, preferring to treat it as a form of irrationality or 'Wednesbury unreasonableness' (see *R.* v. *Secretary of State for the Home Department, Ex parte Brind* [1990] 2 WLR 787, CA; [1991] 2 WLR 588, HL: Lord Ackner, at p. 735; Lord Lowry, at pp. 738–9; cf. Lords Bridge and Roskill; for a further brief discussion of the grounds for judicial review, see Chapter 7; Jowell and Lester, 1987).

The courts in the UK are quite unable to develop criteria, operating on a case-by-case basis without a Constitution or a Bill of Rights or a developed doctrine of proportionality, for deciding when, for example, the value given to freedom of expression and freedom of association should outweigh the value attached to national security if they come into conflict. In the 'Spycatcher' (*Attorney General* v. *Guardian Newspapers Ltd (No. 2)* [1988] 3 WLR 776) and GCHQ (*Council of Civil Service Unions* v. *Minister for the Civil Service* [1985] AC 374) cases, where exactly this issue arose, the judges were divided on where the balance should be struck and for the most part did not resolve it by reference to fundamental principles.

It is not surprising that differences of view emerge in these cases. The outcomes of the GCHQ case (the ban on trade unions was upheld) and of the Spycatcher case (the injunction was discharged principally because it was too late: the lifelong duty of confidentiality that a civil servant owes to the Crown was upheld; see Chapter 10 for further discussion), suggest that judges do tend to put the public interest, as defined by the government, before civil liberties.

It is in the lack of guidance about constitutional values and how they should be weighed against one another if they conflict that the judges in the UK differ from those of the USA, Canada and other countries with Constitutions and Bills of Rights. A Bill of Rights would require a court dealing with this type of issue to be satisfied by evidence and argument rather than by assertion or assumption that public interests should prevail over civil liberties. The burden would be on the state to justify its intervention, not on individuals to prove their rights. A Bill modelled on the ECHR would define the public interest arguments that were relevant (i.e. depending on the Article, necessity in a democratic society, in the interests of national security, territorial integrity, public safety, prevention of disorder or crime, protection of health or morals, protection of the rights and freedoms of others and so on) and exclude irrelevant considerations when the balancing of civil liberties and public interests takes place.

The problem of judicial power under a Bill of Rights

Further objections to a Bill of Rights are that it might well stimulate a considerable volume of litigation that would attract public controversy, many cases would raise highly political questions – this may lead to the 'politicization' of the judiciary – judges would find themselves exposed to allegations of political bias in their decisions on the interpretation of the Bill; and allegations of judicial bias, even if ill-founded, do no good to public confidence in the system.

There is indeed a possibility that judges will be in a position to give effect to their own political preferences when dealing with Bill of Rights cases. This could amount to the exercise of power being unchecked. But this line of argument is flawed in a number of respects. In evaluating the point, we have to take into account the extent to which the sort of power judges would be reviewing under a Bill of Rights is at present subject to legal or political checks. Those who object to a Bill of Rights often focus on the power of judges to override an Act of Parliament. Other countries with written Constitutions and Bills of Rights have learned to live with this possibility; indeed, to take pride in it. But in practice, most decisions and actions that interfere with civil and political rights are not expressly authorized by Parliament but are taken by officials, local authorities and the police. At present, the political checks against abuses of power by these bodies are feeble and often ineffective (see Chapters 3, 4, and 5) and so, it is suggested, additional legal checks are needed.

Secondly, a problem of judicial power already exists under the present system (Lacey, 1989, p. 155). The position would in practice be improved rather than exacerbated if the ECHR or a Bill combining the ECHR and the IC were incorporated into English law, with guidelines for its interpretation that set out the rationales for civil and political rights. This would enable judges to avoid making party political decisions in line with their own preferences, since they would be applying the provisions and provisos of a Bill of Rights to a problem instead of having to resort to their own ill-assorted predispositions and judicial precedents, as is currently the position (Dworkin, 1990, pp. 51–6). Judicial training (see Chapter 7) could also serve to prevent the judiciary from misunderstanding their functions in relation to a Bill of Rights.

Thirdly, the accusation that, unlike politicians, the courts exercise unchecked power, is an exaggeration of the position. In practice, politicians and administrators do exercise considerable unchecked power. Unlike most administrators, ministers and local councillors, judges operate in public in open court; they give reasoned judgments and they are subject to appeal and to public comment and criticism. They are in effect subject to a considerable degree of public and legal accountability (see Chapters 2 and 7). These, though not perfect, are real checks on their power.

Fourthly, judges would very rapidly learn to recognize their own prejudices and take care not to allow their preferences to influence them when applying a Bill of Rights. Many of the political views of judges, as of most individuals, are unarticulated and unconscious, but the bench would with experience come to recognize that some of their political assumptions were controversial and not self-evidently correct, and would therefore have to rationalize them or suppress them.

The terms of the Bill of Rights would provide the criteria by which the judges were to weigh up the arguments, and this in itself would reduce the scope for political preferences to influence the outcome. If necessary, procedures could be established to enable the social and political implications of a case to be investigated (for a discussion of the procedures in public law cases, see Griffith, 1985). In the USA, this is achieved through the use of the 'Brandeis brief', enabling views other than those of the parties to the case to be put. In this country, there have been proposals for a Director of Civil Proceedings who could perform this role, having an independent constitutional status comparable to that of the Director of Public Prosecutions (see Woolf, 1990, ch. 4). And finally, it is suggested, even the aberrant judgment influenced by irrelevant considerations, but delivered in open court after argument by the parties is preferable to unchallengeable actions, often taken in secret, by state or private institutions in breach of the provisions of the ECHR and of the rationales of civil and political rights, which is the present position.

In summary, the fear of judicial bias and politicization is exaggerated and outweighed by the considerable benefit to the quality of public administration and the rights of individuals that would flow from a Bill of Rights. As William Brennan (1989), senior justice of the US Supreme Court put it, 'Whatever the danger of a politicised bench, it hardly seems sufficient to justify scrapping incorporation altogether.'

Conclusions

A Bill of Rights would enhance the legal accountability of government and guarantee the civil and political rights of citizenship. But the adoption of a Bill of Rights should be put in context in the constitution. Some commentators have assumed that supporters of a Bill of Rights regard it as a 'panacea of all our problems' and regard the idea as 'glib' (Ewing and Gearty, 1990, p. 275). This is unfair to the case. While some commentators have advocated a Bill of Rights and nothing else, most see it as part of a programme of constitutional reform that would include some or all of the following: public rights of access to official information, proportional representation, decentralization, reform of the second chamber. This is the approach of Charter 88, of the Social and Liberal Democrats and of many academic writers on the constitution (see Chapter 11). But even if a Bill of Rights were adopted without any other reforms, it would not be simply a 'cosmetic change' (Ewing and Gearty, 1990, p. 275); it would alter the ethos of public administration and public expectations, it would reinforce the status of citizenship and the processes for holding government legally and publicly accountable.

10

Open government

The UK has one of the most secretive governmental systems among those countries which claim to be democratic. Unlike many of the countries in Western Europe and the old Commonwealth, it does not have any form of general right of access to government information. There is freedom of information legislation in Denmark, Finland, France, Greece, Netherlands, Norway and Sweden, and Austria proposes to adopt such legislation. Of the 24 Council of Europe countries, 8 have freedom of information legislation. And although a great deal of official information is disclosed voluntarily by the UK Government, an even greater amount is not (for an account of the law, see Birkinshaw 1990b).

The need to increase openness in government through freedom of information is recognized in the written Constitution produced by Tony Benn and the Institute of Public Policy Research Constitution. Labour and the Liberal Democrats are committed to a Freedom of Information Act. Public opinion is also strongly in favour of reform: the MORI *State of the Nation* poll (MORI, 1991) found that 77 percent of respondents favoured a Freedom of Information Act, and only 9 percent were opposed.

The case for open government

Why is openness in government supposed to be desirable? First, open government allows the public to hold the government accountable for its actions in order to enhance its responsiveness, efficiency and effectiveness. The need to make government genuinely accountable is, as we saw in Chapter 2, central to the UK political system, indeed to the political systems of all democracies. But the public, its representatives in Parliament, the pressure groups which look after the interests of particular sections of the community, and the interest groups which monitor specialist areas of policy cannot carry out their roles in imposing accountability if they do not know what government is up to. In the words of Sir Douglas Wass (1984, pp. 83–4), formerly Permanent Secretary to the Treasury and Joint Head of the Home Civil Service:

> Raising the quality of public debate, and providing the public with the material on which to make an informed judgment on matters of public policy are two major requirements if we are to make the government process operate efficiently and responsively.

Wass has also stressed the need for checks and balances, including access to government information, in order to enhance the protection of society from the state. In his view, the existing safeguards against arbitrary and inefficient policy making by government are insufficient and in need of reinforcement in this and other ways (Wass, 1987, p. 181).

Secondly, 'freedom of information is a *consumer* issue' (Delbridge and Smith, 1982, p. 1). A great deal of public information relates to consumer affairs, including housing, education, the environment, transport, planning and local government, product testing, welfare benefits and energy. The consumer case for access to information is that this sort of information would be invaluable to consumers if it was publicly available. Its collection has been paid for by consumers through taxation and rating. Consumers should have a *right* to such information unless there are good reasons (such as national security, trade secrets and personal privacy) against its release (Delbridge and Smith, 1982, p. 1).

Thirdly, access to information enables individuals to make informed decisions about their own welfare or that of their families. Much information is held by government and regulatory bodies about matters such as environmental pollution, health and safety, and if this is withheld from those affected by dangers they are deprived of the opportunity to protect themselves, the very thing that regulatory agencies were set up to promote in the first place. When, for example, the extent of the leak of radiation from a nuclear processing plant is not made public, people living in the area are denied the opportunity to decide to move elsewhere, or to sue the plant if they become ill as a result of the leak (Michael, 1982). Thus access to information is also an environmental issue.

Public bodies hold large amounts of information about individuals. Access by the individuals concerned to this information is important so that they can have an opportunity to correct any inaccuracies in the information that might affect their treatment by the state: the right to correct information is one way of protecting social citizenship rights (see Chapter 2), since publicly held personal information forms the basis for state bodies to determine such matters as rights to welfare benefits, housing, education, rights to vote, and to receive grants of various kinds.

Citizenship is not only about holding the state to account and securing the rights and performing the obligations of citizenship. It is also about opportunities to participate in governmental and other decisions (see Chapters 1, 2, 5 and 6). The value of public participation is much less if undertaken from a position of ignorance than informed understanding of the business of government.

The importance of openness in the sense of public access to official information is recognized by international organizations. The UN General Assembly passed a resolution in 1946 affirming that 'Freedom of information is a fundamental human right and is the touchstone for all the freedoms to which the United Nations is consecrated' (Resolution 59(2), 14 December 1946). The United Nations Declaration of Human Rights (Article 19), the International Covenant on Civil and Political Rights (Article 19(2)) and the European Convention on Human Rights (Article 10) declare the right of everyone to receive and impart information and ideas (see Chapter 9). The Committee of Ministers of the Council of Europe has adopted a recommendation on access to information held by public authorities (Council of Europe R(81) 19, 25 November 1981).

But in the UK, the right to receive and impart information is subject to legal and operational limitations which mean that the system falls far short of internationally recognized standards. This impedes accountability. Accountability in this context denotes first, the political and public accountability of elected representatives in Whitehall, Westminster and the town halls and, secondly, pressure on officials in central and local government and in the outposts of government, notably the regulatory agencies set up to monitor activity in the private sector – such as the Director-General of Fair Trading, the Industrial Air Pollution Inspectorate, the Atomic Energy Authority – to be efficient and effective. Disclosure of information about the activities of all these public bodies should enable informed judgements to be made about the wisdom and effectiveness of government policy and the effectiveness and efficiency of administration. But government in the UK has a longstanding tradition of secrecy and impenetrability.

Access to official information in the United Kingdom

In response to growing awareness of the difference between the UK and other countries with which we are naturally compared in the matter of open government – other member states of the European Community and former dominions to which we have exported variations on the Westminster system (Marsh, 1987; Chapman and Hunt, 1987; Civil Service Department 1979) – the political parties have given promises in the last 20 years to open up government in a range of respects. The Conservative Party manifesto in 1970 promised to 'eliminate unnecessary secrecy concerning the workings of government', and other parties' manifestos since then have made pledges in similar often vague terms. It has become almost expected of parties in opposition that they will be converted to the cause of open government, only to lapse on coming to power. In effect, almost nothing has been achieved in the direction of legal provision for openness in central government in the last 20 years, though as we shall see some progress has been made in local government.

The natural tendencies of politicians and bureaucrats to hide their operations from public scrutiny are buttressed by the law. Until the Official Secrets Act

1989 came into force, all government information was protected from unauthorized disclosure by section 2 of the Official Secrets Act 1911. This protection applied no matter how trivial or unimportant the information might be, and in practice no matter how strong a case might be made out on public interest grounds for disclosure to be made.

The Ponting case and the culture of secrecy

Although the notorious section 2 has now been repealed, it is important to have a picture of how it operated in order to appreciate the culture of secrecy that it represented and which still pervades public administration. In principle, all unauthorized disclosures of official information were criminal. But the section purported to protect those who made unauthorized disclosures on public interest grounds from prosecution by exempting the communication of information to 'a person to whom it was the defendant's duty in the interest of the state to disclose it'. In practice, however, this provision gave no protection at all to disclosures made 'in the public interest'. In the *Ponting* case (*R. v. Ponting* [1985] Criminal Law Review 319), the defendant had disclosed information that indicated that the government was deliberately misleading the House of Commons Select Committee on Foreign Affairs in its inquiries into the circumstances of the sinking of the Argentine vessel the *General Belgrano* during the Falklands conflict. Ponting's defence to a charge of unauthorized disclosure of information contrary to section 2 of the Official Secrets Act 1911 (now repealed by the 1989 Act) was that the disclosure was covered by the exemption, but he failed.

The judge ruled that Ponting could not escape conviction on the grounds that he honestly and reasonably believed that the communication was in the interests of the state; and that the court had no power to substitute its own assessment of the interests of the state for those of the government: '. . . the interests of the state meant what was in the interests of the State according to its recognised organs of government and the policies as expounded by the particular Government of the day' (*R. v. Ponting* [1985] Criminal Law Review 319, per McCowan J). It would seem to follow from this direction that disclosures not authorized by the government as a matter of deliberate policy could never be covered by this exemption, which therefore rendered the exemption almost meaningless. (The Ponting jury was not convinced by the judge's direction on the law, and they returned a verdict of not guilty; the verdict was, however, clearly perverse from a legal point of view: for further discussion of this case, see Chapter 4).

The issue in the Ponting leak was not whether the government's policy decision to order the sinking of the *General Belgrano* was itself in the public interest – one can quite accept that it cannot be for the courts of for an individual civil servant to make decisions about this sort of substantive public interest; those are normally matters for the government and Parliament. The issue was whether it was in the public interest for Parliament to be misled by a minister when conducting an inquiry into government action. There may of course be good reasons for denying Parliament evidence, e.g. if there had been any question of the Argentines benefiting militarily from disclosures about the sinking of the *General Belgrano*, but this consideration should not be taken to justify positively misleading the House. It is difficult to accept that it could ever be in the public as opposed to the government's interest for Parliament to be deceived. The need for Parliament to receive truthful evidence is a different kind of public interest from public interests that are raised by substantive policies. It should have been regarded by the judge as one of those presumed public interests about which there can be no dispute.

Section 2 of the 1911 Act attracted widespread criticism. The Franks Committee (1972, para. 88) found that it was 'a mess'. It was far too wide, liability was strict, it was not clear when or by whom disclosure could be authorized and juries were reluctant to convict. The section has now been repealed and replaced by the Official Secrets Act 1989. But it remains the law that it is not part of the duty of civil servants to disclose the fact that a minister is misleading Parliament; indeed, it could be a breach of their duties to the Crown as civil servants if they were to do so (see Chapter 4). The reform of the section was introduced only after the Ponting affair made clear to the government that section 2 was in effect a dead letter. But the Act does not establish any rights of access to public information. It merely reduces the scope of the criminal law, leaving other aspects of the law which protect official information from disclosure intact.

The Official Secrets Act 1989

The new Act has a far more open approach to the question of criminal liability for unauthorized disclosures of most official information; only disclosures of specific categories of such information now attract criminal penalties. These include information relating to security and intelligence, defence, international relations, crime and special investigation powers, and information entrusted in confidence to the government by other states or international organizations. In principle, these categories are not controversial.

In all but two of these categories, the Act provides that there is no offence unless the disclosure causes harm, so unauthorized disclosures in such cases are not criminalized. However, strict liability regardless of harm applies to any disclosure of information about interception of communications, and any disclosure of security information by a serving or former security service person. In effect, the breach of confidence itself may be taken to be harmful. The disclosure of the name of Anthony Blunt as the third man in the Burgess–MacLean scandal by Andrew Boyle in his book *The Climate of Treason* in 1981, would be an offence under the Act despite the fact that no harm flowed from it. The government refused to allow the inclusion in the Act of a general public interest defence. Disclosure of information received in confidence from foreign governments and organizations may also be taken to be harmful. Third parties to whom disclosures are made are also liable, sometimes strictly so, for passing on the information if it is damaging.

Although the 1989 Act is unduly restrictive in some respects, it is a good deal more liberal than its predecessor. But it does not of course institute anything like a public right of access to official information. All it does is to decriminalize most disclosures. Government practice, the civil service code of discipline and the operation of the civil law of confidence continue to promote a highly secretive ethos (Palmer, 1990).

The civil servant's duty of confidentiality

The law of confidence was developed by the courts to protect personal relationships where obligations of secrecy arose (notably marriage: *Argyll* v. *Argyll* [1967] Ch. 302; *Prince Albert* v. *Strange* (1894) 1 Mac. and G 25) and contractual and other commercial relationships in which a duty of confidence was expressly or impliedly present. An important aspect of this duty of confidentiality is that the courts have jurisdiction to enforce it by granting injunctions preventing disclosure of confidential information.

In the Crossman Diaries case (*Attorney-General* v. *Jonathan Cape* [1976] QB 75), the duty of confidentiality was extended to 'public' secrets (if that is not a contradiction in terms). The Lord Chief Justice in that case decided that the court had jurisdiction to restrain the publication of official information if it could be shown that publication would be a breach of confidence, that the public interest required that the publication be restrained, and that there were no other facets of the public interest contradictory of and more compelling than that relied upon. This extension of the legal protection of official secrecy into the area of civil law, especially by the use of prior restraint, makes the relaxation of the criminal law under the Official Secrets Act less important than it might otherwise be, since the government can invoke the protection of private law against the disclosure of information.

Use of the private law of confidence is more attractive than the criminal law relating to unauthorized disclosures to a government bent on suppressing the publication of information for a number of reasons (Austin, 1989, 1990). The burden of proof in civil proceedings is the balance of probabilities, whereas in criminal proceedings the Crown has to prove its case beyond reasonable doubt. In criminal cases, the facts are found by the jury and juries are notoriously unwilling to convict in cases where the merits are not on the government's side, as the Ponting trial showed. In civil cases, the decision rests with the judiciary and they have shown themselves to be sympathetic to claims that publication of information would be prejudicial to the public interest, especially in national security. Criminal cases can only be brought after the event and make no provision for prior restraint, whereas the courts, as we see in the Crossman Diaries case and Spycatcher, will grant injunctions preventing publication, which is what the government's principal concern will be in these cases. So much for the maxim 'Publish and be damned' (Scofield, 1990).

But we must not exaggerate the extent of the obligation of confidentiality as it affects government information. This was one of the major issues in the Spycatcher litigation (*Attorney-General* v. *Guardian Newspapers Ltd* [1987] 1 WLR 1248; *Attorney-General* v. *Guardian Newspapers Ltd (No. 2)* [1990] 1 AC 109; *Attorney-General* v. *Newspaper Publishing plc* [1988] Ch. 333; Pannick, 1990). Here the House of Lords concluded that in principle members of the security services owed an almost absolute and lifelong duty of confidentiality to the Crown. But only almost absolute. The duty might be displaced by the public interest in the disclosure of iniquity, but only if the member had exhausted all methods short of publication to deal with the iniquity (*Attorney-General* v. *Guardian Newspapers Ltd (No. 2)* [1990] 1 AC 109, pp. 268–9, per Lord Griffiths). But the government would not be entitled to an injunction protecting confidential information from disclosure unless it could show a detriment to the public interest in publication (*Attorney-General* v. *Guardian Newspapers Ltd (No. 2)* [1990] 1 AC 109, p. 270).

The duty of confidentiality follows the information into the hands of third parties such as newspapers. But in order to obtain a remedy where the disclosure has been made by a third party such as a newspaper, the Crown would have to show not only that the information was confidential but that there was a public interest in preventing its disclosure and that this public interest was not outweighed by other public interests in disclosure, such as the freedom of the press:

> A communication about some aspect of government activity which does no harm to the interests of the nation cannot, even where the original disclosure has been made in breach of confidence, be restrained on the ground of a nebulous equitable duty of conscience serving no useful practical purpose (*Attorney-General* v. *Guardian Newspapers Ltd (No. 2)* [1990] 1 AC 109, pp. 256–7, per Lord Keith of Kinkel).

Eventually in the Spycatcher litigation, given that the information had lost its quality of confidentiality, since it had been published worldwide and was readily available in the UK, the Law Lords were not prepared to continue injunctions preventing its publication.

In the light of the Spycatcher decision, the duty of confidentiality is only enforceable by injunction if there is a public interest in the information remaining secret. The comment may be made that judges are very ready to accede to government pleas that the public interest in national security is at stake in cases of this kind. But subject to this reservation about national security, which cannot arise in most areas of government activity where access to information is in issue, the Spycatcher decision sets important limits to the government's right to invoke the civil law and in particular prior restraint in aid of its secrecy. One of the Law Lords endorsed the statement made by one of the Australian judges dealing with an earlier case of confidentiality, to the effect that the principle of confidentiality

> has been fashioned to protect the personal, private and proprietary interests of the citizen, not to protect the very different interests of the executive

government. It acts, or is supposed to act, not according to standards of private interest, but in the public interest . . . it can scarcely be a relevant detriment to the government that publication of material concerning its actions will merely expose it to public discussion and criticism. It is unacceptable in our democratic society that there should be a restraint on the publication of information relating to government when the only vice of that information is that it enables the public to discuss, review and criticise government action (per Mason J., in *Commonwealth of Australia* v. *John Fairfax and Sons Ltd* (1980) 147 CLR 39, pp. 51–2).

One important lesson to be drawn from the Spycatcher fiasco is that, as Sir Nicolas Browne-Wilkinson, the Vice-Chancellor put it, 'in the contemporary world of electronics and jumbo jets, news anywhere is news everywhere' (*Attorney-General* v. *Guardian Newspapers Ltd* [1987] 1 WLR 1248, p. 1269) – one could add a reference to photocopiers. To concede the practical impossibility of concealing large parts of government information from the public and thus to take positive steps to make it available in a comprehensible and usable form, would be to make a virtue of necessity (always the mark of the great politician).

In addition to the limited protection of government information afforded by the law of confidence, the code of conduct of civil servants, discussed in Chapter 4, imposes duties of non-disclosure which attract disciplinary sanctions. These sanctions are likely to be powerful deterrents against detectable disclosures, since they can seriously damage a civil servant's career prospects and even lead to dismissal (see Chapter 4).

The extent of open government

It would be a mistake to infer from this brief account of the legal position that no information is disclosed to the public by government (Birkinshaw, 1988a, 1990b; Austin, 1989). Green Papers are commonly published before firm policy decisions are taken and these provide useful information for interested members of the public. Royal Commissions, committees of inquiry and various other bodies are set up to report on matters of concern and their reports are published. The Central Office of Information publishes statistics and large quantities of other information.

Administrative directions are issued from time to time to encourage the disclosure of information: the 'Croham directive' of 1977 issued by the head of the Home Civil Service decreed that the background material relating to policy studies and reports should be published unless ministers explicitly decided that it should not be (this directive fell into disuse after 1979). But all of these channels leave scope for the government to contrive that information that it wishes to conceal from the public shall not be disclosed, and this is often precisely the information that the public has an interest in receiving.

The secrecy of central government has provoked unsuccessful attempts at reform over the years. Ultimately, as we have seen, the Official Secrets Act has narrowed the scope of the criminal law in this area. But this still leaves no positive rights of access to government information. Clement Freud MP introduced an Official Information Bill into the House of Commons in 1978 but it was lost with the dissolution of Parliament in May 1979. Since then, little progress has been made in improving rights of access to central government information for the public, save in relation to medical reports and health records (Access to Medical Reports Act 1988 and Access to Health Records Act 1990).

Seen in this light, the powers of the select committees of the House of Commons to call for the production of papers and the attendance of witnesses is one of the few lines of attack on government secrecy. But as we saw in Chapter 3, these powers are limited in practice by the reluctance of the government to disclose sensitive information or allow civil servants to give evidence: the enforcement powers of the Commons when faced with stonewalling by government are weak (for a discussion of the powers of select committees of the House of Commons, see Chapter 3). However, even if the powers of the select committees were improved, this would not satisfy all demands for access to information. After all, these committees are able to look into only relatively few areas of policy each year and many others need public scrutiny.

Openness in local government

Local authorities are not governed by the Official Secrets Act, although the common law of confidentiality applies in principle to disclosures of their information as it does in central government. However, the legal regime of secrecy to which the 1911 Official Secrets Act gave rise infected local government too. The instincts of the politician and the bureaucrat naturally lean towards secrecy. However, secrecy in local government has been eroded by a series of statutes passed in the last 30 years which have opened up the town halls to a much greater extent than Whitehall.

By the Public Bodies (Admission to Meetings) Act 1960, council meetings were required to be open to the press and the public. Under this measure (introduced as a private member's bill by Margaret Thatcher MP), the minutes of council and committee meetings must be published. By the 1972 Local Government Act, council committee meetings must be open to the press and the public. The Local Government (Access to Information) Act 1985 increases public rights of access to council meetings, minutes and background papers. Since the Local Government Act 1933, the accounts of local authorities are open to inspection and audit and the authorities must supply community charge payers with information about how the council's revenue is spent.

The Local Government (Access to Information) Act 1985 improves public rights of access to local authority information, save where specific confidential matters are in question. The categories of exempt information include personal and financial information about council employees, tenants and social service clients. The Proper Officer in the authority is charged with deciding upon exempt information, but there is no statutory appeal or complaint mechanism if his or her decisions are challenged. Judicial review would sometimes be available. Government circulars and the *National Code of Local Government Conduct* also encourage authorities to be open.

A number of local authorities operate voluntary policies of openness. School pupils and social service clients are allowed access to their personal files. The Access to Personal Files Act 1987 sets up the framework for individuals to have the right to obtain access to personal files in respect of them held by local authorities, but the implementation of these rights depends upon regulations being made by government and few steps have been taken by government to do so, save in the areas of school and housing files. When regulations are made, there will no doubt be safeguards to protect the privacy of others and some provision for protecting subjects from serious physical or mental harm (Birkinshaw, 1988a, pp. 218–21). Meanwhile, and pending the making of regulations, the Department of Health and Social Security has encouraged local authorities to grant access to personal files. For example, Circular LAC 83/14, *Personal Social Service Records – Disclosure of Information to Clients* (Department of Health and Social Security, 1983), invites authorities to grant access, although allowing refusal, exceptionally, in order to protect the client (whether parent or child) or sources of confidential information. Where children and parents are concerned, the circular concludes that parents should not have an absolute right of access to records about their children.

The Data Protection Act 1984 gives 'data subjects' – those to whom information relates – the right of access to information held on computers, but local authority personal files will not normally be covered as they are either (1) manual or (2) the authority can rely on section 29(2), which enables the Secretary of State to exempt personal data held for social work purposes where access 'would be likely to prejudice the carrying out of social work'.

There are a number of specific measures about rights of access. The Town and Country Planning Act 1971 (s. 34) provides for access to planning applications and relevant files and plans. The Commissioner for Local Administration has the right to inspect papers (Local Government Act 1974). And councillors have a right of access to council information if they can establish a 'need to know' (*R. v. Birmingham City District Council, Ex parte O* [1983] AC 578; *R. v. Hackney LBC, Ex parte Gamper* [1985] 1 WLR 1229; *R. v. Sheffield City Council, Ex parte Chadwick* (1986) 84 LGR 563).

The collection of measures requiring openness in local government in effect add up to a Public Right of Access to Local Government Information Act for these authorities, although there is also evidence of some local authorities not complying with their duties of disclosure (Birkinshaw, 1988b). As Birkinshaw (1988a, p. 91) comments: 'there is an immediate irony in the fact that it (the Local Government (Access to Information) Act 1985) was passed with the approval of the Government, which had steadfastly refused such legislation for itself'.

The experience of authorities practising open government both before and since the passage of the 1985 Act indicates that the fact of legislating does not of itself produce effective open government. Bradford, for example, adopted an open government policy in 1984, and though it has been quite successful the policy has been found to require consistent implementation in all council departments which can be encouraged by the promulgation of codes of practice by officers. For rights of access to be effective, the information must be readily available to the public, e.g. in local libraries; keeping it in the town hall will reduce access. The local population also needs to be informed and educated about how the council operates if it is to make use of information to try to influence local authority decisions. And the staff dealing with members of the public need to be trained both in their attitudes to the public and in retrieving the information that is sought (Clipson, 1987).

Secrecy in local government

Despite the fact that local government is subject to a regime that requires a welcome degree of openness in its operation, councils are still unduly closed in some respects. The meetings of party caucuses (which often determine the outcome of council meetings) that normally take place before a committee meets and makes decisions about how the party group should vote, are regarded as private.

This aspect of local government decision making has attracted attention from the courts in recent years (Oliver, 1988, pp. 81–5). They have criticized any arrangement whereby councillors allow caucuses composed of non-councillors as well as elected members to bind the councillors in their decisions (*R. v. Waltham Forest LBC, Ex parte Waltham Forest Ratepayers' Action Group* [1987] 3 All ER 671, p. 673) and they have held that councillors from the minority political parties who can establish a 'need to know' have a right to see reports prepared for the ruling group by officers of the council (*R. v. Sheffield City Council, Ex parte Chadwick* (1986) 84 LGR 563; *R. v. Hackney London Borough Council, Ex parte Gamper* [1985] 1 WLR 1229). The government refrained from legislating on the matter when securing the passage of the Local Government and Housing Act 1989, Part I of which gives effect to some of the Widdicombe Committee recommendations, and to the government's response to that report.

Legal requirements of openness in meetings of a party caucus would be unenforceable in practice and would only drive the caucuses underground (this point was received sympathetically by the court in *R. v. Sheffield City Council, Ex parte Chadwick* (1986) 84 LGR 563). But a greater degree of openness about decision making in this kind of meeting could be achieved if, for example, a 'question time' system were introduced in local government at which councillors of the ruling group could be questioned about the considerations that led to their decisions. Something along these lines has been instituted informally in Bradford in their 'open government' policy referred to above – members of the public have a right to ask questions of a named councillor if they submit it in writing in advance (Clipson, 1987).

The case against open government

Having considered the extent to which government, especially central government, remains closed, let us now examine the reasons why politicians and public servants are reluctant to disclose information. To avoid unnecessary controversy, it must be stressed that there is general agreement that certain categories of information should not be disclosed to the general public, including information relating to defence and the security services, to foreign relations, to the investigation and detection of crime, to advice given by civil servants and ministers and thus to Cabinet discussions, to sensitive commercial information and to personal information. It does not of course follow that all such information should be kept secret or that there should be no processes of accountability in respect of these matters, and much needs to be done to enhance the accountability of the security services, the Foreign Office and other organs operating in sensitive areas (the security services are now on a statutory footing: Security Service Act 1989; see Norton-Taylor, 1990; Ewing and Gearty, 1990, ch. 6; Leigh and Lustgarten, 1989). But after these exceptions are taken into account, there remains a vast amount of official information which at present is protected by the law relating to confidentiality and the civil service disciplinary code, but which could well be disclosed without damaging the public interest and which would enhance the accountability of government.

The reasons commonly tendered for non-disclosure of information that does not fall within the exempt categories set out broadly above are first, expense and time. Disclosure would be expensive, it would take up a large part of the time of the civil service; it would mean that new systems of recording files and documents would have to be instituted. This has indeed been the experience of the USA, Canada, Australia and New Zealand in operating their Freedom of Information Acts (Thomas, 1987; Civil Service Department, 1979) and of local authorities such as Bradford which operate open government policies. It is a consideration which must be weighed against the advantages that would flow from greater openness. But the projected costs have in some cases been grossly exaggerated; much of the information requested is in personal files and this is relatively cheaply obtained.

Secondly, disclosure could be abused, with requests for information being made not in order to call the government to account for its conduct but in order to obtain information on business competitors or other individuals. This has been a problem in the USA, for example, where a high proportion of requests for information are made for this reason. The Food and Drugs Administration receives 80 percent of its requests from businessmen seeking information about other, rival businesses (Thomas, 1987). But this problem can be avoided by excepting this sort of information from the right of access, as is done in Canada (Thomas, 1987).

Another form of 'abuse' of information, it is sometimes said, would be the possibility that it might be misunderstood and cause unnecessary panic or anxiety or even damage the economy. The circumstances of the resignation of Edwina Currie from her position as a health minister in 1988 illustrate the problem (Doig, 1989). She had made statements about the extent of the risk of infection from salmonella in eggs. Her remarks, taken literally, were accurate but they were ambiguous, they were misunderstood and they resulted in the collapse of the egg market and in considerable and unnecessary alarm.

This is an essentially paternalistic objection. There is of course a possibility that information may be misunderstood on occasions, but this does not necessarily mean that it should not be disclosed. Edwina Currie's disclosure did attract public attention to a real problem and the Select Committee for Agriculture found that egg producers were at fault and that the policing of the industry by the Ministry of Agriculture had been ineffective (Agriculture Committee HC 108-II, 1988–89). If much more information were regularly disclosed it is likely that the public would adopt a more sanguine attitude to this sort of information and would read the good news along with the bad. Problems such as salmonella infection of egg production would surface in public discussion much sooner and action to solve them could be taken before the problem became serious enough to cause panic and material damage to the industry.

Ministerial responsibility and open government

Public access to information is said to be a breach of ministerial responsibility to Parliament, which is in turn said to be one of the pillars of the constitution. The aspect of ministerial responsibility which is supposed to be endangered by greater openness in government is the convention that ministers are responsible to Parliament for all that is done in their departments, in the sense that they and not their civil servants must answer questions, defend policies or promise to make amends when things have gone awry (see Chapters 2 and 4). The rationale for this aspect of ministerial responsibility is said to be the need to protect the anonymity of civil servants to enable them to serve under successive governments and to give frank advice to ministers. The public's protection against inefficiency and abuse of power on the part of the civil service is supposed to be Parliament's ability to compel ministers to make amends, or discipline their officials.

If we unpick this argument, we find that it is full of holes and frayed at the edges. None of the well worked out proposals for open government suggest that advice tendered to ministers by civil servants should be disclosed. Where other matters are subject to criticism, ministers have at their disposal a wide range of excuses for refusing to answer questions – it should not be assumed that the obligation of ministers to account to Parliament provides in any way a comprehensive net to catch mistakes or misjudgements in public administration. The anonymity of the civil service has been eroded in a number of ways in the last 30 years. Select committees frequently take evidence from civil servants who thus become identified in the public mind or informed circles with particular policies and actions. Correspondence from government departments is normally carried on by named officials. Formal inquiries report on events in which individual civil servants may be found to have been at fault in various ways, and the Parliamentary Commissioner for Administration regularly makes findings of maladministration which implicate particular officials (Marshall, 1984, pp. 66–77). In practice, the shield of anonymity for civil servants that ministerial responsibility to Parliament is supposed to provide has become less effective.

The ineligibility of civil servants to answer questions before select committees or to defend themselves when subjected to parliamentary criticism if ministers refuse to allow them to do so, as happened in the Westland Affair, may mean that Parliament is unable to get to the bottom of what went wrong and who was to blame when carrying out its investigations. In the Westland Affair, the civil servants involved in the improper disclosure of the Solicitor-General's letter were not permitted to testify to the Select Committee on Defence and, consequently, were not given an opportunity to exonerate themselves. Nor were the ministers involved prepared to give details (Oliver and Austin, 1987; Defence Committee HC 519, 1985–86). And experience shows that ministers will not always discipline officials who have erred: after the Westland Affair, the officials involved were not disciplined even though there may have been impropriety on their parts. And the anonymity of the civil service is eroded considerably by a variety of practices which reveal who is responsible for what in departments. Ministerial responsibility is rather a smokescreen than a pillar of the constitution when used to justify government secrecy.

Despite the fact that this justification for secrecy is wheeled out like a rusty cannon when the fortress of official secrecy is being defended, it is not really believed in and has not been for many years. The Fulton Report on the Civil Service (1968, vol. I, p. 93) argued that: '. . . the concept of anonymity should be modified and civil servants as professional administrators, should be able to go further in explaining what their departments are doing'. As we saw in Chapter 4, the new autonomous agencies that will be operating at arms length from Whitehall will inevitably impose a greater degree of direct responsibility on those working in them and this will require effective measures to secure the accountability of the managers for their work. Openness would be one such measure. *The Citizen's Charter* (1991, Cm. 1599) also promises a welcome degree of openness about standards, procedures, and the identity of civil servants.

The fourth reason, which is not explicitly advanced but which is the underlying reason why governments (and civil servants) object to the idea of freedom of information, is that it would expose ministers and their officials to criticism and embarrassment (Ranelagh, 1987). As James Callaghan put it candidly to the Franks Committee (1972, vol. 4, p. 190):

. . . frankly half the people in this country are concerned to find things that will redound to the discredit of the Government, every day. It is inevitable in this case that a Government is going to have some defensive reaction and say, "We are not going to tell you anything more than we can about what is going to discredit us".

Though this explanation for secrecy has the appeal of any admission of human frailty, it is not an attractive or convincing justification.

How could open government be introduced in the United Kingdom?

If a greater degree of public access to official information were to be conceded as desirable, the next issue would be how it should be achieved. The main choice is between the passage of legislation – a Freedom of Information Act (Birkinshaw, 1990a) or a Public Right of Access Act or a series of separate Acts which, taken together, would introduce a right of access regime such as has been achieved more or less in local government – the use of informal administrative measures such as a code of practice (a new 'Croham Directive') or a combination of administrative measures and piecemeal legislation.

As we saw earlier, there is sufficient knowledge of the pitfalls that have been encountered by other countries with Freedom of Information regimes for a general Act to be passed for the UK which would provide for rights of access and the necessary exemptions from disclosure in such a way as to avoid the need for amending legislation which can often follow from radical measures such as this would be. For a government committed to open government, there would be political attractions in having one Act to cover the ground, possibly providing for the details to be filled in by codes of practice and statutory instruments, rather than a series of Acts passed in successive parliamentary sessions which would build up a freedom of information regime incrementally. Enforcement could be either through the courts or, probably more appropriately, through an independent Information Commissioner whose decisions would be subject to judicial review on the usual grounds (see Chapter 7).

But the experience of other countries is seldom regarded by British politicians or civil servants as persuasive in favour of action (though it may be invoked as a reason for inaction), and a more likely approach would be a mixture of administrative measures and piecemeal legislation. This would have the advantage of flexibility in that practice could be altered to meet problems as they arise. But administrative measures could have the disadvantage of unenforceability unless provision were made, for example, for an independent Information Commissioner, accountable perhaps to the Treasury and Civil Service Committee as the Parliamentary Commissioner for Administration is to the Select Committee, to determine disputes about requests for disclosure.

Whatever system were introduced, it is clear from overseas experience and closer at hand, for example the open government experiment in Bradford referred to earlier, that its manner of implementation must be well thought out and supervised if it is to be effective in promoting the objectives of openness discussed above – accountability and effectiveness in government, consumer protection, the protection of individual privacy and autonomy, and the promotion of citizenship. The sudden availability of a mass of undigested and indigestible information would be of no use to the individual or to pressure groups and other organizations with special interests in the subject matter. Information in government files would have to be systematically registered; a consistent policy in the form of codes of practice on dealing with requests for information would have to be devised and its implementation monitored. Some right of appeal to an independent body where disputes about disclosures arise would be essential. So the introduction of statutory rights of access to public information would need to be carefully thought out; but there would be great benefits in terms of accountability, efficiency and effectiveness, and enhanced citizenship in the introduction of open government.

PART IV

Conclusions

11

A written Constitution?

'The United Kingdom needs a new constitutional settlement, enshrined in a written constitituon.' These are the opening words of the Liberal Democrats' Green Paper 'We the People . . .' – Towards a Written Constitution (1990) (see also the Institute of Public Policy Research Constitution, 1991; Tony Benn's Commonwealth of Britain Bill, 1991; Vibert, 1991; Haseler, 1991). There have been other calls for a Constitution in addition to a set of constitutional reforms in the last 15 years or so, notably from Charter 88, Lord Scarman (1974) and Lord Hailsham (1978). But by no means all of those who advocate radical institutional and political reform along the lines considered in Parts II and III of this book would go so far as to recommend a written Constitution.

Three main reasons are given by its advocates for a written Constitution: first, the need to limit the sovereignty of Parliament by entrenching certain aspects of the constitution to prevent them from being repealed or altered for partisan party political reasons by the government of the day (this would 'institutionalise the theory of limited government': Hailsham, 1978, p. 226); secondly, the need to improve accessibility of information about the constitution and in particular the rights of citizens that a Constitution would provide. Thirdly, the need for a thorough 'review and overhaul' (Vibert, 1991) of the system. We shall start by considering each of these in turn.

Parliamentary sovereignty and a written Constitution

The Liberal Democrat paper 'We, The People . . .' – Towards a Written Constitution (1990, p. 7) gives as a reason for a Constitution that by entrenching fundamental rules it would help provide stability, coherence and certainty to the political process. The ability of the UK Parliament to legislate on any subject matter is seen as posing a threat to citizens and to democracy, rather than as an expression of the wishes of citizens and of democratic ideals, as it is sometimes portrayed as doing. An often heard objection to written

Constitutions is that anything that limits the legislative competence of the democratically elected legislature is itself undemocratic – democracy involves the people having the power to pass any laws that they desire.

This argument against a written Constitution for the UK is open to a number of objections. First, Parliament is not in fact democratically elected. As we have seen in Chapter 8, strong criticisms can be made of the electoral system; and the second chamber is undeniably not a democratic institution, whatever other qualities it might have. But even if the electoral system were reformed and even if the second chamber were made democratic, it is far from clear that it would be undemocratic for the sovereignty of Parliament to be restricted by a Constitution.

In considering this aspect of the issue, we need to be clear about what 'the sovereignty of Parliament' implies. In its simplest form, it means that the legislature has the power under the legal system to pass legislation on any subject matter. It is not constrained by the standards of international law, or by any form of 'natural law' or reason or wisdom (*Cheney* v. *Conn* [1968] 1 WLR 242). Most legislatures of independent states possess sovereignty in this form. However, this version of the doctrine of parliamentary sovereignty is far from uncontroversial in the UK. The Parliament of Scotland before the Treaty of Union of 1707 did not claim absolute sovereignty and there is some discontent in Scotland with the assumption that the Westminster Parliament inherited the English character of sovereignty rather than the Scottish concept of limited power.

Although most legislatures of independent states have the power to legislate on any subject matter, many are prevented from passing legislation, especially legislation that alters the Constitution, unless they follow particular procedures or use particular forms of words (see, e.g. the case from Ceylon, *Bribery Commissioners* v. *Ranasinghe* [1965] AC 172; for a discussion, see Marshall, 1971, ch. III). The most common form of procedural entrenchment is a requirement that a special majority be won for the measure in the legislature, such as two-thirds of those voting in the Parliament. This provision figures in a number of the Constitutions of Commonwealth countries and makes it legally impossible for constitutional amendments to be made without substantial support. In federal systems such as the USA, there may be a need to win the support of two-thirds of the states for an amendment.

Some Constitutions, for example that of the Republic of Ireland, require the holding of a referendum to approve a change to the Constitution. Tony Benn's Commonwealth of Britain Bill (Benn, 1991) also envisages referendums before amendment of the Constitution. But there are a number of problems with the use of referendums for this purpose (Bogdanor, 1981, part II). They are only appropriate where the issue is clear. And there is always a risk that the electorate will take the referendum as an opportunity to express a view about the government of the day rather than about the issue at stake. Bogdanor's conclusion in his discussion of the referendum is that it is of value in resolving disputes in clearly circumscribed situations, but it cannot of itself yield the will to agreement where none exists: 'It can articulate a submerged consensus, but it cannot create one' (Bogdanor, 1981, p. 91). Often the losing side will not accept the result with good grace, as happened after the referendum on whether the UK should remain in the European Community in 1975. On the other hand, a referendum can lay to rest a constitutional dispute for a time, as happened after the devolution referendums of 1979 after which Scottish and Welsh nationalism became quiescent for nearly a decade (see Chapter 6). And the use of referendums can provide protection against a government attempting to use its majority in Parliament to implement changes that do not have popular support. This case for the use of referendums has particular force if the electoral system should remain unchanged (Holme, 1987, p. 139).

Yet another entrenching device, used for example in Canada to protect the Charter of Rights, is the 'notwithstanding clause' that was discussed in Chapter 9 in relation to a Bill of Rights.

There are no such protections of legislation against repeal in the UK at present. Parliament may legislate on any subject matter by simple majority, and the most recently passed Act of Parliament will impliedly repeal any provision in an earlier Act or in statutory instruments, rules of the the common law and any other form of law, save where European law is concerned (*Ellen Street Estates* v. *Minister of Health* [1934] 1 KB 590; *R.* v. *Secretary of State for Transport, Ex parte Factortame (No. 2)* [1990] 3 WLR 56; Collins, 1990). If the House of Lords withholds its consent, then a Bill may receive the Royal Assent on the consent of the Commons only (Parliament Acts 1911, 1949). But it is worth noting at this juncture a point to which we shall return, that an exception to the Parliament Acts 1911 and 1949 requires the consent of the second chamber to a Bill to prolong the life of Parliament beyond 5 years. This is an example of a form of 'entrenchment' of a measure of central constitutional importance in the present system.

The question arises, then, of whether procedural restraints or 'notwithstanding clauses' are undemocratic. To maintain, as defenders of the UK version of parliamentary sovereignty often do, that democracy demands that a legislature should be able to legislate on any subject matter by simple majority, has a strange ring about it when the nature of the legislatures around the world that do not have that freedom are considered. To reduce democracy to a right to legislate by a simple majority is to equate it with majoritarianism. As we saw in Chapter 9, there are strong arguments for the view that democracy involves keeping the political process open and protecting minorities, and majoritarianism should not be allowed to subvert these aspects of a democratic system.

Although there are some legal arguments in favour of the view that it would be possible to entrench legislation of the UK Parliament by procedural means, a view that is called the 'new view of sovereignty' (Heuston, 1964, ch. 1), there could be no guarantee that judges in our courts would uphold such provisions and we have to proceed on the assumption that procedural entrenchment by special majority requirements would not be legally effective under the present unwritten constitution of the UK. This difficulty over entrenchment under the present system is why the argument for a written constitution generally entails the inclusion of entrenching provisions.

The educational case for a written Constitution

> Of course, no written constitution can guarantee good government or civil liberties: these depend, above all else, upon the traditions, education and habits of mind of governors and governed alike. But written Constitutions can play a crucial role in forming such habits and traditions (Liberal Democrats, 1990, p. 7).

These words express the case for a Constitution on educational grounds. A complaint that is commonly heard about the UK constitution is that information about how it is supposed to operate and in particular about the rights of citizens is inaccessible, and indeed that much of the system is excessively obscure, consisting of unwritten conventions and practices as well as a mixture of Acts of Parliament, some of them in archaic language, and of decided cases. This problem was voiced by the Speaker's Commission on Citizenship (1990), which saw the obscurity of the constitution as presenting an obstacle to the teaching of citizenship. The commission concluded that a review and codification of the law relating to the legal rights, duties and entitlements of the citizen and the obligations of citizenship was urgently needed (Speaker's Commission, 1990, p. 18; Gardner, 1990, p. 74).

Many of the rights of citizens would be set out in a Bill of Rights (see Chapter 9) if one were enacted, so this particular aspect of the case for accessibility could be met in that way without requiring additionally the adoption of a written Constitution. But of course it is true that information about the working of the system and the values and principles underlying it are complex and difficult to find or define. But whether a Constitution would meet the need for accessibility would depend on how the Constitution was drafted. If the document were short and clear, then its provisions would be easily understood and this would meet some of the needs for accessibility. But such a document could read rather blandly and paint only an incomplete picture of the system, which would not in practice be very informative and could be positively misleading. If it set out only the basic principles, there would have to be a great deal of further legislation to fill in the gaps.

One solution to the need to fill in the gaps would be to refer to much of the legislation that was already in force before the Constitution was adopted, but this would mean that the details of the system could only be found by reading the Constitution and probably large quantities of other legislation, some of it pre-dating and some post-dating the Constitution. In other words, there would continue to be problems of inaccessibility.

To take an example of how a short 'framework' Constitution might read, John Macdonald QC (1990) of the Liberal Democrats produced a draft in 1990 which was appended to the party's paper '*We, The People . . .*' – *Towards a*

Written Constitution. This draft is some 79 articles in length, divided into eight chapters. Chapter 2 is the Bill of Rights, based on the European Convention on Human Rights, and runs to 26 articles. The other articles are necessarily brief. For example, all that is said about the civil service is in Article 78:

> There shall be a professional independent Civil Service. The power to appoint and remove people from the Civil Service shall be vested in a Public Service Commission independent of the government of the United Kingdom. The Public Service Commission shall be appointed by a joint committee of Parliament chosen by the Speaker of the House of Commons and the President of the Senate.

This Constitution is admirably brief and clear in drafting style, but it conveys only the bare bones and fundamentals of the system. The Bill of Rights section would be useful to citizens anxious to know what their rights were (though there is no mention of the social element of citizenship there), but it does not indicate what the duties of the citizen are, nor the duties of the state. This is not a criticism of Macdonald's Constitution, but it does illustrate the sort of shortcomings that any Constitution that is supposed to have an educational function may suffer from. Another Constitution could of course set out these matters, and in detail, but to do so would make the document very much longer and more technical and would in the course of that reduce its comprehensibility to the non-lawyer. This is likely to be a problem with the Institute of Public Policy Research Constitution. There are therefore doubts about the value of a Constitution in making the rules of the Constitution accessible to citizens. In the USA, for example, the terms of the Constitution are not well known or understood (Kammen, 1986, referred to in Holme and Elliott, 1988, p. 36).

Overhauling the system of government

Although the principal proposals for reform of the UK constitution that are near the top of the political agenda are relatively few in number – electoral reform, a Bill of Rights, decentralization, reform of the second chamber, freedom of information and a Ministry of Justice – there are in fact a large number of reforms under discussion, some of which have been considered in these chapters. One argument for a written Constitution might be that it would present an opportunity to overhaul many aspects of the system in one fell swoop. This is the approach adopted by the Institute of Public Policy Research (1991), and, to a lesser extent, by Tony Benn's Commonwealth of Britain Bill (Benn, 1991). The Institute of Public Policy Research Constitution (1991) seeks to provide, in addition to the subjects mentioned above, for citizenship, Cabinet government, the civil service, public finance, political parties, the judiciary, the armed forces and national security, and to effect reforms in each of these areas.

One major problem raised by this approach, if it were adopted, would be the difficulty in achieving consensus over such a wide range of material. Another is the inaccessibility to the public of such a long and detailed document.

Disadvantages of a written Constitution

As we have seen, the principal advantage of a Constitution would be in limiting the ability of Parliament to alter fundamental aspects of the system of government (e.g. the terms of a Bill of Rights, the status of local government or national and regional assemblies, the electoral system, the status of the civil service) by imposing constraints in the form of procedures or notwithstanding clauses. What might be the disadvantages of a Constitution?

Much would depend upon how detailed the Constitution was. Under the present system, important elements of the system are found in conventions regulating the use of power, unwritten understandings and written – though not always published – codes such as the guidance for ministers (*Questions of Procedure for Ministers*; see Chapters 3 and 4) and civil servants appearing before select committees (The Osmotherly Rules; see Chapters 3 and 4). Although of course there are complaints that conventions are not obeyed and the spirit of them is flouted (in refusals by ministers to answer questions fully before select committees, for example), the spirit of these conventions is understood and by and large accepted in principle, although considerations of expediency present irresistible temptations to break them on occasions. It is my view that if a Constitution (or legislation passed to give flesh to a skeleton Constitution) were to seek to put these informal rules into statutory form, this could be seen as an invitation to ministers and others to adopt a legalistic approach, to look to getting round the letter of the law rather than to comply with the spirit of the rules.

Another reservation about the campaign for a written Constitution is that it could divert energy from the more important issues of debating how the substance of the Constitution should be reformed. Richard Holme (1987, p. 140) has suggested that the approach should be 'Reform first, codification later', and in my view this is the right approach. It would in all probability take many years for a programme of reforms such as argued for in this book to be put into effect and concentration on drawing up a written Constitution could lead to insufficient attention being paid to individual reforms.

It is said, too, that the system could become unduly inflexible if a written Constitution with entrenched clauses were adopted. While this is theoretically possible, its disadvantages should not be exaggerated: most Western democracies have such clauses in their Constitutions and it can hardly be said that they all suffer from inflexibility. In practice, flexibility depends as much on the political culture as on the terms of a Constitution (Wheare, 1966, pp. 16–19).

The content and drafting of a written Constitution

This book has focused on a number of important issues that one would expect to find dealt with in a written Constitution for the UK. Any written Constitution would be expected to provide for the legislature, the executive and the judiciary, sub-national government, civil and political rights, and elections (see Wheare, 1966, ch. 3). But there are other matters which might need to be covered. Questions about whether to include reference to arrangements under the present system that would continue under a written Constitution are considered shortly; but other issues, where reform might be considered but which have not been referred to in earlier chapters include, for example: the retention or abolition of the monarchy; the succession to the throne; whether the common law prerogatives of the Crown should be abolished and replaced where appropriate by statutory powers; whether the Church of England should be disestablished. There might be a Preamble reciting where sovereignty lies, probably with 'the people': this would represent a departure from the present position, where sovereignty lies with 'the Queen in Parliament'.

Many of these issues could prove highly controversial, and if it were felt right to include reference to them in a written Constitution, it is to be expected that the whole enterprise might be jeopardized by delays and wrangles over these matters, which could well arouse stronger passions and push people into more entrenched positions than issues such as the Bill of Rights or electoral reform could do. It may have been for this reason that Macdonald's Constitution referred to earlier chose, wisely in my view, not to say anything about these issues.

A number of decisions about drafting style would have to be made if a Constitution for the UK were to be produced. How much detail should the Constitution contain? These matters have to be determined in part by reference to the objectives of enacting such a document; if it is to have an educative function then it should be simply and clearly expressed, for the inclusion of too much detail could serve to conceal the most important principles and provisions from the public or cause confusion. On the other hand, if the prime purpose of the document is to 'map out' the system of government, allocating powers, setting up mechanisms of accountability and effectiveness and giving expression to the status and role of the citizen, then more detail might be indicated. And if the Constitution were used to undertake a thorough overhaul of the system, it could be more detailed still.

Alternatively, a brief framework could be sketched into the Constitution, to be filled out by further legislation; but then the question would arise whether any of that further legislation needed to be entrenched or whether only the articles in the Constitution itself required such protection.

Other decisions that have to be made when drafting a Constitution are to what extent the document and legislation passed to fill it out is intended to be an exhaustive codification and reform of the system, the source of the whole of the law of the constitution, and to what extent there is room for the continuance of the existing system, but subject to the overriding force of the Constitution.

The way in which this decision affects the drafting of a Constitution may be illustrated by reference to Macdonald's Constitution in 'We, The People . . .' (Liberal Democrats, 1990). Article 1 reads:

This Constitution is the supreme law of the United Kingdom of Great Britain and Northern Ireland. It derives its validity from the people of the

United Kingdom with whom sovereignty lies and provides the framework through which alone the power of government may lawfully be exercised. The Constitution is binding on the Crown and any law or prerogative rule that is inconsistent with the provisions of the Constitution is, to the extent of the inconsistency, of no force or effect.

This Article, assumes but does not itself provide for, the retention of the Monarchy with the present rules for succession, the present powers including prerogatives, save to the extent that other provisions alter them. The Constitution is silent about the Church of England and the European Community and many other matters, and so in these respects the system would continue as at present. The document allows, then, for the continued operation of many existing laws, both statutory and common law rules, and makes no reference to fundamental provisions such as the Act of Settlement, the Acts of Union, the Bill of Rights 1689, and so on. Later chapters deal with rights and freedoms, Parliament, executive powers, a supreme court, decentralization to the nations and regions, the civil service, and amendment of the Constitution.

This approach has much to commend it, since an attempt to incorporate these fundamental Acts into a written Constitution would make it very long, and there would always be a risk of a constitutional lacuna if some rules were omitted by an oversight. The Institute of Public Policy Research Constitution (1991) attempts an exhaustive statement of the system and becomes in places very detailed and technical. On the other hand, Macdonald's Constitution does not perform an educational task that might be considered important in that it does not set out even the basic rules about the monarchy, succession to the Crown, the union of Scotland, England and Wales, and Northern Ireland, or the status of local government (the intention on this latter point being that this should be dealt with in part by ordinary legislation passed at Westminster and in part by the new national and regional assemblies).

It is to be expected that most of the provisions in a Constitution would be protected by some form of entrenchment – two-thirds majorities, a requirement for the consent of both Houses, a referendum, notwithstanding clauses. But not all laws of a constitutional nature need be so entrenched. For example, Macdonald's Constitution does not refer to a freedom of information act in so many words (although Article 15 in the Bill of Rights chapter gives a right to receive and impart information and ideas). But the Liberal Democrats have committed the party to the introduction of a Freedom of Information Act and this would be in the form of ordinary legislation that could be amended from time to time without the protection of entrenching clauses. Similarly, as indicated above, the actual structure and powers of local government are not set out in Macdonald's Constitution, and further Acts would have to be passed by the UK Parliament or the assemblies to deal with these matters. (Macdonald's Constitution envisages that there should be single-tier principal authorities below the national and regional assemblies, but that the decision which tier that should be – district or county councils, for example – should be taken locally by the assemblies and not imposed from the centre.)

In a Constitution of this kind, there would be a complex hierarchy of laws in the UK, with the Constitution prevailing over legislation passed by the assemblies and the UK Parliament, but with UK legislation prevailing over some assembly measures, and some assembly legislation prevailing over UK Acts. There would also continue to be various grades of subordinate legislation (statutory instruments, orders in council) emanating from central government and from the assemblies. The institutional structure would also vary depending on what decisions each nation or region made about local government in its area. (But to secure a degree of uniformity in matters of service provision, the Macdonald draft provides that: 'it shall be the duty of the United Kingdom Parliament to define basic levels of service provision which shall bind National Parliaments and Regional Assemblies'.)

Macdonald's Constitution, then, provides an interesting example of a relatively simple straightforward document that could radically alter the operation of the system of government while leaving in place many of the existing structures. But this is not by any means the only way in which a Constitution could be drafted. At the other extreme, in length and detail, a Constitution could include the provisions of the Act of Settlement and other legislation relating to the Crown, remove prerogatives, disestablish the Church of England, provide for Cabinet government and ministerial responsibility to Parliament, provide for the Parliamentary Commissioner for Administration, recognize the roles of political parties, and so on. This, as indicated above, is the approach adopted by the Institute of Public Policy Research Constitution (Institute of Public Policy Research, 1991). This approach involves a far more explicit statement of the nature and functioning of the system of government, and it implies an increased degree of regulation of large areas of activity such as the conduct of Cabinet which are currently only informally regulated. It could also require decisions to be made and recorded in the Constitution as to which of the rights and duties set out in the document were to be legally enforceable and which were not. The Constitution prepared by the Institute of Public Policy Research (IPPR) provides, in this respect, an interesting contrast with Macdonald's Constitution.

The procedure for constitutional reform or for adopting a written Constitution

If it were decided in principle that a written Constitution should be adopted, or that a particular measure of constitutional reform – proportional representation for example – should be introduced, the question would arise whether any special procedure ought to be followed to secure general agreement about the desirability of the measure, or to prevent reforms being pushed through by a party to secure for itself an in-built advantage in the working of the system.

An example of the sort of procedure that could be adopted is provided by the

Written Constitution Bill, a private member's Bill introduced into the House of Commons in March 1990, which would have required the Speaker of the House of Commons to convene a Speaker's Conference to consider the matter of a Constitution for the UK and to draw up a draft of such a Constitution. The draft would have been laid before each House of Parliament in the form of a Bill, and if passed there would have been a referendum before it was put into effect.

This Bill had no chance of making progress in the House and it was introduced as a means of drawing attention to the issue. But it was unusual in that it envisaged the introduction of a Constitution that would itself reform the system rather than first reforming the system by a series of measures and then consolidating reforms in a Constitution, which is an approach that is more frequently suggested.

Lord Scarman (1974, p. 76), the first commentator to give serious consideration to the question, did not feel that anything as formal as a constituent assembly was necessary. He felt that a programme of constitutional reform should be phased in over a period of years, and that Parliament should consult a wide range of interests, including Scottish and Welsh nationalists and politicians in Northern Ireland, trade unionists and others, and that the introduction of a written Constitution should not be embarked upon without this lengthy process.

Lord Hailsham, in the days when he was committed to constitutional reform, was in favour of a gradual approach, and proposed setting up a commission, subject to parliamentary supervision, to 'map out' the constitution and draft one reforming measure at a time, each of which would be submitted to a referendum once passed by Parliament. Once ratified by Parliament, each measure should be amendable only by the same process. He felt that certain measures, for example to reform the second chamber, should be dealt with sooner than others. He spoke of the system of government that would result from such a programme as being a written Constitution 'in the technical sense', since the power of Parliament to alter or amend it would to the extent of the requirement for a referendum be restrained (Hailsham, 1978, ch. 36).

When he delivered the Hamlyn lectures in 1974, which drew the attention of lawyers to the case for constitutional reform, Lord Scarman was not convinced that it was necessary for the constitution to be written in one document or a set of documents (Scarman, 1974; p. 76). But he has since then come round to the view that we do need a Constitution (Scarman, 1988, pp. 109–110). In recognition of the fact that this would take some time to achieve, he now proposes two interim measures which would represent a half-way house to a full-blown written Constitution, namely the incorporation of the European Convention of Human Rights into our law, and a new Parliamentary Act requiring the assent of both Houses of Parliament to the amendment of certain scheduled Acts. The Schedule should include the new Bill of Rights, all legislation promoting racial equality and equal rights for women, the structural legislation establishing local government, and other legislation, notably the Habeas Corpus Acts and

Magna Carta, which are considered to be of constitutional importance. However, the ultimate goal would remain:

> a constitution which is based on a true and legally enforceable separation of the powers of the government, which declares and defines our constitutional rights and freedoms, and which establishes a court having jurisdiction on challenge by any person or group of persons to review the constitutionality of executive action and legislation and to give the appropriate relief if either be held to be contrary to the constitution (Scarman, 1988, p. 110).

The Liberal Democrats (1990) have produced the most detailed 'Reform Timetable' for the introduction of a constitution in recent years. They see as a precondition the election of a reform-minded House of Commons. Before the election that would produce such a House, a Proportional Representation Bill and a Constituent Assembly Bill would have been prepared. Parliament would then incorporate the ECHR into UK law, enact a Proportional Representation Act and Acts setting up assemblies in Scotland and Wales, a Freedom of Information Act, a Judicial Service Commission Act, and an Act providing for fixed-term Parliaments. Work would start on fixing boundaries for English regions and House of Lords reform.

A Constituent Assembly Bill would also be passed enabling the next House of Commons to sit as a constituent assembly as well as its normal functions. At the end of this first Parliament, elections to the House of Commons would be by proportional representation. The new House of Commons in its role as a Constituent Assembly would have been charged by the Constituent Assembly Act with drawing up a Constitution. This it would do and the Commons would pass Acts creating regional assemblies in England, establishing single-tier local authorities in England, and reforming the House of Lords to create a Senate. Elections would then be held for the Senate and to English regional assemblies.

Finally, a Constitution would be adopted by an affirmative vote of at least two-thirds of its members in their role as members of the Constituent Assembly, and this would come into force, with the establishment of a Supreme Court, and entrenchment of proportional representation, the principles of home rule and decentralization and the Bill of Rights by a two-thirds majority requirement. It would be for the Constituent Assembly to decide on its own procedure and to decide whether a referendum should be held before the Constitution is adopted. The authors of the paper felt that a referendum would not be necessary, since the proposals would have been the subject of extensive debate over two general elections and the Constitution would have had to command the support of two-thirds of the Constituent Assembly who would in turn have been elected by a similar proportion of the voters.

Whatever one's views about the need for a Constitution and for particular reforms, the document is interesting in indicating the sort of time-scale that would be needed for the project and for its attempts to deal with issues of popular consent and legitimation of the process.

There are other procedures in the system which have been used in the past when constitutional reform has been under discussion. One is the Speaker's Conference (Lyon and Wigram, 1977; Wade, 1980, ch. 1), which was used on a number of occasions between 1969 and 1973 to consider electoral reform. This institution usually has some 30 members drawn from the principal parties in the House of Commons, but it is not given its terms of reference by Parliament, but by the government (indeed, it has not always been given terms of reference), and these terms will not necessarily be debated in Parliament. Sir William Wade (1980, p. 3) concluded in his Hamlyn lectures of 1980 that this was at its best only 'a frail advisory mechanism, at the mercy of the government of the day'.

Another approach would be to establish a Royal Commission to consider the whole issue of a written Constitution or particular proposals for reform: this was proposed by Lord Hailsham (1978) in *The Dilemma of Democracy*. But often these commissions are used by politicians as excuses to put an issue on the back-burner and it is unlikely that this would satisfy those who are convinced that the case for constitutional reform is clear, that much of the groundwork has been done and that ultimately the decision to seek to introduce a particular reforming measure or set of measures is for politicians and not for members of a Royal Commission. The fact that a decision of this kind is essentially political does not mean that there should not be wide consultation and a special legitimating procedure for some reforms of the sorts discussed above.

A Constitutional court?

Certain of the reforms that have been discussed in this book would result in an increase in litigation and the reference to the courts of cases with important constitutional implications, often highly party political in nature. This would be a likely result of the introduction of a system of national and regional assemblies, where there would be likely to be disputes about the competence of local government, the national and regional assemblies and central government. The introduction of a Bill of Rights would also lead to an increase of litigation in which the propriety of government action and the compatibility of Westminster legislation and the acts of the regional and national assemblies with the Bill of Rights would be raised.

This prospect raises a number of issues about the fitness of the judiciary to deal with these issues (see discussion in Chapter 9): whether they should be dealt with in the ordinary course of litigation in the ordinary courts, and whether there should be a special constitutional court.

A Constitutional court could take the form of the present Judicial Committee of the House of Lords or of the Privy Council. If the second chamber were reformed, then the Judicial Committee of the House of Lords might disappear, but the Judicial Committee of the Privy Council could continue in being, unless the Privy Council were also abolished in a scheme of constitutional reform. But it would have to be borne in mind that the Judicial Committee of the Privy Council is the last court of appeal for a number of Commonwealth countries and they might not wish to see it abolished. If the House of Lords were abolished, the Judicial Committee of the Privy Council could take on the functions of the present Judicial Committee of the House of Lords as the final court of appeal in the UK, and of a Constitutional court.

An alternative approach would be to set up a separate court from the final court of appeal on non-constitutional matters, possibly composed of a combination of judges, former civil servants and other people with suitable experience, along the lines of the Conseil Constitutionnel or the Conseil d'Etat in France. Appointment to such a court need not be by the Judicial Services Commission (or the Lord Chancellor if he or she were to retain responsibility for judicial appointments), but by some other method, such as recommendation by the Prime Minister subject to parliamentary approval. In this way, the ordinary courts would continue to be insulated from political pressures, but appointments to the Constitutional court or council would have a political input designed to secure as far as possible that the members did not over-reach themselves in exercising what could be considerable power.

The disadvantages of establishing a special constitutional court on these lines are great. Delay would be introduced into litigation if all cases raising constitutional issues had to be referred to such a court. The appointment of members of the court could become highly politicized, as is the case in the USA, where Presidents attempt to appoint politically sympathetic judges to the Supreme Court, and the nominees are cross-questioned on their political views by Congress. The appointment process could be used to 'pack' the court with judges sympathetic to a particular political ideology.

A further disadvantage of the Conseil Constitutionnel model is that the Conseil does not have the power to strike down Acts of Parliament as being unconstitutional. All the council can do is to scrutinize legislation before it comes into effect and report on its compatibility with the French Constitution. This has not prevented it from taking an active role in extending its interpretation of what is a 'constitutional matter', but its powers are nevertheless limited. There is no possibility of questioning the constitutionality of a *loi* once promulgated, and in particular no possibility of incidental or concrete review. So if the French Parliament should decide to go ahead and enact a law which the Conseil Constitutionnel has pronounced unconstitutional, neither the Conseil nor the courts have power to annul it. This approach is quite different from that adopted by the US Supreme Court since the decision in *Marbury* v. *Madison* (1803) 1 Cranch 103, which permits the courts to strike down unconstitutional legislation. To approach the question of the justiciability of constitutional issues in the way adopted by the Conseil Constitutionnel would be a departure from the English common law tradition encapsulated in the tag *ubi jus, ibi remedium*: a right without remedy is a contradiction in terms. If a Constitutional court were set up, it is more likely to follow the US than the French model.

It is suggested that it would be preferable for all courts to have jurisdiction to deal with issues over the interpretation and application of constitutional measures in the ordinary course of litigation, as they are with all points of law at present. Appeals would lie to the Supreme or Constitutional court, but delays in litigation and expense caused would be minimized if ordinary courts had this jurisdiction.

Conclusions

There is at present in the UK much less support for a written Constitution than there is for constitutional reform. The cases for a Constitution are not the same as those for reform, and it is suggested that Holme (1987, p. 140) was right to express the fear that talk of a written Constitution could serve to divert public interest and political energy from the more important issues of how the constitution should be reformed. There are several ways in which major measures of constitutional reform could be protected from repeal, the appropriateness of each depending on the nature of the reform and on what other reforms were in place. If the European Convention on Human Rights were incorporated into UK law, then it would be well protected by the fact of its international status and so a 'notwithstanding clause' requirement would suffice to protect it as is the case with the Charter of Rights in Canada. There is every reason to suppose that the UK courts would give effect to such a clause notwithstanding the decision in *Ellen Street Estates* v. *Minister of Health* [1934] 1 KB 590 (see Chapter 9 and the discussion earlier in this chapter). Other measures could be protected in other ways which would be effective even without a Constitution, such as requiring the consent of the second chamber, as is presently the case with Bills to extend the life of Parliament.

If national and regional assemblies were set up, it could be provided that no Bill to alter their powers could be presented to Parliament without the consent of a proportion of the assemblies, say two-thirds. Although this might not be strictly enforceable (i.e. the UK courts might not be willing to order that a Bill should not be presented to Parliament), measures to this effect would set up very powerful political obstacles in the way of a government at Whitehall seeking to alter the powers of assemblies without a strong degree of consensus. The very introduction of reforms such as a Freedom of Information Act, national and regional assemblies and proportional representation, would alter the political climate so as to make repeal or amendment of constitutional measures politically difficult. There are disadvantages in resorting to the use of referenda on constitutional matters which may be highly complex, and requirements for two-thirds majorities in the legislature could introduce undue inflexibility into the system – after all, we have to accept the possibility that some of these reforms would need refining over the years or might even become unpopular and damaging to the system.

The reality of the matter is that the adoption of a Constitution is unlikely to become politically attractive for many years, if at all, and indeed if the reforms advocated in this book were adopted, the case for a Constitution would become weaker and attractive to fewer people as they saw the operation of the system improving so that there seemed less point in bothering to codify the system and adopt a Constitution. The case based on the educational value of a Constitution is weak, especially if a Bill of Rights were to be adopted, since this relatively short document would contain the basic principles about which citizens are most concerned and which they have most need to know. It is much to be preferred that the energies of reformers be directed at individual measures of reform, about which there is a growing consensus.

12

A programme for constitutional renewal: Towards accountability, effectiveness and citizenship

We have seen in this book how the accountability of government, its effectiveness and the status of citizenship are closely interrelated, and how defective present arrangements are in securing these three essentials to good government. MORI's *State of the Nation* poll (1991) found strong public support for a range of reforms that would increase the accountability and effectiveness of government and improve citizenship rights. Let us start this concluding chapter, then, by reviewing the arguments surrounding these three themes and their relevance to the institutions of the state and the operation of the political process.

The argument in this book has been that the institutions of the state are in many respects insufficiently accountable – politically, publicly, legally and administratively – both for their *modus operandi* (the ground rules of the system of government) and for the substance of what they do. Accountability of government to Parliament is one of the cornerstones of the constitution, but there is a major problem in the relationship between Parliament and the government and the difficulties in achieving the appropriate balance between the two. The fact that the Executive is the dominant party in this relationship means that the accountability of government to Parliament and to the public is weak, and the public interest, which it is the prime duty of government to promote, suffers. But the dilemma is that measures that made Parliament the dominant partner might undermine the effectiveness of government. While it has been argued that an adjustment in the relationship is required, it should not be such as to make effective government impossible.

Parliament and the Executive

The weakness of Parliament in its relations with the Executive has been attributed to a range of factors. In particular, the balance of the parties in the

House of Commons, which almost invariably gives the government a majority – and generally a safe one – means that the government can get away with failing to give a full account of its policies and administration and can also avoid having to take corrective action or make amends if its activities are found to be unwise or oppressive. It also means that there are insufficient pressures on government to respond to the needs and wishes of the citizenry. Procedural reform in Parliament cannot on its own secure the necessary change in the political process. The balance of the parties in Parliament needs to be redressed to provide a fairer reflection of the balance of public support for different political philosophies and strategies for government and to revitalize the operation of the political process in Parliament. This can only be achieved by electoral reform. In this respect, institutional and political reform are closely linked.

But it has been a thread of the argument in this book that no single reform can solve the problems of the system of government. Electoral reform alone would not secure an effective political process that encouraged accountability, effectiveness and citizenship. Any parliamentary majority, whether formed by a single party or by a coalition or pact, has the power to secure the passage of legislation that suppresses accountability or undermines the effectiveness of the citizenry in participating in the political process: any government may be tempted to use its majority to suppress freedom of speech or association, for example, both important in promoting accountability and citizenship. So proposals for legislation, protected in some way from repeal by a temporary majority acting for its own purposes, that protects fundamental rights, especially those to do with the openness of the political process, have a place in the prescriptions for improving the accountability of government. That accountability has to be secured not only in Parliament, but also outside it through other mechanisms than the conventions of ministerial responsibility.

The other aspect of the relationship between government and Parliament which poses problems for accountability is the role of the second chamber. There is no longer support, as there was in some quarters in the 1970s, for a single-chamber legislature. But the search for a suitable set of functions for the second chamber and a composition that would not have the effect of frustrating the government in the Commons or of reducing rather than enhancing the checks and balances within which government has to operate, has as yet been unsuccessful.

Many of the members of the present House of Lords perform a useful function in reviewing government legislation and scrutinizing policy and this is a role that a second chamber should perform. But the unrepresentative composition of the House and its own lack of public accountability mean that it is not in a strong position to demand that government respond to its demands or recommendations. In addition, the fact that the Conservative Party has an in-built majority in the Lords by way of hereditary peerages means that Conservative administrations have an unfair advantage over Labour governments. So a way needs to be found to eliminate the in-built advantage and to enhance accountability without undermining the effectiveness of government.

The ethos of secrecy

The weak accountability of government in the system as it operates at present is added to by the ethos of secrecy backed up by law, which denies to Parliament and to the public information about government activity which could form the basis of informed and constructive criticisms. The secrecy of public administration in the UK, particularly in central government, not only limits its accountability to Parliament and to the public for the substantive policies that it pursues, but it also allows government to operate according to ground rules that do not promote effectiveness and efficiency in government, and which frustrate the efforts of citizens to make a contribution to the political process.

In referring to the secrecy surrounding the ground rules of the system, we can point to the fact that the rules of ministerial and Cabinet conduct are not published. The *Questions of Procedure for Ministers*, which contains many of these rules, is confidential; ministers are not permitted under the conventions of collective responsibility to disclose how Cabinet is organized, what committees it has and what their terms of reference are. Nor are there adequate provisions for securing that even the most basic ground rule, that ministers should not deceive Parliament, is complied with, as the Ponting case showed. The *Questions of Procedure* that govern ministers and the Osmotherly Rules according to which civil servants operate when appearing before select committees, pay only lip-service to the accountability of the Executive to Parliament and give more attention to the situations in which duties of accountability do not arise. Although it is not suggested that ministerial accountability could or should be enforced through the courts, other devices, such as the requirement for the publication of ground rules which would expose them to criticism and ministers too if they were not obeyed, should have an effect in practice in putting government under pressure to accept its accountability to Parliament. In this way again, openness has an important role to play in affecting the political process and thus enhancing accountability.

Secrecy surrounds the substance of what government does as much as the ground rules according to which it operates; and this secrecy shields government from accountability to Parliament, to the public at large and to special publics – consumers of government services, the press and special interest groups. But secrecy poses problems beyond the realms of political and public accountability. Where government invokes public interest immunity in court, secrecy also protects it from legal accountablity. Hence the case for improved rights of access to official information is based on the need to improve all forms of accountability.

The arguments against such rights of access are expressed largely in terms of protecting citizens from intrusions in their privacy (a claim that is persuasive in many instances) and in promoting effectiveness (a claim that requires careful examination, since it is all too often an euphemistic way of claiming immunity from accountability).

The public accountability of government

The public accountability of government is supposed to secure, among other things, that it is responsive to and therefore effective in meeting, the needs of those affected by its actions. In this context, it has to be acknowledged that if government is too much exposed to pressures to meet the demands of powerful consumers or would-be consumers of its services, then the public interest may fall victim to private interests. Again a balance has to be found between the two sets of interests. This requires openness about the operation of government and about the workings of private interests, and the exposure of both to public comment and criticism and a degree of legal control. The recognition of the need to prevent the 'capture' of government by private interests forms part of the case for disclosure of interests by MPs (and for publication by private bodies of information about their contributions to political parties and other political causes). The increased democratic and public legitimacy of Parliament and of government that would result from a reformed electoral system, ought also to increase the authority of government to resist pressures from special interests at the expense of the public interest.

The centralized nature of the system of government makes for the adoption of policies that are often unresponsive to the needs of those living away from the metropolis. And the fact that there is a north–south divide, both in the prosperity of the UK and in the levels of support for the two main parties, provides backing for the view that the government in London has not been sensitive to the needs of the north of the country since the late 1960s, when the Royal Commission on the Constitution was established in response to this problem.

Of course, no system of government is ideally responsive and the reaction of some might be that if centralization is a problem, it is not one that requires institutional or political reform: a wise government will recognize the claims of the regions and nations of the UK and if the electorate in some regions and nations feels that a government is neglecting their needs, then those voters can elect another government at the next opportunity.

This is the sort of response that is liable to be made to most complaints about the operation of the system. Often the chance to elect another party or set of parties to power will provide sufficient redress for those who are discontented with things as they are. But this is not by any means always the case, and in the case of the nations and regions of the UK it is suggested, the problem does require an institutional solution. The opportunity to elect another government has not provided a real outlet for the aspirations of the Scots in practice in the 1980s. Although Labour is by far the strongest party in the country, with only some 10 percent of the population of the UK, their votes have relatively little impact on the colour of the flag metaphorically flown in Whitehall.

A sense that centralization is a sufficiently serious problem to call for a solution is clear in the pressures from Scotland for a Parliament for that country. The case for decentralization to national assemblies or parliaments in Scotland, Wales and Northern Ireland, and to regional assemblies in England is a response to this sense. For Scotland and Wales, the case may also be based on the internationally recognized right to self-determination, but it has to be said that it is not yet clear that this is a right which the people of those countries are claiming, and it is not generally regarded as a right that ought to be thrust upon people against their will.

Overload

Another aspect of the case for decentralization is the problem of overload at the centre. This is undoubtedly a factor that has contributed to ineffectiveness in government's ability to devise policies for the whole country over the full range of state activity. There are many elements in the loads which ministers bear – departmental responsibilities for policy and administration, constituency work, and responsibility for Cabinet decisions and the overall strategy of government. That this is a problem that should be tackled has been recognized in some of the reforms of the civil service, especially *The Next Steps* programme, which will remove responsibility for large areas of administration from ministers. But they are clinging to their accountability to Parliament for these agencies and therefore forfeiting some of the benefits that should flow to them from the reduction in their workloads. Here again, the place of the doctrines of ministerial responsibility in thinking about the constitution provides obstacles against reform: what needs to be appreciated is that political accountability, especially in the form of ministerial responsibility, is not and never has been very effective and that other techniques for securing accountability – legal, administrative and public – have an important potential for enhancing the effectiveness of the system and reducing ministerial overload at the same time.

Overload could also be reduced by the decentralization of large parts of government business to national and regional assemblies, and this consideration forms an important part of the case for this reform. If such a system were instituted, central government could concentrate on complex areas such as economic and fiscal policy, relations with the European Community, foreign affairs, defence, environmental and national transport policy, equalization between the nations and regions, and the maintenance and definition of minimum standards of public service and welfare benefits throughout the UK.

The accountability of local government

Local government, too, suffers from poor accountability to its electorate and the consumers of its services. Its weak accountability to its voters is in part due to the longstanding problem of low turn outs in local elections. But we must ask why the turn out in those elections is low. There are a range of explanations. One is that many voters are little affected by what their local authorities do and see no benefit in voting as long as their rubbish is collected and streets swept and lit. But some voters who do see the importance of local services have little faith in the capabilities of local authorities or in their willingness to take account of the wishes of the electors and despair of being able to influence this by voting. This is a comment on the operation of the electoral system in local government, since in many areas one party has a safe majority and is unlikely to be ousted in an election. (This problem can be exaggerated and there have been dramatic examples of solid majorities being overturned.) But the working of the electoral system would alter if a system of election by single transferable vote were introduced in local government, for then local parties would have to be more responsive to their voters' wishes.

To an extent, the unwillingness of voters to turn out in local elections is a reflection on the undoubtedly poor quality of some local government; but this itself may be explained by the fact that the status of local government is not such as to attract into its service councillors of high calibre. The deterioration in the status of local government over the last two decades or so is attributable in large part to reductions in the freedom of action of local government in deciding how its services should be delivered and what its priorities should be; its financial autonomy has also been progressively eroded by government-imposed limitations on its spending levels and reductions in its ability to raise what sums it thinks appropriate for local sources, first the rates and now the community charge. What has happened in the last decade or so is that the local government's accountability to its electors has been replaced by political accountability to government. This has added to the problems of centralization.

In this respect, local government has been victim of a vicious circle: the poor quality of some local authority services has been due in part to its lack of accountability to its voters. The response of the Conservative government in the 1980s was not to enhance this accountability through electoral reform, but to reduce its freedom of action. This in turn lowered its status, so that it appeared to be less deserving of the freedoms and autonomy that it demanded. And this in turn discourages voters to turn out and further undermines public accountability. On the other hand, the accountability of local authorities has been increased to its consumers in a range of important ways, but these have for the most part depoliticized many of its functions. The response of government in the 1980s in this and other fields was to depoliticize activity by transferring functions to market or surrogate market forces, and to regulate political activity in local government closely. It has been to smother rather than to foster the political process.

The role of the courts

Legal accountability is an important aspect of the range of accountability mechanisms. This has been an area neglected by Parliament and government over the years. In many respects, it is weaker in the UK than in other comparable countries. This is because our courts lack both the constitutional legitimacy and the necessary principles and criteria against which to impose legal accountability.

This is an aspect of the problem of the 'unprincipled constitution' to adapt David Marquand's phrase. Parliament has never defined the role of the courts in the constitution, and so the judges have sought to define it for themselves. While they have no particular claim in democratic terms to do so, and they are not publicly or politically accountable for how they have done it, it is suggested that it is better that they should have a role defined by themselves than no role at all. It is always open to Parliament to redefine that role if it wishes to do so. But here the problem of neglect of the legal system has been acute, since Parliament and successive governments have shied away from defining the role of the judges in imposing legal accountability and have not, for example, codified the grounds for judicial review.

Since the relationship between the courts and government has developed in a piecemeal way, the rules that the courts apply in judicial review cases are in many respects unclear and unpredictable. In particular, the judges' problems derive from the absence of a written Constitution that would articulate what was expected of government, and a Bill of Rights which would supply substantive criteria against which the acts of government could be measured and adjudicated upon.

In this respect and in others, administrative law in the UK is weak. But administrative law is not only about legal accountability and judicial review; it is also about openness, explicit codes of conduct and ground rules, internal review procedures, audit, ombudsmen, and a whole range of procedures that together belong under our fourth form of accountability – administrative. This has an important role not only in promoting efficiency and effectiveness, to which we return shortly, but also in promoting responsiveness, transparency, responsibility in government. Even if public and political accountability were strengthened through the introduction of a system of proportional representation and public rights of access to official information, accountability would not be adequate. Even if the legal system were also reformed, with the grounds for judicial review codified, the independence of the judiciary secured, a Ministry of Justice given responsibility for the system, individual citizens and consumer groups would not be sufficiently protected. A far more sophisticated system of administrative law would be required for those problems to be solved.

Improving efficiency and effectiveness

Efficiency and effectiveness in government cannot be guaranteed. But the view expressed by some that the way to secure better government is simply to vote for another party suggests that there is nothing wrong with the system, only with the people who operate it. There is, however, a strong case for saying that the system itself contributes to the problem. The acute overload from which ministers suffer makes it hard for them to give policy the attention that it deserves. The overload extends to the actual volume of work for which they are responsible and to the political pressures to which they are subject from within government and party and from pressure groups and lobbyists. Hence there have been repeated adjustments or reversals of policy to take account of difficulties that ministers should have anticipated. This point is well illustrated by the case of local government legislation, which has been repeatedly repealed and revised in the last decade or so in ways that could have been avoided if policy work had been done properly in the first place.

The Cabinet system is supposed to involve collective decision making, and this should promote good government. The theory is that if all ministers in the Cabinet are responsible for policy, then they should all take an interest in it; and discussion in Cabinet should allow for doubts to be expressed and taken into account and a better decision to emerge from this process. Not only should individual decisions on policy be better and more effective under such a system, but government policy overall should be more coherent and consistent – it should have a sense of direction and strategy.

In practice, as experience under Mrs Thatcher in the 1980s indicated, the Cabinet system is very flexible, and collective decision making is not a necessary element of Cabinet government. The introduction of a more presidential style of government in the Thatcher years was made possible partly by the secrecy surrounding the system, so that the ground rules could be changed without public accountability being engaged. And it is by no means clear that the relative lack of accountability for the way in which the system operated made for more effective policies emerging from Cabinet in those years – the opposite is more likely to have been the case.

Part of the problem over the effectiveness of government strategy arises from the under-resourcing of the system. Neither the Cabinet as a whole nor ministers individually have the support of staff that could enable them to take a strategic view of government policy, or indeed of the policy in their own departments. Although some ministers have political advisers, these are for the most part small in number. Nor does the Cabinet as a whole have a substantial support staff when it comes to matters of strategy. The Prime Minister has a Policy Unit, but this is no substitute for support for the Cabinet as a body. Here, as in many areas, government in the UK is conducted on a shoestring. The case for improving the institutional arrangements for dealing with this problem, whether through a Cabinet Department with this responsibility or some other arrangement, is strong.

Problems over the policy-making process, however, are not confined to government. They often originate in the quality of work done by opposition parties preparing for government. The political parties are hindered in preparing realistic policies that could succeed by their lack of resources. They lack not only information, but the money and the staff necessary to enable them to research alternative policies thoroughly and produce realistic alternatives. They are also limited in their ability to make informed and constructive criticisms of the government, and the lack of such responses to government makes it less pressing for government to react to parliamentary criticism from the opposition by reviewing its policies. This problem is also contributed to by the balance of the parties in Parliament as referred to above.

Management problems

The administration of government policy also has its faults. The efforts of the civil service and outposts of government – the nationalized industries, the NHS and a range of quangos – have been hindered over the years by political meddling by ministers. In this context, the contrast between two forms of political accountability – ministerial and parliamentary – and their impact on efficiency and effectiveness is significant. The power of ministers to call bodies to account lays itself open to be abused for partisan party political or short-term advantage. The right of parliamentary select committees to call the civil service and other administrative bodies to account is not in general used as a vehicle for partisanship or short-term goals, and is more likely to be directed at promoting the general public interest. On the other hand, the authority of government could be undermined if it were felt that the administration, the civil service, owed duties to Parliament as well as or in place of their duties to their ministers, as has sometimes been suggested, especially after the experiences of the Ponting and Westland affairs in the 1980s. But here a distinction may be made between the civil servant's duty of obedience, which should surely be owed to the minister, subject to safeguards against abuse, and the duty to account, explain and inform, which should surely be owed both to ministers and to Parliament (and indeed to the courts and to administrative bodies), subject again to safeguards that would protect civil servants and other administrators from party political pressures.

Civil servants are shielded from political and public accountability and ministers tend not to be particularly interested in efficiency and effectiveness, and so the effectiveness of administration has been neglected over the years. The introduction of executive agencies is therefore an important innovation and one which, properly managed and protected from ministerial meddling by a regime of openness, should improve the quality of administration, whatever party is in power.

Central–local relations

The inefficiencies and ineffectiveness of many local authorities have been contributed to by the problems of accountability referred to above. Local government has also suffered from underfunding by central government which, taken with the reduction of freedom to raise revenue from the rates and now the community charge, has meant that many local government services are of poor quality. This is not to say that local government does not have its own problems of inefficiency, but here again problems of accountability have made it difficult for complaints about inefficiency to be met with improvements in services. To meet this problem, the freedom of local government to raise revenue needs to be restored with suitable safeguards for taxpayers and consumers of services in the form of improved electoral and administrative accountability.

Hence accountability and effectiveness are closely connected to one another, and the principal respect in which the two may be incompatible is where there is scope for elected politicians – ministers in central government, majority party groups in local government – to use their power over their administrations in the name of political accountability in ways that undermine the effectiveness of that administration. Ways need to be found to counter this tendency and at the same time to improve the public, legal and administrative accountability of administration.

Citizenship in the United Kingdom

Out third theme has been the quest for the elements in a mature, active status and practice of citizenship in the conditions of the UK in the late years of the twentieth century. As we have seen, many of what should be the civil, political and social rights that make up the status of citizens are lacking in our system. Not only does the law not recognize rights as such, only liberties, the government and the courts have sanctioned the erosion of important liberties in the last decade or so. This has been particularly marked in the areas of freedom of expression (especially of the media) and peaceful assembly (especially in industrial disputes). The former may be put down in large part to the excessively secretive ethos of government. In both areas, there have been demonstrations of intolerant, authoritarian attitudes on the part of government, local authorities and the courts to dissidents and to criticism of government policy.

Even the political right to vote has been devalued in recent years. This has resulted partly from government policy, such as the introduction of the community charge, which has built into it a disincentive to register to vote; but it has also been a side-effect of social changes, which have altered the distribution and level of support for the two main political parties and thus the operation of the electoral system. Election results have increasingly under-rated the support for smaller parties with evenly distributed support, so that the balance of the parties in the House of Commons does not fairly represent the support for different parties, interests and views in the electorate. Thus the political rights of citizenship have suffered serious erosion.

Social rights, too, have declined to the point where large numbers of people live in such poverty that they are unable to participate in the mainstream of national life or even of the life of local and functional communities. The senses of belonging to the community and of national cohesion which are essential to citizenship are also damaged by discrimination against ethnic and other minorities and against women. The trend in the 1980s to reduce public expenditure and to encourage voluntary work contributed to the exclusion of many citizens through poverty from the community, since the objective in encouraging active citizenship was not that it should serve as an addition to public provision of essential social services, but often as a substitute for them. Hence 'active citizenship' has to some extent superseded the citizenship of entitlement of the post-war period, but not in a way that adequately secures the social rights of those in need. Voluntary work in the community does have the effect of cementing community ties between the givers and the recipients of these services, but this cannot of itself justify the erosion of social rights that has taken place.

Citizenship is not only about voluntary action in the community and the social, civil and political entitlements referred to above. It is also about the participation of citizens in the political process, their role in holding government to account. Here the trend in the 1980s has been to depoliticize activity in the community and to discourage political activity such as membership of pressure groups. This has further undermined the idea of citizenship as a political status, and thus the public accountability of government.

Towards constitutional reform

It has been in response to the perceived need for improvements in the arrangements for encouraging accountability, effectiveness and citizenship that many of the proposals for constitutional reform that have been considered here have been put forward. But in considering these proposals and our reaction to them, we have to bear in mind the complexity and subtlety of the UK's system of government. The system is far from perfect, but it has developed incrementally over a period of many centuries and is finely balanced. The different aspects of it are closely intertwined with one another. And so, it is suggested, no single measure can deal with all, or even most, of the areas that are in need of reform. On the other hand, the system is sufficiently flexible to be able to accommodate a series of individual reforming measures; it is not essential to introduce a whole programme of reform in one fell swoop through a new constitutional settlement or a written Constitution. Indeed, it is part of the argument in this book that it would be unwise to do so.

How, then, can the defects in the system that have been briefly summarized above and discussed at greater length in previous chapters be remedied? The strategy may be seen as two-fold involving both institutional and political reform.

Institutional reform

A whole range of institutional reforms is possible to improve accountability, effectiveness and citizenship and, although it is not my aim to put forward a detailed programme, the guiding principles may be set out. As far as Parliament is concerned, some further procedural reforms are desirable, especially in relation to the powers of the select committees, but it would be a mistake to place too much faith in this sort of reform. The future of the second chamber must depend on what other reforms are introduced, but if a scheme of regional and national decentralization were introduced, then the second chamber could have an important role in representing the interests of the nations and regions. It could also have a role in representing interests that are not and could never be represented in the House of Commons, but not, it is suggested, through a machinery for the election of members by groups such as trade unions, academics or others. Instead, the procedure for appointment of life peers could be rationalized and their tenure, even titles, reformed, so as to allow for representation of these interests in the second chamber.

The second chamber also has a potential role as constitutional watchdog, which the House of Lords has occasionally taken upon itself, and which could and should be developed if important reforms such as the introduction of a Bill of Rights and decentralization were introduced. The second chamber could be given delaying or veto powers where such measures were threatened with repeal or alteration by the Commons.

The question of decentralization is one of the most difficult in the current debates about institutional reform. The case is largely put as a response to pressures coming from Scotland, based on the right to self-determination. Decentralization to the regions of England cannot be based on that argument, and is proposed partly to avoid a lopsided arrangement that would emerge from decentralization to Scotland alone, partly to reduce the overload on central government and partly to encourage a more active political culture and therefore more effective government of the regions. Overload at the centre could be reduced by other measures, such as executive agencies being set up in the civil service, and the increase in policy strategy back-up for the Cabinet considered earlier. But these measures could not deal with the problem of unresponsiveness. So the case for national and regional government is not as strong as the case for other reforms, particularly since there is at present not strong pressure from the regions or from Wales for the decentralization of power, and devolution to Northern Ireland would be unworkable if it did not command the consent of both communities there. There could be disadvantages in decentralization which would need to be set off against the advantages. Decentralization, whether to Scotland alone or to Wales and the regions as well, could provide the conditions for conflict between the centre and the regions and nations over a wide range of issues (in particular finance) and inequalities in powers (e.g. legislative and revenue raising) between different nations and regions, which could be damaging to the sense of national community.

Local government's role must depend to some extent on whether decentralization is introduced. If it were, then there would be a strong case for establishing a single tier of local government, perhaps according to the wishes of national and regional parliaments. But a view is gaining ground that a single-tier local government system might in any event be better, more effective and more transparent than the present two-tier system that prevails in most of the country. There is also a strong case for giving back to local government freedom to raise revenue without the threat of 'capping' by Whitehall. But here the issue of the political accountability of local government enters into the picture, and so the political process and institutional reform are again interdependent. The case for introducing the single transferable vote in local government and for encouraging the organization of authorities into neighbourhood committees is based on recognition of the need to increase the accountability and responsiveness of local government to its electors and consumers, rather than to central government, and thereby also setting in place structures that should promote efficiency and effectiveness.

Reform of the political process

As suggested earlier, institutional reform alone cannot achieve the necessary improvements in the accountability and effectiveness of government and the status and practice of citizenship. The political process needs to be revitalized with the relationship of dominance between government and Parliament adjusted in favour of the latter and the encouragement of political involvement of the citizenry. This cannot happen for so long as the present electoral system is retained, and this is one of the strongest arguments for the introduction of the single transferable vote for elections to the House of Commons.

But, as suggested earlier, proportional representation should not be regarded as the panacea for the problem of accountability. First, it would not improve administrative or legal accountability. Nor would it improve the accountability of government and the civil service to particular groups affected by their actions. And it would not itself give members of the House of Commons all of the resources needed to impose political accountability on government. Further reforms to this end would have to include a public right of access to official information and rights to be consulted on matters of policy. But here the question arises whether the rights of citizens to participate in government decisions and their scrutiny can be secured in a system as centralized as ours. The question of decentralization is, again, intimately mixed in with that of the accountability of government to its consumers.

As suggested in Chapter 2, accountability and effectiveness are not always compatible, but as a general rule public accountability and accountability to Parliament (as opposed to government) may be expected to promote efficiency and effectiveness. Of the four main processes of accountability (political, public, legal and administrative) however, administrative processes are particularly designed to promote effectiveness. Here administrative law is currently weak and it is suggested there is a need to strengthen it in a range of ways. Again it would be misleading to suggest that any one reform would solve the problem. The drawing up and publication of codes of good administrative practice, the codification of the grounds for judicial review, the hiving off of functions to agencies governed by framework documents, the development of forms of effectiveness and value for money audit, the introduction of 'performance agreements' between executive agencies and departments and of contracts stipulating standards in local government, the introduction of various forms of self-government and consumer choice, all have a contribution to make to improving effectiveness.

Finally, the issue of a Bill of Rights. The rights of citizens both to respect for their private lives and to participate in the political process through the exercise of the right to free speech, to associate and to demonstrate peacefully have all been eroded in the last decade and more; the case for a Bill of Rights, then, rests both on the need to protect and enhance the status of citizenship and on securing the public accountability of government through the freedom of the media and the activities of citizens. The weakness of the protection for these rights under the present system is a result of a range of factors: the fact that governments can rely on parliamentary majorities to push through measures that interfere with civil and political rights; the fact that the courts have no fixed priorities when called upon to make difficult decisions between the interests of the state and of individuals. The case against a Bill of Rights is largely founded on mistrust of the judges, but the very existence of such a Bill should provide the courts with the sense of priorities and principles which the present system does not provide.

Another objection, that it is undemocratic for Parliament to be prevented by a Bill of Rights from legislating as it wishes, is demonstrably ill-founded since democracy does not mean majoritarianism, and in any event the provisions of a Bill of Rights which protect free speech and freedom of association are designed to give protection to the democratic political process – it cannot be undemocratic to prevent interference with such measures.

Given that a model Bill of Rights is available in the form of the European Convention on Human Rights, which could be improved if thought necessary by the addition of some elements of the International Covenant, there should be a ready political consensus on the content of such a Charter once agreement in principle on the need for a Bill of Rights was achieved. Since the ECHR already binds the government of the UK in international law, the issues about entrenchment that would arise if another model were adopted can be avoided by incorporation of the Convention.

But again, the adoption of a Bill of Rights could not alone provide a panacea for the ills of the constitution: its existence would transform the political process by making the citizenry more aware of its role and importance and the attitudes of politicians and administrators would likewise change for the better. But the measure would not deal with the problems of a dominant executive, centralization, poor policy making and so on, from which the system suffers.

Conclusions

What is required, then, is a wider consciousness of the defects of the system as it operates at present and an appreciation of the complexities of the process of reform. The political parties and campaigning groups such as Charter 88 have an important role to play in securing that these issues receive the attention that they deserve. The need to improve accountability, effectiveness and citizenship ought not to divide the political parties, if only they could appreciate the nature of the arguments for them. While it is understandable that a party in power will resent attempts to make it more accountable, parties in opposition recognize that need. Our politicians should have the commitment and courage to secure that necessary reforms are undertaken, without which the sad history of policy failures of the post-war years is likely to continue. While a vital, effective, accountable political system and a mature citizenry cannot guarantee successful government, a system that lacks those three is doomed to failure.

Appendix: The European Convention for the Protection of Human Rights and Fundamental Freedoms

Article 1
The High Contracting Parties shall secure to everyone within their jurisdiction the rights and freedoms defined in Section 1 of this Convention.

SECTION 1

Article 2
1. Everyone's right to life shall be protected by law. No one shall be deprived of his life intentionally save in the execution of a sentence of a court following his conviction of a crime for which this penalty is provided by law.
2. Deprivation of life shall not be regarded as inflicted in contravention of this Article when it results from the use of force which is no more than absolutely necessary:
   (a) in defence of any person from unlawful violence;
   (b) in order to effect a lawful arrest or to prevent the escape of a person lawfully detained;
   (c) in action lawfully taken for the purpose of quelling a riot or insurrection.

Article 3
No one shall be subjected to torture or to inhuman or degrading treatment or punishment.

Article 4
1. No one shall be held in slavery or servitude.
2. No one shall be required to perform forced or compulsory labour.
3. For the purpose of this Article the term 'forced or compulsory labour' shall not include:

(a) any work required to be done in the ordinary course of detention imposed according to the provisions of Article 5 of this Convention or during conditional release from such detention;
(b) any service of a military character or, in case of conscientious objectors in countries where they are recognized, service exacted instead of compulsory military service;
(c) any service exacted in case of an emergency or calamity threatening the life or well-being of the community;
(d) any work or service which forms part of normal civic obligations.

Article 5
1. Everyone has the right to liberty and security of person. No one shall be deprived of his liberty save in the following cases and in accordance with a procedure prescribed by law:
   (a) the lawful detention of a person after conviction by a competent court;
   (b) the lawful arrest or detention of a person for noncompliance with the lawful order of a court or in order to secure the fulfilment of any obligation prescribed by law;
   (c) the lawful arrest or detention of a person effected for the purpose of bringing him before the competent legal authority on reasonable suspicion of having committed an offence or when it is reasonably considered necessary to prevent his committing an offence or fleeing after having done so;
   (d) the detention of a minor by lawful order for the purpose of educational supervision or his lawful detention for the purpose of bringing him before the competent legal authority;
   (e) the lawful detention of persons for the prevention of the spreading of infectious diseases, of persons of unsound mind, alcoholics or drug addicts, or vagrants;
   (f) the lawful arrest or detention of a person to prevent his effecting an unauthorized entry into the country or of a person against whom action is being taken with a view to deportation or extradition.
2. Everyone who is arrested shall be informed promptly, in a language which he understands, of the reasons for his arrest and of any charge against him.
3. Everyone arrested or detained in accordance with the provisions of paragraph 1 (c) of this Article shall be brought promptly before a judge or other officer authorized by law to exercise judicial power and shall be entitled to trial within a reasonable time or to release pending trial. Release may be conditioned by guarantees to appear for trial.
4. Everyone who is deprived of his liberty by arrest or detention shall be entitled to take proceedings by which the lawfulness of his detention shall be decided speedily by a court and his release ordered if the detention is now lawful.
5. Everyone who has been the victim of arrest or detention in contravention of the provisions of this Article shall have an enforceable right to compensation.

Article 6
1. In the determination of his civil rights and obligations or of any criminal charge against him, everyone is entitled to a fair and public hearing within a reasonable time by an independent and impartial tribunal established by law. Judgement shall be pronounced publicly but the press and public may be excluded from all or part of the trial in the interest of morals, public order or national security in a democratic society, where the interest of juveniles or the protection of the private life of the parties so require, or to the extent strictly necessary in the opinion of the court in special circumstances where publicity would prejudice the interests of justice.

2. Everyone charged with a criminal offence shall be presumed innocent until proved guilty according to law.
3. Everyone charged with a criminal offence has the following minimum rights:
   (a) to be informed promptly, in a language which he understands and in detail, of the nature and cause of the accusation against him;
   (b) to have adequate time and facilities for the preparation of his defence;
   (c) to defend himself in person or through legal assistance of his own choosing or, if he has not sufficient means to pay for legal assistance, to be given it free when the interests of justice so require;
   (d) to examine or have examined witnesses against him and to obtain the attendance and examination of witnesses on his behalf under the same conditions as witnesses against him;
   (e) to have the free assistance of an interpreter if he cannot understand or speak the language used in court.

Article 7
1. No one shall be held guilty of any criminal offence on account of any act or omission which did not constitute a criminal offence under national or international law at the time when it was committed. Nor shall a heavier penalty be imposed than the one that was applicable at the time the criminal offence was committed.
2. This Article shall not prejudice the trial and punishment of any person for any act or omission which, at the time when it was committed, was criminal according to the general principles of law recognized by civilized nations.

Article 8
1. Everyone has the right to respect for his private and family life, his home and his correspondence.
2. There shall be no interference by a public authority with the exercise of this right except such as is in accordance with the law and is necessary in a democratic society in the interests of national security, public safety or the economic well-being of the country, for the prevention of disorder or crime, for the protection of health or morals, or for the protection of the rights and freedoms of others.

Article 9
1. Everyone has the right to freedom of thought, conscience and religion: this right includes freedom to change his religion or belief, and freedom, either alone or in community with others and in public or private, to manifest his religion or belief, in worship, teaching, practice and observance.
2. Freedom to manifest one's religion or beliefs shall be subject only to such limitations as are prescribed by law and are necessary in a democratic society in the interests of public safety, for the protection of public order, health or morals, or for the protection of the rights and freedoms of others.

Article 10
1. Everyone has the right to freedom of expression. This right shall include freedom to hold opinions and to receive and impart information and ideas without interference by public authority and regardless of frontiers. This Article shall not prevent States from requiring the licensing of broadcasting, television or cinema enterprises.

2. The exercise of these freedoms, since it carries with it duties and responsibilities, may be subject to such formalities, conditions, restrictions or penalties as are prescribed by law and are necessary in a democratic society in the interests of national security, territorial integrity or public safety, for the prevention of disorder or crime, for the protection of health or morals, for the protection of the reputation or rights of others, for preventing the disclosure of information received in confidence, or for maintaining the authority and impartiality of the judiciary.

Article 11

1. Everyone has the right to freedom of peaceful assembly and to freedom of association with others, including the right to form and to join trade unions for the protection of his interests.
2. No restrictions shall be placed on the exercise of these rights other than such as are prescribed by law and are necessary in a democratic society in the interests of national security or public safety, for the prevention of disorder or crime, for the protection of health or morals or for the protection of the rights and freedoms of others. This Article shall not prevent the imposition of lawful restrictions on the exercise of these rights by members of the armed forces, of the police or of the administration of the State.

Article 12

Men and women of marriageable age have the right to marry and to found a family, according to the national laws governing the exercise of this right.

Article 13

Everyone whose rights and freedoms as set forth in this Convention are violated shall have an effective remedy before a national authority notwithstanding that the violation has been committed by persons acting in an official capacity.

Article 14

The enjoyment of the rights and freedoms set forth in this Convention shall be secured without discrimination on any ground such as sex, race, colour, language, religion, political or other opinion, national or social origin, association with a national minority, property, birth or other status.

Article 15

1. In time of war or other public emergency threatening the life of the nation any High Contracting Party may take measures derogating from its obligations under this Convention to the extent strictly required by the exigencies of the situation, provided that such measures are not inconsistent with its other obligations under international law.
2. No derogation from Article 2, except in respect of deaths resulting from lawful acts of war, or from Articles 3, 4 (paragraph 1) and 7 shall be made under this provision.
3. Any High Contracting Party availing itself of this right of derogation shall keep the Secretary-General of the Council of Europe fully informed of the measures which it has taken and the reasons therefor. It shall also inform the Secretary-General of the Council of Europe when such measures have ceased to operate and the provisions of the Convention are again being fully executed.

Article 16

Nothing in Articles 10, 11 and 14 shall be regarded as preventing the High Contracting Parties from imposing restrictions on the political activity of aliens.

Article 17
Nothing in this Convention may be interpreted as implying for any State, group or person any right to engage in any activity or perform any act aimed at the destruction of any of the rights and freedoms set forth herein or at their limitation to a greater extent than is provided for in the Convention.

Article 18
The restrictions permitted under this Convention to the said rights and freedoms shall not be applied for any purpose other than those for which they have been prescribed.

PROTOCOL 1: ENFORCEMENT OF CERTAIN RIGHTS AND FREEDOMS NOT INCLUDED IN SECTION I OF THE CONVENTION

The Governments signatory hereto, being Members of the Council of Europe.

Being resolved to take steps to ensure the collective enforcement of certain rights and freedoms other than those already included in Section I of the Convention for the Protection of Human Rights and Fundamental Freedoms signed at Rome on 4 November 1950 (hereinafter referred to as 'the Convention').

Have agreed as follows:

Article 1
Every natural or legal person is entitled to the peaceful enjoyment of his possessions. No one shall be deprived of his possessions except in the public interest and subject to the conditions provided for by law and by the general principles of international law.

The preceding provisions shall not, however, in any way impair the right of a State to enforce such laws as it deems necessary to control the use of property in accordance with the general interest or to secure the payment of taxes or other contributions or penalties.

Article 2
No person shall be denied the right to education. In the exercise of any functions which it assumes in relation to education and to teaching, the State shall respect the right of parents to ensure such education and teaching in conformity with their own religious and philosophical convictions.

Article 3
The High Contracting Parties undertake to hold free elections at reasonable intervals by secret ballot, under conditions which will ensure the free expression of the opinion of the people in the choice of the legislature.

PROTOCOL 4: PROTECTING CERTAIN ADDITIONAL RIGHTS

The Governments signatory hereto, being Members of the Council of Europe.

Being resolved to take steps to ensure the collective enforcement of certain rights and freedoms other than those already included in Section I of the Convention for the Protection of Human Rights and Fundamental Freedoms signed at Rome on 4 November 1950 (hereinafter referred to as 'the Convention') and in Articles 1 to 3 of the First Protocol to the Convention, signed at Paris on 20 March 1952.

Have agreed as follows:

Article 1
No one shall be deprived of his liberty merely on the ground of inability to fulfil a contractual obligation.

Article 2
1. Everyone lawfully within the territory of a State shall, within that territory, have the right to liberty of movement and freedom to choose his residence.
2. Everyone shall be free to leave any country, including his own.
3. No restrictions shall be placed on the exercise of these rights other than such as are in accordance with law and are necessary in a democratic society in the interests of national security or public safety, for the maintenance of 'ordre public', for the prevention of crime or for the protection of the rights and freedoms of others.
4. The rights set forth in paragraph 1 may also be subject, in particular areas, to restrictions imposed in accordance with law and justified by the public interest in a democratic society.

Article 3
1. No one shall be expelled, by means either of an individual or of a collective measure, from the territory of the State of which he is a national.
2. No one shall be deprived of the right to enter the territory of the State of which he is a national.

Article 4
Collective explusion of aliens is prohibited.

References

Aglietta, M. (1979). *A Theory of Capitalist Regulation*. London, New Left Books.

Alexander, E. R. (1989). The Canadian Charter of Rights and Freedoms in the Supreme Court of Canada. *Law Quarterly Review*, 105, 561–81.

Amery, L. S. (1947). *Thoughts on the Constitution*. Oxford, Oxford University Press.

Amnesty International (1991). *United Kingdom Human Rights Concerns*. London, Amnesty International.

Ancram, M. (n.d.). *Devolution – Why Not*. London, Aims of Industry.

Armstrong, H. (1989). Community regional policy. In Lodge, J. (ed.), *The European Community and the Challenge of the Future*. London, Pinter, pp. 167–85.

Armstrong, Sir Robert (1985). *The Duties and Responsibilities of Civil Servants in Relation to Ministers: Note by the Head of the Home Civil Service*, 1985, HC *Official Report* vol. 74, 1984–85. London, HMSO.

Ashdown, P. (1989). *Citizens' Britain*. London, Fourth Estate.

Association of Community Health Councils (1991). *Health and Welfare: A Review of Health Inequalities in the United Kingdom*. London, Association of Community Health Councils.

Association of District Councils (1987). *Closer to the People*. London, Association of District Councils.

Audit Commission (1991). *Response to the Government's Consultation Paper 'A New Tax for Local Government'*. London, Audit Commission.

Austin, R. (1986). Public order prophylactics. *Current Legal Problems*, 1986, 227–36.

Austin, R. (1989). Freedom of information: The legal impact. In Jowell, J. and Oliver, D. (eds), *The Changing Constitution*, 2nd edn. Oxford, Clarendon Press, pp. 409–50.

Austin, R. (1990). The Spycatcher saga: Public secrecy from private rights. In Kingsford-Smith, D. and Oliver, D. (eds), *Economical with the Truth: The Law and the Media in a Democratic Society*. Oxford, ESC, pp. 27–42.

Bagehot, W. (1963). *The English Constitution*. Glasgow, Fontana/Collins.

Barry, B. (1967). The public interest. In Quinton, A. (ed.), *Political Philosophy*. Oxford, Oxford University Press, pp. 112–26.

Beer, S. (1982a). *Modern British Politics*. London, Faber and Faber.

Beer, S. (1982b). *Britain Against Itself*. London, Faber and Faber.

Bell, J. (1983). *Policy Arguments in Judicial Decisions*. Oxford, Clarendon Press.

Benn, S. I. (1978). Human rights – for whom and for what. In Kamenka, E. (ed.), *Human Rights*. London, Edward Arnold, pp. 59–73.

Benn, T. (1981). *Arguments for Democracy*. Harmondsworth, Penguin.

Benn, T. (1991). *Commonwealth of Britain Bill*. London, HMSO.

Bew, P. and Patterson, H. (1985). *The British State and the Ulster Crisis from Wilson to Thatcher*. London, Verso.

Birkinshaw, P. (1985). *Grievances, Remedies and the State*. London, Sweet and Maxwell.

Birkinshaw, P. (1988a). *Freedom of Information: The Law, the Practice and the Ideal*. London, Weidenfeld.

Birkinshaw, P. (1988b). Open government – local government style. *Public Policy and Administration*, 1988, 46–55.

Birkinshaw, P. (1990a). *Reforming the Secret State*. Milton Keynes, Open University Press.

Birkinshaw, P. (1990b). *Government and Information*. London, Butterworth.

Blackburn, R. (1989). Parliamentary opinion on a new Bill of Rights. *Political Quarterly*, 60, 469–80.

Blackstone (1825). *Commentaries on the Laws of England*, 16th edn. London, J. Butterworth.

Bloch, A. (1991). *The Community Charge in England and Wales: Local Authority Experience*. York, Joseph Rowntree Foundation.

Blunkett, D. (1981). Towards a socialist social policy. *Local Government Policy Making*. Birmingham, University of Birmingham.

Blunkett, D. and Green G. (1984). *Building from the Bottom*. London, Fabian Society.

Bogdanor, V. (1979). *Devolution*. Oxford, Oxford University Press.

Bogdanor, V. (1981). *The People and the Party System: The Referendum and Electoral Reform in British Politics*. Cambridge, Cambridge University Press.

Boyle, A. (1979). *The Climate of Treason*. London, Hutchinson.

Bradley, A. W. (1989). The sovereignty of Parliament – in perpetuity? In Jowell, J. and Oliver, D. (eds), *The Changing Constitution*, 2nd edn. Oxford, Clarendon Press, pp. 25–52.

Brazier, R. (1988). *Constitutional Practice*. Oxford, Clarendon Press.

Brazier, R, (1989). Government and law: Ministerial responsibility for legal affairs. *Public Law*, 64–94.

Brazier, R. (ed.) (1990). *Constitutional Texts*. Oxford, Clarendon Press.

Brennan, W. (1989). H. L. A. Hart Lecture. *The Independent*, 23 May 1989.

Breton, A. (1974). *The Economic Theory of Representative Government*. London, Macmillan.

Browne-Wilkinson, Sir Nicolas (1988). The independence of the judiciary in the 1980s. *Public Law*, 44–57.

Bryce, Viscount (1918). *Report of the Conference Chaired by Viscount Bryce*, Cd. 9038. London, HMSO.

Buchan, N. and Sumner, T. (eds) (1989). *Glasnost in Britain?* London, Macmillan.

Buchanan, J. (1965). *The Inconsistencies of the National Health Service*. London, Institute of Economic Affairs.

Buckland, P. (1981). *A History of Northern Ireland*. New York, Holmes and Meier.

Butt, R. (1967). *The Power of Parliament*. London, Constable.

Cabinet Office (1980). *Select Committees: Memorandum of Guidance for Officials* (the Osmotherly Rules). London, HMSO.

Caldecote, Lord (1980). *Industry Needs Electoral Reform*. London, Conservative Action for Electoral Reform.

Callaghan, J. (1987). *Time and Chance*. London, Collins.

Carter, N. (1991). Learning to measure performance: the use of indicators in organizations, *Public Administration* **69**, 85–101.

Chapman, R. A. and Hunt, M. (eds) (1987). *Open Government*. London, Croom Helm.

Civil Service Department (1979). *Disclosure of Official Information: A Report on Overseas Practice*. London, HMSO.

Civil Service Department (1980). *Select Committees: Memorandum of Guidance for Officials* (The Osmotherly Rules). London, Civil Service Department.

Clipson, A. (1987). Bradford's 'open government' experience. In Chapman, R. A. and Hunt, M. (eds), *Open Government*. London, Croom Helm, pp. 123–33.

Coates, K. (ed.) (1979). *What Went Wrong?* Nottingham, Spokesman.

Collins, L. (1990). *European Community Law in the United Kingdom*, 4th edn. London, Butterworths.

Coombes, D. (1982). *Representative Government and Economic Power*. London, Heinemann Educational.

Coulson, A. (1990). *Devolving Power: The Case for Regional Government* (Fabian Society Tract no. 537). London, Fabian Society.

Crick, B. R. (1964). *The Reform of Parliament*, revised 2nd edn. London, Weidenfeld and Nicolson.

Crick, B. R. (1977). Commentary in *Political Quarterly*, **48**, 249–59.

Crick, B. R. (1988). Sovereignty, centralism and devolution. In Holme, R. and Elliott, M. (eds), *1688–1988: Time for a New Constitution*. London, Macmillan, pp. 57–80.

Crick, B. R. (1989). Beyond parliamentary reform. *Political Quarterly*, **60**, 396–9.

Crosland, A. (1956). *The Future of Socialism*. London, Jonathan Cape.

Curtice, J. and Steed, M. (1982). Electoral choice and the production of government. *British Journal of Political Science*, 12, 249–98.

Dahrendorf, R. (1988). Citizenship and the modern social conflict. In Holme, R. and Elliott, M. (eds), *1688–1988: Time for a New Constitution*. London, Macmillan, pp. 112–25.

Daintith, T. C. (1989). The executive power today: Bargaining and economic control. In Jowell, J. and Oliver, D. (eds), *The Changing Constitution*, 2nd edn. Oxford, Clarendon Press, pp. 193–218.

Daltrop, A. (1986). *Political Realities: Politics and the European Community*, 2nd edn. London, Longman.

Deakin, N. and Wright, A. (eds) (1989). *Consuming Public Services*. London, Routledge.

Debnam, G. (1989). Adversary politics in Britain 1964–1979: Change of government and the climate of stress. *Parliamentary Affairs*, **42**, 213–29.

Delbridge, R. and Smith, M. (eds) (1982). *Consuming Secrets*. London, Burnett.

d'Entreves, A. P. (1967). *The Notion of the State*. Oxford, Clarendon Press.

Department of Health and Social Security (1983). *Personal Social Service Records – Disclosure of Information to Clients*, Circular LAC 83/14. London, HMSO.

Department of the Environment (1991a). *A New Tax for Local Government*. London, Department of the Environment.

Department of the Environment (1991b). *The Structure of Local Government in England*. London, Department of the Environment.

Department of the Environment (1991c). *The Internal Management of Local Authorities in England*. London, Department of the Environment.

Doig, A. (1989). The resignation of Edwina Currie. *Parliamentary Affairs*, **42**, 317–29.

Donaghy, P. J. and Newton, M. T. (1987). *Spain: A Guide to Political and Economic Institutions*. Cambridge, Cambridge University Press.

Donnelly, J. (1985). *The Concept of Human Rights*. London, Croom Helm.

Donoughue, B. (1987). *The Prime Minister: The Conduct of Policy under Harold Wilson and James Callaghan*. London, Cape.

Downs, A. (1967). *An Economic Theory of Democracy.* New York, Harper and Row.

Drewry, G. (1983). Lord Haldane's Ministry of Justice – Stillborn or strangled at birth? *Public Administration,* 61, 396–414.

Drewry, G. (1987a). JUSTICE Report on the Administration of the Courts. *Modern Law Review,* 50, 354–60.

Drewry, G. (1987b). The debate about a Ministry of Justice – A Joad's eye view. *Public Law,* 502–509.

Drewry, G. (ed.) (1989a). *The New Select Committees,* 2nd edn. Oxford, Clarendon Press.

Drewry, G. (1989b). Select committees and backbench power. In Jowell, J. and Oliver, D. (eds), *The Changing Constitution,* 2nd end. Oxford, Clarendon Press, pp. 141–63.

Drewry, G. (1990). Next Steps: The pace falters. *Public Law,* 322–9.

Drewry, G. and Butcher, T. (1988). *The Civil Service Today.* Oxford, Blackwell.

Dummett, A. and Nicol, A. (1990). *Subjects, Citizens, Aliens and Others.* London, Weidenfeld and Nicolson.

Dunleavy, P. (1990). Reinterpreting the Westland affair: Theories of state and core executive decision making. *Public Administration,* 68, 29–60.

Dworkin, R. (1987). *Taking Rights Seriously,* 5th impression. London, Duckworth.

Dworkin, R. (1990). *A Bill of Rights for Britain.* London, Chatto and Windus.

Efficiency Unit (1988). *Improving Management in Government: The Next Steps.* London, HMSO.

Efficiency Unit (1991). *Making the Most of Next Steps: The Management of Ministers' Departments and their Executive Agencies.* London, HMSO.

Elder, N. C. M. (1973). Regionalism and the publicity principle in Sweden. In *Report of the Royal Commission on The Constitution 1969–73,* Cmnd. 5460–I. London, HMSO.

Ewing, K. D. (1987). *The Funding of Political Parties in Britain.* Cambridge, Cambridge University Press.

Ewing, K. D. and Gearty, C. A. (1990). *Freedom under Thatcher.* Oxford, Clarendon Press.

Finer, S. E. (ed.) (1975). *Adversary Politics and Electoral Reform.* London, Anthony Wigram.

Finnie, W. (1991). Anti-terrorist legislation and the European Convention on Human Rights. *Modern Law Review,* 54, 288–93.

Finnis, J. (1980). *Natural Law and Natural Rights.* Oxford, Clarendon Press.

Fishman, N. (1989). Extending the scope of representative democracy. *Political Quarterly,* 60, 442–55.

Franklin, M. N. (1985). *The Decline of Class Voting in Britain: Changes in the Basis of Electoral Choice 1964–1983.* Oxford, Clarendon Press.

Franks, Lord (1972). *Report of the Departmental Committee on Section 2 of the Official Secrets Act 1911,* Cmnd. 5104. London, HMSO.

Fulton, Lord (1968). *Report of the Committee on the Civil Service,* Cmnd. 3638. London, HMSO.

Galbraith, J. K. (1983). *The Anatomy of Power.* Boston, Houghton Mifflin.

Gamble, A. (1988). *Free Economy – Strong State.* London, Macmillan.

Ganz, G. (1990). The depoliticisation of local government: The Local Government and Housing Act 1989, Part I. *Public Law,* 224–42.

Gardner, J. P. (1990). What lawyers mean by citizenship. In *Encouraging Citizenship: Report of the Commission on Citizenship* (Speaker's Commission). London, HMSO, pp. 63–78.

Garrett, J. and Sheldon, R. (1973). *Administrative Reform: The Next Steps* (Fabian Tract No. 426). London, Fabian Society.

Geekie, J. and Levy, R. (1989). Devolution and the tartanisation of the Labour Party. *Parliamentary Affairs*, **42**, 399–411.

Giddens, A. (1981). *A Contemporary Critique of Historical Materialism*, Vol. I. London, Macmillan.

Giddens, A. (1982). *Profiles and Critiques in Social Theory*. London, Macmillan.

Giddens, A. (1984). *The Constitution of Society*. Cambridge, Polity Press.

Goldsworthy, D. (1991). *Setting Up Next Steps*. London, HMSO.

Goodson-Wickes, C. (1984). *The New Corruption*. London, Centre for Policy Studies.

Graham, D. and Clarke, P. (1986). The New Enlightenment. London, Macmillan.

Grant, M. (1986). *Rate Capping and the Law*, 2nd edn. London, Association of Metropolitan Authorities.

Grant, M. (1988). Introductory commentary on the Local Government Finance Act 1988. In *Current Law Annotated Statutes 1988*. London, Sweet and Maxwell.

Grant, W. (1989). The erosion of intermediary institutions. *Political Quarterly*, **60**, 10–21.

Green, Sir Guy (1985). The rationale and some aspects of judicial independence. *Australian Law Journal*, **59**, 135–50.

Griffith, J. A. G. (1979). The political constitution. *Modern Law Review*, **42**, 1–21.

Griffith, J. A. G. (1985). Judicial decision-making in public law. *Public Law*, 564–82.

Griffith, J. A. G. (1991). *The Politics of the Judiciary*, 4th edn. Glasgow, Fontana.

Griffith, J. A. G. and Ryle, M. (1989). *Parliament: Functions, Practices and Procedures*. London, Sweet and Maxwell.

Gyford, J. (1985). *The Politics of Local Socialism*. London, Allen and Unwin.

Gyford, J., Leach, S. and Game, C. (1990). *The Changing Politics of Local Government*. London, Unwin Hyman.

Hailsham, Lord (1976). *Elective Dictatorship*. London, British Broadcasting Corporation.

Hailsham, Lord (1978). *The Dilemma of Democracy*. London, Collins.

Haldane, Lord (1918). *Report of the Machinery of Government Committee*, Cd. 9230. London, HMSO.

Hambleton, R. (1988). Consumerism, decentralization and local democracy. *Public Administration*, **66**, 125–47.

Hansard Society (1976). *Report of the Commission on Electoral Reform*. London, Hansard Society.

Hansard Society (1979). *Politics and Industry – The Great Mismatch*. London, Hansard Society.

Hansard Society Commission (1990). *Women at the Top*. London, Hansard Society.

Hart, W. O. and Garner, J. F. (1973). *Hart's Introduction to the Law of Local Government and Administration*, 9th edn. London, Butterworth.

Haseler, S., (1991). *Britain's Ancien Régime. The Need for a New Constitutional Settlement*. London, The Radical Society.

Hayek, F. A. von (1960). *The Constitution of Liberty*. London, Routledge and Kegan Paul.

Head of the Home Civil Service (1987). *The Duties and Responsibilities of Civil Servants in Relation to Ministers: A Note by the Head of the Home Civil Service*, 123 HC Deb. 572–5 (Written Answers 2 December 1987). London, HMSO.

Heater, D. (1990). *Citizenship: The Civic Ideal in World History, Politics and Education*. London, Longman.

Heath, A., Jowell, R. and Curtice, J. (1985). *How Britain Votes*. Oxford, Pergamon Press.

Heath, A., Jowell, R. and Curtice, J. (1986). Understanding electoral change in Britain. *Parliamentary Affairs*, **39**, 150–64.

Held, D. (1989). *Political Theory and the Modern State*. Cambridge, Polity Press.

Hennessy, P. (1986). *Cabinet*. Oxford, Blackwell.

Hennessy, P. (1989a). *Whitehall*. London, Martin Secker and Warburg.

Hennessy, P. (1989b). Thatcher declines to disclose rules of the ministerial game. *Independent*, 1 May.

Hennessy, P. (1990). *Evidence*. Treasury and Civil Service Committee, Eighth Report, HC 481, 1989–90, Appendix I.

Henney, A. (1982). *Inside Local Government*. London, Sinclair Browne.

Heuston, R. V. F. (1964). *Essays in Constitutional Law*, 2nd edn. London, Stevens and Son.

Hirst, P. (1988). Representative democracy and its limits. *Political Quarterly*, 59, 190–205.

Hirst, P. (1989). *After Thatcher*. London, Collins.

Hollis, C. (1949). *Can Parliament Survive?* London, Hollis and Carter.

Holme, R. (n.d.). *A Democracy which Works*. London, Parliamentary Democracy Trust.

Holme, R. (1987). *The People's Kingdom*. London, Bodley Head.

Holme, R. and Elliott, M. (eds) (1988). *1688–1988: Time for a New Constitution*. London, Macmillan.

Hoskyns, Sir John (1983). Whitehall and Westminster: An outsider's view. *Parliamentary Affairs*, 36, 137–47.

House of Lords Select Committee on a Bill of Rights (1978). *Report*. House of Lords Paper 176 (1977–8). London, HMSO.

Institute of Public Policy Research (1991). *The Constitution of the United Kingdom*. London, IPPR.

Jackson, W. E. (1966). *The Structure of Local Government in England and Wales*, 5th edn. London, Longman.

Jaconelli, J. (1980). *Enacting a Bill of Rights*. Oxford, Clarendon Press.

Jaconelli, J. (1988). The European Human Rights Convention. *Political Quarterly*, 59, 343–57.

Jennings, Sir Ivor (1959). *The Law and the Constitution*, 5th edn. London, University of London Press.

Johnson, N. (1977). *In Search of the Constitution*. Oxford, Pergamon Press.

Johnston, R. J. (1985). *The Geography of English Politics: The 1983 General Election*. London, Croom Helm.

Johnston, R. J., Pattie, C. J. and Allsopp, J. G. (1988). *A Nation Dividing? The Electoral Map of Great Britain 1979–1987*. London, Longman.

Joint Liberal/SDP Alliance Commission on Constitutional Reform (1982). *Electoral Reform: Fairer Voting in Natural Constituencies*. London, Joint Liberal/SDP Alliance Commission on Electoral Reform.

Jones, G. and Stewart, J. (1985). *Case for Local Government*, 2nd edn. London, George Allen and Unwin.

Jowell, J. and Lester, A. (1987). Beyond *Wednesbury*: Substantive principles of administrative law. *Public Law*, 368–82.

Jowell, J. and Lester, A. (1988). Proportionality: Neither novel nor dangerous. In Jowell, J. and Oliver, D. (eds), *New Directions in Judicial Review*. London, Sweet and Maxwell, pp. 51–69.

Jowell, J. and Oliver, D. (eds) (1988). *New Directions in Judicial Review*. London, Sweet and Maxwell.

Jowell, J. and Oliver, D. (eds) (1989). *The Changing Constitution*, 2nd edn. Oxford, Clarendon Press.

JUSTICE (1986). *The Administration of the Courts*. London, JUSTICE.

JUSTICE (1989). *Miscarriages of Justice*. London, JUSTICE.

Justice-All Souls Review (1988). *Administrative Justice: Some Necessary Reforms*. Oxford, Clarendon Press.

Kamenka, E. (ed.) (1978). *Human Rights.* London, Edward Arnold.
Kammen, M. (1986). *A Machine that Would Go of Itself.* New York, Knopf.
Kapteyn, Judge, P. J. G. (1990). *Community Law and the Principle of Subsidiarity.* Annual lecture delivered to the Kings College London European Community Law Association, 2 November 1990. Unpublished.
Kellas, J. (1990). The constitutional options for Scotland. *Parliamentary Affairs*, 43, 426–34.
Keynes, J. M. (1936). *The General Theory of Employment, Interest and Money.* London, Macmillan.
Kilbrandon, Lord (1973). *Report on the Royal Commission on the Constitution 1969–73*, Cmnd. 5460, 5460-I. London, HMSO.
King, D. S. (1987). *The New Right: Politics, Markets and Citizenship.* London, Macmillan.
Kingsford-Smith, D. and Oliver, D. (eds) (1990). *Economical with the Truth: The Law and the Media in a Democratic Society.* Oxford, ESC.
Labour Party (1989). *Meet the Challenge: Make the Change.* London, Labour Party.
Labour Party (1990). *Looking to the Future.* London, Labour Party.
Labour Party (1991a). *Opportunity Britain. Labour's Better Way for the 1990s.* London, Labour Party.
Labour Party (1991b). *Opportunity, Quality, Accountability. The Better Way for Local Government.* London, Labour Party.
Labour Party (1991c). *The Charter of Rights. Guaranteeing Individual Liberty in a Free Society.* London, Labour Party.
Lacey, N. (1989). Are rights best left unwritten? *Political Quarterly*, 60, 433–41.
Lakeman, E. (1974). *How Democracies Vote*, 4th revised edn. London, Faber.
Lansley, S., Goss, S. and Wolmar, C. (eds) (1989). *Councils in Conflict: The Rise and Fall of the Municipal Left.* London, Macmillan.
Lash, S. and Urry, J. (1987). *The End of Organised Capitalism.* Cambridge, Polity Press.
Laver, M. (1981). *The Politics of Private Desires.* Harmondsworth, Penguin.
Layfield, F. (1976). *Report of the Committee of Inquiry into Local Government Finance*, Cmnd. 6453. London, HMSO.
Layton, C. (1990). *The Healing of Europe.* London, Federal Trust for Education and Research.
Lee, S. (1987). Against a Bill of Rights? In Neuberger, J. (ed.), *Freedom of Information . . . Freedom of the Individual?* London, Papermac, pp. 58–83.
Legal Aid Advisory Committee (1984). *33rd Annual Report for 1982/83*, HC 137, 1983–84. London, HMSO.
Leigh, I. and Lustgarten, L. (1989). The Security Service Act 1989. *Modern Law Review*, 52, 801–840.
Lester, A. (1984). Fundamental rights: The United Kingdom isolated? *Public Law*, 46–72.
Lester, A. and Bindman, G. (1972). *Race and Law in Great Britain.* Cambridge, Mass., Harvard University Press.
Lester, A. *et al.*, (1990). *A British Bill of Rights* (IPPR Constitution Paper No. 1). London, Institute of Public Policy Research.
Liberal Democrats (1990). *'We the People . . .' – Towards a Written Constitution* (Federal Green Paper No. 13). Dorchester, Liberal Democrat Publications.
Liberal Democrats (1991a). *Citizens' Britain.* London, Liberal Democrats.
Liberal Democrats (1991b). *Shaping Tomorrow, Starting Today*, Dorchester, Liberal Democrat Publications.
Lodge, J. (ed.) (1989). *The European Community and the Challenge of the Future.* London, Pinter.

Lord Chancellor's Department (1986). *Judicial Appointments*. London, HMSO.
Loughlin, M. (1986). *Local Government in the Modern State*. London, Sweet and Maxwell.
Lyon, E. and Wigram, A. (1977). *The Speaker's Conference*. London, Conservative Action for Electoral Reform.
Macdonald, J. (1990). Draft constitution. In *"We, The People . . ." – Towards a Written Constitution* (Liberal Democrat Federal Green Paper No. 13). Dorchester, Liberal Democrat Publications.
Mackay, Lord (1991). *The Lord Chancellor in the 1990s*. Inaugural Mishcon lecture delivered at University College London, 6 March 1991. Unpublished.
Markesinis, B. (1990). Our patchy law of privacy – time to do something about it. *Modern Law Review*, 53, 802–809.
Marquand, D. (1988). *The Unprincipled Society*. London, Jonathan Cape.
Marquand, D. (1989). Regional devolution. In Jowell, J. and Oliver, D. (eds), *The Changing Constitution*, 2nd edn. Oxford, Clarendon Press, pp. 385–407.
Marsh, I. (1990). Liberal priorities, the Lib-Lab pact and the requirements for policy influence. *Parliamentary Affairs*, 43, 292–321.
Marsh, N. S. (ed.) (1987). *Public Access to Government-held Information: A Comparative Symposium*. London, British Institute of International and Comparative Law.
Marshall, G. (1971). *Constitutional Theory*. Oxford, Clarendon Press.
Marshall, G. (1984). *Constitutional Conventions*. Oxford, Clarendon Press.
Marshall, G. (1987). Overriding a Bill of Rights. *Public Law*, 9–11.
Marshall, G. (ed.) (1989). *Ministerial Responsibility*. Oxford, Oxford University Press.
Marshall, T. H. (1950). *Citizenship and Social Class*. Cambridge, Cambridge University Press.
Maud, Sir John (1967). *Report of the Committee on the Management of Local Government*. London, HMSO.
Maude, Sir Angus and Szemerey, J. (1982). *Why Electoral Change? The Case for PR Examined*. London, Conservative Political Centre.
McAuslan, J. P. W. B. (1988). Public law and public choice. *Modern Law Review*, 51, 681–715.
McCrudden, C. (1989). Northern Ireland and the British Constitution. In Jowell, J. and Oliver, D. (eds), *The Changing Constitution*, 2nd edn. Oxford, Clarendon Press, pp. 297–342.
Meacher, M. (1979). Whitehall's short way with democracy. In Coates, K. (ed.), *What Went Wrong?* Nottingham, Spokesman, pp. 170–86.
Mead, L. (1986). *Beyond Entitlement*. New York, Free Press.
Meadowcroft, M. (1982). *Liberalism and the Left*. London, Liberator.
Meredith, P. (1989). Educational reform. *Modern Law Review*, 52, 215–31.
Michael, J. (1982). *The Politics of Secrecy*. London, National Council for Civil Liberties.
Middlemas, K. (1979). *Politics in Industrial Society*. London, Deutsch.
Miliband, R. (1961, 1972). *Parliamentary Socialism: A Study in the Politics of Labour*. London, Merlin Press.
Miliband, R. (1984). *Capitalist Democracy in Britain*. Oxford, Oxford University Press.
Miller, W. (1986). Local electoral behaviour. In *The Conduct of Local Authority Business, Research Volume III*, Cmnd. 9800. London, HMSO.
Miller, W. (1988). *Irrelevant Elections? The Quality of Local Democracy*. Oxford, Clarendon Press.
Morgan, J. P. (1975). *The House of Lords and the Labour Government 1964–70*. Oxford, Clarendon Press.
MORI (1991). *State of the Nation*. London, MORI.
Mueller, D. C. (1979). *Public Choice*. Cambridge, Cambridge University Press.

National Curriculum Council (1990). *Curriculum Guidance 8: Education for Citizenship*. York, National Curriculum Council.

National Economic Development Office (1976). *A Study of UK Nationalised Industries*. London, HMSO.

Neuberger, J. (ed.) (1987). *Freedom of Information . . . Freedom of the Individual?* London, Papermac.

Niskanen, W. A. (1971). *Bureaucracy and Representative Government*. Chicago, Aldine.

Norton, P. (1978). *Conservative Dissidents*. London, Temple Smith.

Norton, P. (1980). *Dissension in the House of Commons 1974–79*. Oxford, Clarendon Press.

Norton, P. (1981). *The Commons in Perspective*. Oxford, Martin Robertson.

Norton, P. (1985). *The British Polity*. London, Longman.

Norton-Taylor, R. (1990). *In Defence of the Realm? The Case for Accountable Security Services*. London, Civil Liberties Trust.

Oldfield, A. (1990a). *Citizenship and the Community: Civic Republicanism and the Modern World*. London, Routledge.

Oldfield, A. (1990b). Citizenship: An unnatural practice? *Political Quarterly*, 61, 177–98.

Oliver, D. (1981). The constitutional implications of the reforms of the Labour party. *Public Law*, 151–63.

Oliver, D. (1986). Politicians and the courts. *Parliamentary Affairs*, 41, 13–33.

Oliver, D. (1988). The courts and the policy making process. In Jowell, J. and Oliver, D. (eds), *New Directions in Judicial Review*. London, Sweet and Maxwell, pp. 73–89.

Oliver, D. (1989). The parties and Parliament: Representative or intra-party democracy? In Jowell, J. and Oliver, D. (eds), *The Changing Constitution*, 2nd edn. Oxford, Clarendon Press, pp. 115–40.

Oliver, D. and Austin, R. (1987). Political and constitutional aspects of the Westland Affair. *Parliamentary Affairs*, 40, 20–40.

Olsen, M. (1965). *The Logic of Collective Action*. Oxford, Oxford University Press.

O'Toole, B. J. (1990). T. H. Green and the ethics of senior officials in British central government. *Public Administration*, 68, 337–52.

Palmer, S. (1990). Tightening secrecy law: The Official Secrets Act 1989. *Public Law*, 243–56.

Pannick, D. (1990). Spycatcher: Two years of legal indignations. In Kingsford-Smith, D. and Oliver, D. (eds), *Economical with the Truth: The Law and the Media in a Democratic Society*. Oxford, ESC, pp. 17–26.

Parkinson, M. (1986). Decision making by Liverpool City Council: Setting the rate, 1985–86. In *Research Volume IV: The Conduct of Local Authority Business* (the Widdicombe Report), Cmnd. 9801. London, HMSO.

Patchett, K. (1975). *Safeguards for Judicial Independence in Law and Practice*. Paper delivered at the Fourth CMA Conference. Unpublished.

Plant, R. (1988). *Citizenship, Rights and Socialism* (Fabian Society No. 531). London, Fabian Society.

Plant, R. (1990). Citizenship and rights. In *Citizenship and Rights in Thatcher's Britain: Two Views*. London, Institute of Economic Affairs, Health and Welfare Unit.

Plant, R. (1991). *The Plant Report*. London, *The Guardian*.

Political and Economic Planning (1974). *Reshaping Britain: A Programme of Economic and Social Reform*. London, Political and Economic Planning.

Pontier, J. M. (1986). La subsidiarité en droit administratif. *Revue du Droit Public et de la Science Politique en France et à l'Etranger*, 102, 1515–37.

Quinton, A. (ed.) (1967). *Political Philosophy*. Oxford, Oxford University Press.

Rallings, C. and Thrasher, M. (1988). Local elections in Britain: Comparing myth with reality. *Parliamentary Affairs*, 41, 182–94.

232   *Government in the United Kingdom*

Ranelagh, J. (1987). Secrets, supervision and information. In Neuberger, J. (ed.), *Freedom of Information . . . Freedom of the Individual?* London, Papermac, pp. 19–37.
Rawlings, H. F. (1988). *Law and the Electoral Process.* London, Sweet and Maxwell.
Rawls, J. (1972). *A Theory of Justice.* Oxford, Oxford University Press.
Redwood, J. and Hatch, J. (1982). *Controlling Public Industries.* Oxford, Blackwell.
Rhodes, R. A. W. (1987). Developing the public service orientation. *Local Government Studies*, 13, 13, 63–73.
Richardson, J. J. (1982). Programme evaluation in Britain and Sweden. *Parliamentary Affairs*, 35, 160–80.
Robertson, G. (1989). *Freedom, the Individual and the Law.* Harmondsworth, Penguin.
Robson, W. A. (1931). *The Development of Local Government.* London, Allen and Unwin.
Rogaly, J. (1976). *Parliament for the People.* London, Temple Smith.
Rose, R. (1976). *The Problem of Party Government.* Harmondsworth, Penguin.
Rose, R. (1984). *Do Parties Make a Difference?*, 2nd edn. London, Macmillan.
Rose, R. (1985). *Politics in England: Persistence and Change*, 4th edn. London, Faber and Faber.
Rose, R. (1986). Law as a resource of public policy. *Parliamentary Affairs*, 39, 297–314.
Rothschild, Lord (1977). *Meditations of a Broomstick.* London, Collins.
Rougemont, D. de (1983). *The Future is Within Us.* Oxford, Pergamon Press.
Ryle, M. (1990). Disclosure of financial interests by MPs: The John Browne Affair. *Public Law*, 313–22.
Scarman, Sir Leslie (1974). *English Law – The New Dimension.* London, Stevens and Sons.
Scarman, Lord (1988). Bill of Rights and law reform. In Holme, R. and Elliott, M. (eds), *1688–1988: Time for a New Constitution.* London, Macmillan, pp. 103–11.
Schelling, T. C. (1978). *Micromotives and Macrobehaviour.* New York, Norton.
Schofield, P. (1990). Bentham on public opinion and the press. In Kingsford-Smith, D. and Oliver, D. (eds), *Economical with the Truth: The Law and the Media in a Democratic Society.* Oxford, ESC, pp. 95–108.
Scott, I. R. (1989). The Council of Judges in the Supreme Court of England and Wales. *Public Law*, 379–88.
Scottish Constitutional Convention (1989). *Towards a Scottish Parliament.* Edinburgh, SCC.
Scottish Constitutional Convention (1990a). *Key Elements of Proposals for Scottish Parliament.* Edinburgh, SCC.
Scottish Constitutional Convention (1990b). *Towards Scotland's Parliament.* Edinburgh, SCC.
Self, P. (1985). *Political Theories of Modern Government.* London, George Allen and Unwin.
Self, P. (1990). What's wrong with government? *Political Quarterly*, 61, 23–35.
Seyd, P. (1987). *The Rise and Fall of the Labour Left.* London, Macmillan.
Shetreet, S. (1976). *Judges on Trial.* Oxford, North-Holland.
Skordali, E. (1991). *Judicial Appointments: An International Review of Existing Models* (Research and Policy Planning Unit of the Law Society). London, Law Society.
Smith, B. (1976). *Policy Making in British Government: An Analysis of Power and Rationality.* Oxford, Martin Robertson.
Smith, J. (1991). *The Public Service Ethos.* London, Royal Institute of Public Administration.
Smith, T. (1972). *Anti-Politics: Consensus, Reform and Protest.* London, Charles Knight.
Social and Liberal Democrats (1989). *Partners for Freedom and Justice* (Federal White Paper No. 2). Hebden Bridge, Hebden Royd.

Speaker's Commission (1990). *Encouraging Citizenship*. London, HMSO.
Spencer, M. (1990). *1992 and All That*. London, Civil Liberties Trust.
Steel, D. (1980). *A House Divided*. London, Weidenfeld and Nicolson.
Thomas, R. (1987). The experience of other countries. In Chapman, R. A. and Hunt, M. (eds), *Open Government*. London, Croom Helm, pp. 135–71.
Thornton, P. (1989). *Decade of Decline: Civil Liberties in the Thatcher Years*. London, National Council for Civil Liberties.
Toussaint, M. (1988). *Report on the Democratic Deficit in the European Community*. Luxembourg, Office of Official Publications of the European Community.
Tower Hamlets London Borough Council (1988). *Decentralisation: A Change for the Better*. London, Tower Hamlets LBC.
Townsend, P. (1979). *Poverty in the United Kingdom*. London, Allen Lane.
Tullock, G. (1965). *The Politics of Bureaucracy*. Washington, Public Affairs Press.
Tullock, G. (1976). *The Vote Motive*. London, Institute of Economic Affairs.
Turpin, C. (1990). *British Government and the Constitution*, 2nd edn. London, Weidenfeld and Nicolson.
Veljanowski, C. (1987). *Selling the State*. London, Weidenfeld and Nicolson.
Vibert, F. (1991). *Constitutional Reform in the United Kingdom – An Incremental Agenda*. London, Institute of Economic Affairs.
Wade, E. C. S. and Bradley, A. W. (1985). *Constitutional and Administrative Law*, 10th edn. London, Longman.
Wade, H. W. R. (1980). *Constitutional Fundamentals*. London, Stevens.
Wade, Sir William (1988). *Administrative Law*, 6th edn. Oxford, Clarendon Press.
Wallington, P. and McBride, J. (1976). *Civil Liberties and a Bill of Rights*. London, Cobden Trust.
Ware, A. (1979). *The Logic of Party Democracy*. London, Macmillan.
Wass, Sir Douglas (1984). *Government and the Governed*. London, Routledge and Kegan Paul.
Wass, Sir Douglas (1987). Checks and balances in public policy making. *Public Law*, 181–201.
Webb, B. and Webb, S. (1920). *A Constitution for the Socialist Commonwealth of Great Britain*. London, Longman.
Wedderburn, Lord (1990). *The Social Charter, European Company and Employment Rights*. London, Institute of Employment Rights.
Wheare, K. C. (1966). *Modern Constitutions*. Oxford, Oxford University Press.
Widdicombe, D. (1985). *Local Authority Publicity* (Interim Report of the Committee of Inquiry into the Conduct of Local Authority Business). London, HMSO.
Widdicombe, D. (1986). *Report of the Committee of Inquiry into the Conduct of Local Authority Business*, Cmnd. 9797. London, HMSO.
Wilke, M. and Wallace, H. (1990). *Subsidiarity: Approaches to Power-Sharing in the European Community* (Royal Institute of International Affairs Discussion Paper No. 27). London, Royal Institute of International Affairs.
Woolf, Sir Harry (1986). Public law, private law: Why the divide? *Public Law*, 220–38.
Woolf, Sir Harry (1990). *Protection of the Public – A New Challenge*. London, Stevens.
Zander, M. (1985). *A Bill of Rights?*, 3rd edn. London, Sweet and Maxwell.

GOVERNMENT PAPERS
(in chronological order)

Report of the Conference Chaired by Viscount Bryce, Cd. 9038 (London, 1918).
Report of the Machinery of Government Committee (The Haldane Report), Cd. 9230 (London, 1918).

Report of the Committee on the Management of Local Government (The Maud Report) (London, 1967).

Report of the Committee on the Civil Service (The Fulton Report), Cmnd. 3638 (London, 1968).

House of Lords Reform, Cmnd. 3799 (London, 1968).

Report of the Departmental Committee on Section 2 of the Official Secrets Act 1911 (The Franks Report), Cmnd. 5104 (London, 1972).

Report on the Royal Commission on The Constitution 1969–73 (The Kilbrandon Report), Cmnd. 5460 (London, 1973).

Report of the Committee of Inquiry into Local Government Finance (The Layfield Report), Cmnd. 6453 (London, 1976).

Disclosure of Official Information: A Report on Overseas Practice (London, Civil Service Department, 1979).

Select Committees: Memorandum of Guidance for Officials (The Osmotherly Rules) (London, Civil Service Department, 1980).

Alternatives to Domestic Rates, Cmnd. 8449 (London, 1981).

Northern Ireland: A Framework for Devolution, Cmnd. 8541 (London, 1982).

Personal Social Service Records – Disclosure of Information to Clients (Department of Health and Social Security Circular LAC 83/14) (London 1983).

Rates, Cmnd. 9008 (London, 1983).

Paying for Local Government, Cmnd. 9714 (London, 1986).

Civil Servants and Ministers: Duties and Responsibilities, Cmnd. 9841 (London, 1986).

Local Authority Publicity (Interim Report of the Committee of Inquiry into the Conduct of Local Authority Business) (London, 1986).

Report of the Committee of Inquiry into the Conduct of Local Authority Business (The Widdicombe Report), Cmnd. 9797 (London, 1986).

The Conduct of Local Authority Business: The Government Response to the Report of the Widdicombe Committee of Inquiry. Cm. 433 (London, 1988).

Improving Management in Government: The Next Steps (Efficiency Unit, London, 1988).

Developments in the Next Steps Programme: The Government Reply to the Eighth Report from the Treasury and Civil Service Committee, Session 1988–89, HC 348, Cm. 524 (London, 1988).

The Government Reply to the Fifth Report from the Treasury and Civil Service Committee, Session 1988–89, HC 348, Cm. 841 (London, 1989).

The Financing and Accountability of Next Steps Agencies, Cm. 914 (London, 1989).

The Working of the Select Committee System. Government Response to the Second Report of the House of Commons Select Committee on Procedure, Session 1989–90, Cm. 1532 (London, 1991).

The Citizen's Charter, Cm. 1599 (London, 1988).

HOUSE OF COMMONS PAPERS
(in approximate chronological order)

Report from the Select Committee on Members' Interests (Declaration), 1969–70, HC 57.

First Report from the Select Committee on Procedure, 1977–78, HC 588-I to II.

Sixth Report from the Home Affairs Committee, 1981–82: *Miscarriages of Justice*, HC 421. London, HMSO.

Liaison Committee 1982–83: *The Select Committee System*, HC 92. London, HMSO.

Seventh Report from the Treasury and Civil Service Committee 1985–86: *Ministers and Civil Servants: Duties and Responsibilities*, HC 92. London, HMSO.

Fourth Report from the Defence Committee 1985–86: *Westland plc: The Government's Decision-Making*, HC 519. London, HMSO.

First Report from the Liaison Committee, 1986–87: *Accountability of Ministers and Civil Servants to Select Committees of the House of Commons*, HC 100. London, HMSO.

The Duties and Responsibilities of Civil Servants in Relation to Ministers: A Note by the Head of the Home Civil Service, 1987, 123 HC Deb. 572–5 (Written Answers, 2 December 1987).

Eighth Report from the Treasury and Civil Service Committee 1987–88: *Civil Service Management Reform: The Next Steps*, HC 494. London, HMSO.

First Report from the Agriculture Committee 1988–89, HC 108–11. London, HMSO.

Select Committee on Procedure 1989–90: *The Working of the Select Committee System*, HC 19–I, 19–i. London, HMSO.

Eighth Report from the Treasury and Civil Service Committee 1989–90: *Progress in the Next Steps Initiative*, HC 481. London, HMSO.

Second Report from the Select Committee on Members' Interests 1989–90, HC 506 (*re* Mr Michael Mates, MP*). London, HMSO.

Third Report from the Select Committee on Members' Interests 1989–90, HC 561 (*re* Mr Michael Grylls, MP). London, HMSO.

Fifth Special Report from the Treasury and Civil Service Committee 1989–90: *The Civil Service Pay and Conditions of Service Code: The Government's Observations on the Fifth Report from the Committee in Session 1989–90*, HC 617. London, HMSO.

First Report from the Select Committee on Members' Interests 1990–91: *The Interests of Chairmen and Members of Select Committees*, HC 108. London, HMSO.

Third Report from the Select Committee on Procedure 1990–91: *Parliamentary Questions*, HC 178. London, HMSO.

Index